LEBANESE CUISINE

Anissa Helou

ST. MARTIN'S PRESS ❧ NEW YORK

To my mother and grandmother

Designed by Judy Linard
Jacket design and illustrations Nicci Walker
Food preparation for photography by Laurice Helou
Photography by Anissa Helou and Kiloran Howard
Art direction and styling Anissa Helou
Dishes, cutlery, wooden objects, surfaces and screen
from Anissa Helou Collection and Robert Young Antiques
Typesetting by Pearl Graphics, Hemel Hempstead

Library of Congress Cataloging-in-Publication Data

Helou, Anissa.
    Lebanese cuisine : more than 250 authentic recipes from the most elegant Middle Eastern cuisine / Anissa Helou.
        p.   cm.
    ISBN 0-312-13111-9
    1. Cookery, Lebanese.   I. Title.
TX725.L4H45   1995
641.595692—dc20   95-3764
                                                                     CIP

First published in Great Britain by Grub Street

First U.S. Edition: June 1995
10 9 8 7 6 5 4 3 2 1

Contents

Acknowledgments

 The person I am most indebted to in the writing of this book is my mother, Laurice Helou. She taught me most of what I know about Lebanese cuisine. She like me learned from her mother and my grandmother acquired her knowledge of food and cookery from her mother and so on, back through the many generations of Lebanese women. My mother was the source of most of the recipes included here and she stayed in London especially to help and advise me throughout. She was also instrumental in providing much of the information about old Lebanese traditions and food.

I would also like to thank Caroline Davidson who, as my agent and friend, was my guide in my first steps as a cookery writer. Her advice and editorial help throughout the making of this book have been invaluable. I am also grateful to her helper, Liz Hursthouse, for testing some of the recipes. My gratitude goes to Donald Munson, my other guide, who patiently helped me edit parts of the manuscript; Mahmoud Alghanim, from Arab Food Services inc, Kuwait for his financial sponsorship; Miriam Polunin for very early advice on how to put a cookery book proposal together; Peregrine and Patricia Pollen, Susannah Pollen, Robert and Josyane Young, Ted and Diana Few, Anne-Marie de Rougemont, Amna Al-Sabah and Liz Walker for their editorial comments at the proposal stage of this book; Kiloran Howard for taking my portrait and the food photographs for the proposal; Charles Perry for sending me all his papers on Arabic cookery for PPC and the Oxford Symposium of food and cookery; Janny de Moor for sending me her paper for the Oxford Symposium on "Eating Out in the Ancient Near East"; Assia Djebbar for sending me *Les Voyageurs d'Orient* from Paris; Mohammad Jouni for sending me recipes from Southern Lebanon and Antoine Mamari for the loan of precious books on the Lebanon and for sending me information on Kefraya and Ksara wines.

4

ACKNOWLEDGMENTS

I would also like to thank all those who lent me their kitchens in order for me to test recipes that I was not so keen to prepare in my own over-cluttered house; Simi Bedford and David Landau; Clare and James Kirkman, who also lent me their ice-cream maker; my sister, Marie Karam, and her family, who moreover supplied me regularly with reference cookery and travel books, as well as special ingredients from Beirut and finally my brother, Joseph Helou and his wife.

My special thanks go to: Zelfa Hourani for her editorial advice, the loan of her kitchen and of her collection of PPCs and other useful books; to her father, Cecil Hourani for reading the introduction to confirm there were no glaring mistakes; Helen Saberi who tested recipes for me and who also, together with Alan Davidson, helped start the investigation to unravel the mystery of *bois de panama*; Alan Davidson for kindly allowing me to consult various books in his extensive library; Loyd Grossman for reading some of the recipes and commenting favourably on them; Marina Coriolano for testing so many recipes and Anne Dolamore, my publisher, for her advice and help with the art direction during the photography of the food.

I would also like to thank everyone at the Green Valley, Zeina and Haddad Brothers food stores as well as Michel Yazbek and others at Fakhreldine restaurant and Clarissa Dickson-Wright formerly at Books for Cooks for their time and patience in answering my questions.

Finally I would like to apologize and thank all those who have helped me and whom I forgot to mention.

A Brief History of the Lebanon

 Since ancient times the Lebanon has held a place in history that is out of all proportion to its size. This small, lush country lies along the eastern coast of the Mediterranean, on the fringe of the fertile crescent where western civilisation began. Its name derives from *lubnan*, the Semitic word for white, to describe the snow covered peaks of the Mount Lebanon range which stops the dry hot easterly winds from reaching the inner and coastal plains while the sea breezes bring with them abundant rains to fertilize the soil. The Lebanon is famous for its temperate climate, cedar, pine and olive trees as well as for the abundance and variety of its agricultural produce.

The first settlers arrived round about 3000 BC. They were Canaanites, a Semitic people, who later became known as Phoenicians. The Greeks called the land Phoenicia, "the land of purple" after the color of a highly prized purple dye that the Canaanites extracted from a mollusc found all along the coastline. The Phoenicians established a string of coastal city-states from where they became the first great navigator-traders fulfilling the function of commercial and cultural intermediaries between East and West. Their trade included spices, grains, dried and preserved foodstuffs and wines. They made a vital contribution to history by developing from Egyptian hieroglyphs the basis of the alphabet used today throughout the western world. Their rich land and their continuous travels must have allowed the Phoenicians to develop a varied cuisine but to date no one has found an early Phoenician recipe, probably because they wrote on papyrus.

The Lebanon's geographical position, at the ancient cross-roads between East and West, its bountiful land and prosperous trade

6

made it prey to regular invasion by a succession of outsiders; a phenomenon that has continued until the present day. The first long term invaders were the Egyptians who ruled for three centuries from 1484 to 1150 BC. After which the Phoenicians experienced their only period of independence which was broken by the arrival of the Assyrians in 857 BC soon to be followed by the Babylonians then the Persians. In 333 BC Alexander the Great swept through the land and brought western influence to people who until then had been under an Egypto-Eastern influence. The Phoenicians assimilated western influences as readily as those of the East and in turn made an enduring impression on their conquerors. The Greeks brought with them a culinary sophistication and some of their cooks, often slaves, are mentioned in the histories. One of the most famous, Cadmos, who was cook to the king of Sidon in Phoenicia, is said to have introduced writing to Greece.

The Romans brought drastic changes to the area by merging all the states that lay between the Taurus and Sinai into one province they called Syria. Thus the Phoenicians no longer existed in name and their language was gradually supplanted by Aramaic. The Romans turned Beirut into a leading provincial cultural centre by establishing a school of law there. The population increased and for the first time in history, people began to move inland and establish towns at the foot and lower slopes of the mountains. Then, as today, these areas were rich in vines, fig trees and a plethora of succulent fruit and vegetables.

The prosperity of the country continued through the Byzantine era until the middle of the sixth century when a succession of severe earthquakes shook the country, nearly annihilating its coastal towns. These once thriving and cosmopolitan towns lay in ruins and began sinking into historical oblivion, no longer the centre of Mediterranean trade.

The advent of Islam changed the political make-up of the whole region but the new Muslim conquerors ignored the Lebanon and it gradually became the home of religious minorities who migrated there in search of a haven for their schismatic orders. The Maronites arrived, towards the end of the seventh century, to settle in the North of the country. Two centuries later a Druze missionary brought his followers to Wadi al-Taym, on the south-western slopes of the Anti-Lebanon range. The Shiites or Matawilah divided themselves between Sidon and Baalbek and the Nosairis settled in the South.

The leading families established feudal seats and rallied many of the surrounding natives to their faith. The Maronites' number was especially increased by incoming Christian and Jewish refugees, fleeing from the persecutions of the Muslim Abbassid caliphs, whose capital was Baghdad. It is safe to say that these new religious settlers brought with them sets of dietetic laws that influenced the cooking trends of the time.

The Crusaders arrived in the eleventh century, re-establishing direct western influence and making the Lebanon part of the kingdom of Jerusalem. By the middle of the thirteenth century, the Egyptian Mameluks reclaimed the country from the European Crusaders and the Lebanon was again under eastern influence. These Mameluks were slaves of Turkish and Circassian origins, who had seized power from their masters, the Ayyubid sultans. Their reign was an unhappy one. The Ottomans who replaced them at the beginning of the sixteenth century found the fertile land ravaged by their predecessors' scorched-earth policy, by the repeated and savage invasions of the Mongol hordes and, as if nature wanted to lend a hand to the cruelty of humans, by a series of earthquakes that again caused widespread destruction. The population was devastated by successive epidemics of plague accompanied by drought and famine.

After the discovery of America, the trade routes shifted from the Mediterranean to the Atlantic and the Lebanese were replaced by the Portuguese as intermediaries in Afro-Asian trade.

It was during the long period of Ottoman rule (1516-1914) that the Lebanon began to take the shape it has now. The unification process began under the leadership of Fakhr el-Deen II (1572-1635), a feudal lord, ruling over the Shoof province in Southern Lebanon. He was given a free hand in local affairs by the Ottoman sultan. He decided to unite the different Lebanese communities by first annexing the surrounding provinces, then he proceeded to conquer the coastal city-states, Beirut, Sidon, Tyre and Tripoli. He opened the country to western trade and education. French, British and Italian agents established trading posts and their religious orders sent missionaries to convert and educate the population. These liberal policies were continued by another feudal lord, Beshir II (1789-1840). Following Beshir's death the country fell victim to its first bout of sectarian fighting and again to another in 1860. The Turks, under the intervention of the Europeans, restored order and after the first tolerant Ottoman mutasarrif (governor), Dawood Basha, the

Lebanon experienced a return to normality and once again to unity and a long period of autonomy.

The Ottoman empire was broken up after the First World War and the French held a mandate over the country from 1920 to 1946. They declared it a republic in 1920, giving it its present frontiers. On 26 November 1941 the Lebanon became fully independent but it was not until 1946 that the last French troops evacuated the country. From that time onwards the country and its people began to regain their long-lost status as commercial and cultural intermediaries between East and West and again prospered until, in 1975, the Lebanon was plunged into the tragic civil war from which it has emerged only recently.

Lebanese cuisine as we know it today has evolved through these successive invasions with each culture leaving its mark. Those who seem to have left the most perceptible signs of influence are the Egyptians, Persians, ancient Greeks and Ottomans. The French, whose culinary influence has spread to almost every corner of the western and Middle Eastern world, had in their mere 25 years in the Lebanon a strong refining influence on the local cuisine. This probably explains why Lebanese food is that much more varied and refined than that of its Middle Eastern neighbours.

Claudia Roden in her excellent, comprehensive Book of Middle Eastern Food has promoted the idea of a collective cuisine. Yet does this notion really make sense? Should one classify Egyptian or Moroccan food as 'Middle Eastern'? Both countries are in Africa and their cuisines are decidedly different. Can one promote the notion of a European cuisine? One just has to consider the potato, a vegetable shared throughout Europe, to see that it is prepared and served in a myriad of different ways throughout the EEC. There is no such thing as a 'European' potato dish. Are stuffed vine leaves a typical Middle Eastern dish? In a sense yes – they are used through-out the Near and Middle East. Yet do they not deserve more differentiation than the fact that they are stuffed? What about the sweet and sour Persian stuffed vine leaves? These are a completely different gastronomic experience from Lebanese ones, vegetarian or non-vegetarian, which have no hint of sweetness to them and these in turn are different from the fat and rather hard Greek or Turkish ones where the stuffing is cooked before it is used.

Challenging the concept of a collective Middle Eastern cuisine leads to the question of whether there is a case for a book on

Lebanese cuisine alone. Is our cuisine sufficiently different from others in the Middle East to warrant a sole volume? What are the influences behind it and have these been assimilated enough to create a distinctive cuisine? Are the principal influences Turkish or Ottoman, as is generally assumed? Or, on the contrary, did the Ottomans take from our cuisine, as well as from others', to develop a way of cooking that they then spread throughout their empire? Unfortunately there is not enough research into the subject for me to provide a complete or convincing answer. All I can do is draw on my personal experience of the food of these countries; Lebanon and Syria, where I grew up, and Egypt, Greece, Turkey, Iran and the Gulf countries which I have visited. This has led me to conclude that, although some dishes are quite similar, there are quite enough overall differences to justify an in-depth exploration of the Lebanese gastronomic experience.

It might be difficult to dissociate our food from that of Syria, Jordan and Palestine but our cuisine is quite distinctive from theirs. There is one main geographical difference between the Lebanon and its neighbours in that there is no desert land and therefore no nomadic Bedouin population with its culinary tradition. It is obvious that any local cuisine is determined by what is fresh and good in the local and nearby markets. Due to the much larger Christian population (until recently the majority) and their Lenten restrictions, as well as the abundance of agricultural produce and shortage of meat in the mountains, we have a wider variety of vegetarian dishes. We also eat an exceptional amount of raw vegetables, either 'au naturel' or in salads or in pickles with a choice of these always present at our table. Unlike our neighbours we use fat sparingly as Freya Stark writes in a letter to her father, describing a meal with the Syrian family she stayed with after leaving the Lebanon:

> "Damascus, 19.3.28.
> It is not all joy living with a native family. Meals, for instance, are a trial: I am given a fork, but otherwise one dips one's bread in the dish, and eats the most deadly food swimming in every variety of fat."
> Freya Stark, *Letters from Syria*, 1942

Some dishes are particularly Lebanese such as *tabbooleh, kibbeh nayeh* and *bil-saniyeh* as well as *burghul bi-d'feeneh, m'jaddarah* and *hindbeh bil-zeyt*; but many more are shared. The Lebanese version

10

of those shared dishes often looks and tastes different from that of its neighboring countries. A great deal of artistry goes into garnishing dishes and laying out a Lebanese *mezze* table and much attention is paid to achieving a fine balance between ingredients in each dish so that the different tastes offset each other delicately. All this contributes to creating a very distinctive culinary tradition that has earned its entry in the Larousse Gastronomique as a thing unto itself. Now let me prove it.

Throughout the text the transliteration has been made to reproduce the Lebanese pronunciation of Arabic words. The symbol ^ should be read as a slight hiccup and replaces the letter q which is not enunciated in the colloquial language. The letters kh should be read as the Scottish ch in "loch", dh as th in "though" and gh as the French r. The symbol ᶜ is for an Arabic letter that has no Western equivalent. It is pronounced from the bottom of the throat and it is very difficult to pronounce for non-Arabic speakers.

The Lebanese Larder
Beyt Al-Moonah Al-Lubnaniyah

"Now his majesty found the entire land of Djani (Lebanese coast) with their orchards filled with fruit. Their wines were found lying in their vats, as water flows, and their grains on their threshing floors. They were more plentiful than the sand of the shore. The army overflowed with their possession."

Inscribed on the walls of the temple of Karnak of one of Thutmose III's campaigns in Lebanon and Syria.

 In contrast to other Arab countries where people go to market to buy most of their food, the Lebanese go to the corner shop for their essential ingredients, a tradition left over from the French protectorate. In dark and over cluttered stores, filled with imported cans of all types, one buys freshly ground Turkish coffee, pine nuts, tahini (sesame cream), and numerous spices from nutmeg to fabulously long cinnamon sticks. Not all ingredients are obtained from these corner shops though; many households have relatives in the country-side who supply them with produce from their lands. As a child in Beirut I remember the arrival of fat canvas bags filled with various grains, large tin cans of extra virgin olive oil and straw baskets brimming with dates. Our supply system was particularly exciting as my father was Syrian and my mother Lebanese, which meant that we got a variety of wonderful produce from both countries. My mother's uncle from a nearby village provided us with our yearly supply of olive oil, kishk, za‘tar (thyme mixture) and tomato paste, while our relatives in Syria sent us our sesame seeds, sumac, bulgur burghul – cracked wheat, shankleesh (fermented cheese), dried figs and many other delicacies. Apart from the seasonal supply we always had luscious surprises when relatives came to visit. It is very much part of the Lebanese tradition to always arrive at somebody's home with some offering, usually food; either some home-made confection or a bowl of figs, prickly pears or other delicious seasonal fruit in perfect condition, more often than not picked straight from the tree or bush.

Although you cannot expect to match this sort of supply system outside the Lebanon, most western cities have shops, usually Greek, Turkish, Cypriot, Iranian or Lebanese, where one can find many of the ingredients necessary for Lebanese cooking.

If you are going to make Lebanese dishes on a regular basis there are key ingredients that you should always have at hand. Tahini, bulgur, dried legumes and white short grain rice are used frequently and you need to have these in the store cupboard, whereas the necessary seasonings are cinnamon sticks and powder, ground allspice and finely ground black or white pepper or a mixture of the two. Another key ingredient is Arabic bread, which is served at every meal and keeps very well in the freezer.

Fresh ingredients to keep in your refrigerator are lemons, spring onions (scallions), parsley and mint. Most herbs will keep for a week or more in the bottom drawer in the refrigerator if they are properly packed. Pack them loosely in plastic bags, seal these and put on top of other vegetables so that the herbs don't get crushed. It is a good idea to turn the bag over every two or three days to shift the condensation inside and let it drop back to the other side. Store spring onions in the same way as herbs.

ALLSPICE
B'har Helo

In Arabic *b'har* means pepper and *helo* sweet. Allspice is called sweet pepper because of its subtle combined flavor that hints of clove, cinnamon and nutmeg. Its aroma is essential in almost all the basic recipes.

ANISE (SEEDS AND POWDER)
Yansoon

Anise seeds are used whole or ground to make infusions or to flavor puddings.

BLACK AND WHITE PEPPER
B'har Harr

B'har Harr literally means hot pepper, but usually refers to finely

13

ground black or white pepper or a mixture of the two, which produces a grey powder.

BOIS DE PANAMA
Shirsh al-Halaweh

The inner bark and surface roots of a perennial South American tree called *Quillaja saponaria* Molina, commonly known as soap bark, quillay bark, China bark, Murillo bark, Seifenholz, saponaria. It is used for its foaming qualities and "bittersweet aromatic flavor"[1] to make *natef* (see p. 211). The bark is also used as a soap to wash carpets in late spring before they are put away for the summer.

BREADS
Al-Khobz

Bread is the staple of Lebanese meals; it is served with every dish as a matter of course with pita bread being the most commonly served. Many of the famous dips and sauces such as *hommus* and *baba ghannooge* are essentially bread dips, although they are just as delicious eaten with raw vegetables if you are on a bread-free diet. The breads listed below freeze very well and I always keep a few packets in the freezer, ready to be taken out when I serve a Lebanese meal. They are all made with the same dough but shaped, flavored or baked differently. They have always been available in Middle Eastern shops and lately have become regulars on supermarket shelves as well.

PITA BREAD
Khobz Arabi

Pita bread is a two-layered flat bread. When the dough is baked it rises like a balloon causing the dough to cook in two thin layers. The bread collapses as soon as you take it out of the oven and, provided you let it cool before piling up the loaves, the layers will easily come apart when you want to open the bread. It is the most commonly

[1] From Esteban Pombo Villar letter to A.E. Davidson about bois de panama revealing the reference to it in "Fenaroli's Handbook of Flavor Ingredients", T.E. Furia and N. Bellanca, eds., CRC Press, Cleveland, 1971, p. 208.

eaten bread in the Lebanon where many people eat with their hands using torn pieces of bread to scoop up their food, as well as wipe their mouth with (the latter is a rather startling custom that is still prevalent among mountain folk).

In the Lebanon pita bread comes in three sizes: a large disc, about 12 inches in diameter for home use; a medium one, about half the size, used for commercial sandwiches; and a third, slightly smaller loaf, that is baked and served in restaurants, always piping hot with a cloud of steam escaping as soon as you tear it open.

HANDKERCHIEF BREAD
Marqooq

This is my favorite of all three breads. I call it handkerchief bread because it is paper thin and unfolds like one, except that it is round. I love to hold it by the middle as with a large handkerchief and arrange a few on a bread tray as if they were soft pyramids. In the U.S. it is commonly called mountain bread.

The making of marqooq is a mountain speciality that requires a special skill which was passed from mother to daughter until modern times reached our mountains and the industrial baking of marqooq became possible. Here is a wonderful description of making it from Freya Stark's Letters from Syria, 1942.

"Brumana 6.1.28

I have just got warm by going downstairs to see our neighbor make the flat sheets of bread I like so much. She sits on the floor with a round flattish cushion on one knee and smooths the balls of dough out on a board with her palms and fingers till they are about the size of a plate. Then she throws them with a very neat quick movement first over one forearm, then over the other. Her arms are very brown, tattooed and with twisted gold bracelets. The round of dough grows and grows miraculously till it is about two-and-a-half feet across and almost transparent. She then tosses it on to her cushion, arranges the edges so as to make it as nearly round as possible, and throws it all in one movement, so as not to crease it, on to a little metal dome which is on the floor and has a few sticks and pine needles burning underneath it. In one minute the whole thing is cooked, and if the fire is well distributed, is nice and crisp all over, and very good. And it has the advantage of being good to eat for a week."

SESAME BREAD
Ka‘k bil-Semsum

Ka‘k bil-Semsum is a thick, small pita bread that is dipped in sesame seeds on both sides before baking. It is either shaped as a small round pita bread or made into a small handbag-like loaf with a thin round handle and a flattish round body. We eat it as a savoury snack with a sprinkling of za‘tar (see p. 32) on the inside. It was, and still is, one of the many foods peddled by hawkers along the corniche in Beirut that used to appeal to us when we were children. Ka‘k is also used to make a sweet breakfast sandwich with the bag end of the loaf cut open and filled with k'nafeh (see p. 228). We bought and ate these sandwiches at sweet shops or sometimes we took the breads together with a tray of k'nafeh home and made the sandwiches ourselves to offer visiting relatives.

BULGUR
Burghul

Bulgur is made from wheat that has been boiled, dried and then ground. It is a staple ingredient of Lebanese food, used sparingly in dishes such as tabbooleh (parsley salad) and kibbeh bil-saniyeh (a baked dish consisting of two thin layers of a meat paste made with cracked wheat and minced lamb in between which is a meat, onion and pine nut filling) or as a main element in mountain dishes such as bulgur bi d'feeneh or bil-banadoorah (cracked wheat with chick peas and meat or in tomato sauce). There are three grades: coarse (kheshin), fine (na‘em) and very fine (f'reyfeerah). These are pre-pared from either brown wheat (ˆameh baladi – local) or white wheat (ˆameh gharbi – western). The former produces bulgur asmar – brown and the latter bulgur abyad – white.

My mother can still remember the making of bulgur in her native village where she spent her summer holidays. Once their newly harvested wheat was delivered to their homes, the women would spend hours picking it clean of little stones and wild grasses. After they sorted the wheat, they washed it, half boiled it in water, drained it and spread it on cotton sheets on the flat roof tops to dry in the sun. They left it there for several days – going back regularly to turn it over – until it was completely dry. Then the men took the dried wheat to special stone mills where they only ground bulgur. The

16

finished product was brought back home and sifted to produce the three different grades. The sifted bulgur was put in canvas bags and labelled according to the grades to last them for the year. In the poorer or more remote houses they did not use communal mills. They boiled, dried and stored their wheat whole and only ground it on the day it was to be cooked. This was done by hand on a millstone and the resulting bulgur was all the same coarse grade.

With modern technology the 'artisanal' way of preparing cracked wheat has mostly vanished. The wheat is now industrially processed. After it is parboiled, it is kiln-dried then passed through two different grade mills to achieve fine and coarse grains. As for the very fine bulgur (*f'reyfeerah*) it is still found in the few homes where they prepare their own and is generally used to make nutritious and tasty vegetarian balls that are stuffed with onions, chick peas and parsley and then fried in olive oil. These are eaten for Lent. Because of the ready availability of commercially produced bulgur, I buy 2 to 5 pounds at a time and store it, away from the light, in a glass jar with a cork top.

CAROB MOLASSES
Dibess Kharroob

A thick dark syrup extracted from carob pods. The long pods are picked when dark and ripe and taken to a special press to extract their juice. *Dibess kharroob* is served with pita bread as a sweet dip and is eaten alone or mixed with tahini. The ripe pods can also be chewed on as a sweet snack, a favorite amongst Lebanese children. In the U.S., this type of molasses is available only in Middle Eastern shops.

CHEESE and DAIRY PRODUCTS
Al-Ajban Wa Al-Alban

BUTTERMILK
Ayran

Real *ayran* is a slightly sour drink which is the liquid left over from when yogurt is churned to produce butter. A much faster version, although not as tasty, is to dilute enough water into yogurt to produce a thin creamy drink which you then salt to taste.

CHEESES
Al-Ajban

Most Lebanese cheeses are made from ewe's or goat's milk. In the spring a fresh goat's cheese (*jibneh khadrah*) is made in the mountains and brought down to be sold in the cities for immediate consumption. Another fresh cheese is a type of curd cheese (^*areesh*) which is made from yogurt and lemon juice. The yogurt is boiled with a little lemon juice until it separates, after which it is taken off the heat and strained. The curdled yogurt is then left to cool before being gathered in a cheesecloth and hung over a sink or bowl to drain overnight. It is then transferred into a covered container and put in the refrigerator where it will keep for a couple of days unsalted, or longer when it is salted. Some people prepare it without lemon juice.

From this curd cheese we make a round fermented cheese called *shankleesh*. The curd cheese is seasoned with salt and a little cayenne pepper then rolled into balls, each the size of a small orange. The balls are spread on a cotton cloth laid over a straw mat and left to dry for five or six days, after which they are put in airtight glass jars and left to ferment for up to a week. After the cheese is moldy all over, the mold is rinsed off under cold water and the balls rolled in plain dried thyme. They are then packed in clean glass jars and are ready to eat within a week; the longer they are kept the softer and stronger in taste they become.

The medium fresh cheeses are two types of feta, a Bulgarian one (*bolghari*) or one made in Tripoli (*jibneh trabolsiyeh*). Both are white, crumbly, salty cheeses. *Halloom* is another salty, but harder, white cheese with an elastic, chewy texture and it is sometimes flavored with black cumin seeds called *habbet el-barakeh* (the grain of grace) in Arabic. It comes in individual squares with rounded corners or shaped in long thick tresses (*jibneh majdooleh*), the latter having a looser, more filamented texture. Both feta and *halloom* need to be soaked in fresh water before eating or cooking to get rid of some of the salty taste. *Akkawi* is a softer, slightly less salted variation of *halloom* that is also used in sweet preparations.

The most popular non-white hard cheese we eat is an imported matured ewe's cheese we call *kashkawan*, which can be either the Romanian *kashkaval*, the Greek *Kasseri* or the Turkish *Kaser*.

LEBBA
Lebbah

Lebbah is the first milk after the cow has given birth which is like very thick cream. It is eaten with a sprinkling of sugar or honey and is utterly delicious. This delicacy is hard to find in the U.S.

YOGURT
Laban

Yogurt is very important in our cuisine both as a refreshing food accompaniment and as a cooking sauce. Many Lebanese people still make their yogurt at home. My mother boils the milk in a plain, stainless steel pan, leaves it to cool to a temperature where she can hardly bear to dip her finger in and counts to ten. She then whisks a little yogurt (3 tablespoons of yogurt for 4½ cups milk) she had kept from the previous batch until it is creamy and stirs it into the milk. She covers the pan, wraps it up in a towel and leaves it for 3 to 4 hours, forbidding anyone to touch it. After that time she very gently unwraps and uncovers the pan without disturbing the yogurt and leaves it to cool completely, for another two to three hours. She then puts it in the refrigerator for another couple of hours before using it. My favorite of commercial yogurts is the organic one that has a yellow creamy skin like that of our home-made one.

From yogurt we make what seems to be a cream cheese but is not, *labneh*. The yogurt is strained in a cheesecloth to varying degrees, ranging from a soft creamy texture to one that is almost like curd cheese. The creamier type is eaten mixed with olive oil as a sandwich spread or dip whilst the dryer one is used as a stuffing in savoury pastries or to make *kabees labneh*.

CHICK PEAS
Hommus

An ancient staple that is much used in our cuisine. You can use either dried or tinned chick peas. The dried ones should be soaked overnight before being cooked for 1-2 hours depending on what you are using them for. You can reduce the cooking time by using a pressure cooker (follow the manufacturer's instructions for best results). Many people find canned chick peas a practical alternative, but I still insist on using the dried ones as I do not like the taste or texture of canned food.

There is a short moment in early summer when chick peas are available fresh in London. Green bunches laden with the peas still in the pod are sold by street hawkers, usually to children who spend hours squeezing each pod open to extract and eat the green chick pea. A very healthy snack.

CINNAMON (STICKS, POWDER)
^Erfeh

There are two types of cinnamon trees, both from the same *lauracea* family that produce two different types of sticks. The thin sheets of the inner part of the bark of *Cinnamomum zeylanicum* are dried and rolled in thin quills to produce real cinnamon. These are sold in the West all cut to the same short length, whereas in the Lebanon they are left uncut and can be found as long as 12 inches. The thick, dark bark of *Cinnamomum cassia* is known as cassia. The latter is the most often used because of its stronger taste and is a required addition to most soups, stocks and stews. The average length of sticks mentioned in the recipes is about 2 inches, although a little more will only make the dish more tasty. You should also have a stock of ground cinnamon, but this does not keep as well as the sticks, so buy the powder in small quantities and restock as and when you need to.

CLARIFIED BUTTER
Samneh

Samneh is made from butter that has been boiled until the fat in the pan is as transparent as a tear (*dam^at el-eyn*). It is then taken off the heat and left to settle before being carefully strained through a fine sieve into sealed containers, where it will keep for a year or more. There is a home-made version which is produced from the skin of boiled milk. The boiled milk is left to rest overnight before the skin is skimmed and cooked in a frying pan until it separates. It is used up very quickly, and, when lightly salted, makes a delicious sandwich spread.

COLOCASIA (TARO)
Qelqass

Colocasia was the potato of the Romans. It is a large brown root vegetable which we fry or boil. It is commonly available from Turkish and Greek shops as well as health food and Middle Eastern groceries.

COUSCOUS
Moghrabbiyeh

Lebanese couscous is quite different from its North African counterpart. The grains made from flour and salted water are the size of small beads, about ¼ inch in diameter. "A bowl of flour is sprinkled intermittently with salted water as the fingers of the right hand rake through it in sweeping, circular movements, causing balls of dough to coagulate. The granules are also rubbed between the palms or against the side of the bowl to shape them, and when complete they are dried."[2] Unlike the many variations of North African couscous, ours is always cooked with chicken and lamb (or either on their own) with only baby onions as the vegetable garnish.

DESERT TRUFFLE
Kamah

A truffle found in the sand which is relatively smooth-skinned. It has no particular aroma (unlike its western counterpart), and a nutty flavour. It is washed very carefully, then peeled, and depending on its size either kept whole or cut into medium-sized cubes and marinated before being grilled; or boiled and then dressed in olive oil and lemon; or made into a stew with meat.

DRIED FIGS
Teen M'yabass

Figs are plentiful in the Lebanon and in pre-1976 Beirut they were brought down, freshly picked, from the mountains and peddled from house to house with the hawkers shouting *yalla a teen men el-jabal* (here are figs from the mountain). As the season nears its end, the last crop is picked and prepared for drying. Each fig is pressed flat, which often causes it to open slightly, and put on straw mats. These

[2] Charles Perry, *Couscous and its Cousins*, Oxford Food Symposium, 1989

21

are laid on flat roofs or in unused fields, protected from the dust, and left to dry in the sun for several days. Once they are completely dry, they are stacked in tin boxes and stored away for later use. Sometimes they are dipped in boiling water flavored with anise seeds to ward off insects, then dried again before being stored. They can also be chopped up and made into a solid jam that is eaten with bread or off the spoon 'to sweeten the mouth' (*tay halli el-temm*) as we put it.

DRIED VEGETABLES
Khodar M'yabasseh or Mo^addadeh

Most dried vegetables are prepared at home and rarely found commercially, at least not outside the Lebanon. I have found dried okra abroad, strung onto cotton threads like necklaces – a rather attractive decoration for the kitchen. The vegetables are trimmed as if they were to be cooked – in the case of eggplants they are also cored – and then spread on cotton sheets and left to dry, green vegetables in the shade to keep their color, and all the others in the sun. Before cooking they are soaked in hot water until they swell back to their original size.

GARLIC
Toom

Garlic is a much used ingredient in our food. We usually crush it in a wooden mortar and pestle reserved for that purpose. The quickest and easiest way to pound a large amount of garlic by hand is to chop it coarsely before putting it in the mortar adding a little salt to absorb the juices during pounding.

GRAPE MOLASSES
Dibess ʿEnab

"All through the summer fruit is plentiful and cheap. I have never eaten such huge and delicious plums as in the Lebanon, and there are besides, fresh figs (white and black), fresh bananas, apples, pears, peaches and the best grapes in the world. Mountain honey, if you can get it, is delicious; so is the grape dibis, or syrup, a honey-like, healthful addition to bread, whether the unleavened Arab loaf or the usually procurable French roll."

E.S. Stevens, *Cedars, Saints and Sinners in Syria*, 1926

This *dibess* is made from cooked grape juice and has a lovely golden brown color. It is eaten in the same way as *dibess kharroob*, the carob molasses but without tahini. Available only from Middle Eastern shops.

M'LOOKHIYEH
M'lookhiyeh

M'lookhiyeh is a plant native to Egypt and India. The leaves are quite large and have strange little whiskers (like those of a catfish) where they join the stalk. They can be used fresh or dried or frozen to make a very distinctive green sauce for chicken or meat. Although fresh *m'lookhiyeh* is not commonly available, and when available, it takes a long time to prepare, I prefer to use it as it is far superior in taste and texture. This vegetable is rarely found in the U.S. It is available in dried form in Middle Eastern groceries.

To prepare fresh m'lookhiyeh leaves
You should allow 2-3 hours to prepare and chop the quantity of fresh *m'lookhiyeh* given in the recipe on p. 161. Pick the *m'lookhiyeh* leaves clean off their stalks, making sure you do not leave any bit of stalk on them. Wash and dry them in a salad dryer, then spread them onto clean paper towels and leave to dry completely. The best way to chop the leaves into very fine slivers is to do it in small batches. Pick up a handful of *m'lookhiyeh* leaves and hold them down onto the chopping board. Cup your hand around the leaves and press your fingers firmly on the tip of the bunch. Use a razor-sharp knife to slice the bunched leaves, as if you were shaving them, into 1/12- or 1/10-inch strips (see chopping of parsley in *tabbooleh*, p. 71). When you finish chopping the leaves, put them in a bowl, cover with a clean kitchen towel and set aside until the broth is ready. You can also use the leaves whole and drop them unchopped in the stock as they do in the south, a good time-saving alternative and an equally delicious variation.

KISHK
Kishk

Kishk looks like a pale ivory flour and is made from bulgur, mixed with yogurt which is naturally fermented and then dried. It is prepared in the autumn as a winter provision and provides the basis for a hearty breakfast or Lenten soup. In my family, where *kishk* is made by hand at home, we use one portion of bulgur to eight of salted yogurt. The bulgur is put into a wide crock and covered with two parts yogurt. It is left to soak for 24 hours, during which time the rest of the yogurt is salted and put in a cloth bag to drain its excess water. The next day the strained yogurt is divided into three parts, one of which is mixed into the bulgur/yogurt mixture and the other two added on successive days. After all the yogurt is included, the mixture is left for a week to ferment until it becomes quite sour. It is then spread, in small lumps, on clean cloths laid over straw mats and put out to dry in the sun. The dried lumps are then rubbed between the palms of the hand until they separate into a coarse powder. The powder is filtered through a coarse sifter and put away in canvas bags. The bigger pieces left in the sifter are mixed with ´awarma, and sometimes *labneh*, and used as a filling for savoury pastries.

Kishk is now made commercially and ground by machine. The result is very fine and of a uniform ivory color, whereas the home-made kind is speckled with lovely golden flecks of ground bulgur. There are several brands of *kishk*, some better than others, although none has the texture of home-made. Available in Middle Eastern groceries.

LUPINE SEEDS
Tormus

This is another ancient legume that was part of the Mediterranean diet as far back as the third century before Christ. *Tormus* has to be soaked for a long time before it becomes edible. The dried seeds are soaked in plenty of fresh water for 24 hours before they are blanched for 5 minutes. They are then drained, rinsed and put to soak again in cold water for 4-5 days. During that time the water is changed about 3-4 times a day. *Tormus* is then drained and chilled before being served salted as a snack or part of a *mezze*. The soaked lupine seeds are round, flat and yellow with a thick opaque skin that you remove before eating the seed.

MAHLAB
Mahlab

Mahlab is the kernel of a black cherry. The grains are small and pear-shaped with a light brown husk and a pale soft core. They are sold whole or ground and are used to add an interesting piquant taste to Lebanese biscuits.

MASTIC
Miskeh

A resin collected from the *Pistacia lentiscus* tree native to Greece, Turkey and other eastern Mediterranean countries. *Miskeh* is used in minute amounts to give an exotic taste to some puddings and ice-creams. It can make the most horrible cracking noises when chewed on its own or with a little wax.

'MOON OF THE RELIGION'
^Amar el-Deen

A sticky sheet of candy made with a sweetened dried apricot purée. This is a Syrian speciality but is used to flavor ice-creams and is the equivalent of a western lollipop for Arab children.

OLIVES
Zeytoon

Olives are probably one of the earliest exports of our ancestors, the Phoenician traders. They are as much of a staple as bread and most Lebanese eat them for breakfast with *labneh*, also to finish off their main meals in the same way the French finish theirs with cheese. It is rare to go into a Lebanese kitchen that does not have a bowl of olives ready to be put on the table for breakfast, lunch and dinner. It is worth buying fresh green or black olives to preserve in your own kitchen as the difference in taste between home-preserved olives and commercial ones is really startling. The most famous olive groves are in Hasbayah, Deir Meymas and Marjaʿyoon in the South of the Lebanon and in the Shoof province, south east of Beirut.

To prepare and preserve green olives (zeytoon akhdar)
There are three different ways of preparing the olives before preserving them. You can crush each olive with a clean stone or pestle to burst the flesh open without breaking the hard stone; or slit each lengthways with a sharp knife; or keep them whole. Whichever way you prepare them, the preserving method is the same although the taste will be quite different.

Put the prepared olives in a bowl, cover with water and leave to soak for two days, changing the water twice a day. Drain the olives then cut a few lemons in thin wedges and wash a few fresh chili peppers (the chili and lemon to taste). Take large sterilised glass jars and spread a thick layer of olives over the bottom, arrange a few lemon wedges on top and continue making similar layers, interspersing each two or three with one or two chilies until you have filled the jar. Cover the olives with water in which you will have diluted a large amount of salt. To check the high salt content, put a whole uncooked egg in its shell in the water; if it floats, the solution is salty enough for the olives not to rot. A method that is called in Arabic *fowshet el-baydah* 'floating of the egg.' The uncut olives will take longest to ripen, about six months, the slit ones will become edible after two months and the crushed ones after three weeks.

To prepare and preserve black olives (zeytoon aswad)
Black olives are preserved in olive oil. Wash them in several changes of water until clean, put them in a large crock and sprinkle liberally with sea salt. Turn them over twice a day for about four days, so that they absorb the salt uniformly, then cover them with extra virgin olive oil, add a little wine vinegar (or not according to taste) and turn over for two more days. Pack in sterilised glass jars and, depending on how ripe they are to start with, eat immediately or after one or two weeks.

Both black and green olives should last for a year at least.

OLIVE OIL
Zeyt Zeytoon

Olive oil is made throughout the Lebanon and consumed in large quantities. Many people buy their yearly supply directly from trusted producers who are either relatives or friends. In my family of seven, my mother bought about 75 quarts each season. The green olives are hand picked and carefully selected to produce three different types of extra virgin oil: the best, known as *khadeer* (green), is extracted from totally unblemished olives, the second best, called *bab awal* (first door), is the pressing from those with slight blemishes, whilst the third, known as *bab thani* (second door), is the oil extracted from the rest of the crop. The olives that have already fallen off the tree are collected and pressed to produce oil for soap.

Although Lebanese extra virgin olive oil is excellent, I would be loath to rely on commercially marketed Lebanese oils as rules and regulations are not always strictly implemented as they are in the West. In the recipes I always specify extra virgin olive oil as it is the purest, but that is not to say you need to use very expensive kinds. Any supermarket brand, some being better than others, will do for both cooked dishes and salad dressings unless you are an *afficionado* and insist on buying a specific area's produce.

ORANGE BLOSSOM WATER
Ma' el-Zahr

A fragrant water distilled from macerated blossom flowers of the Seville orange (*bou-sfayr*). The water has a slightly bitter taste and is used sparingly in puddings. We use it regularly to prepare a delicate, aromatic substitute for real coffee which we serve after meals. We call it white coffee (*qahwah baydah*) and make it by adding a teaspoon of *ma' el-zahr* to a small coffee cupful of boiling water. Orange blossom water is also given in very small quantities, as a reviver to people who have a fainting attack.

PICKLES
Kabees

Lebanese people usually prepare their own pickles from a large variety of raw vegetables. An unusual feature of these pickles is that some are stuffed before preserving, such as eggplant. I have devoted a whole chapter on the making of these, see pp. 197-207.

PINE NUTS
S'noobar

Pine nuts are a produce of several different species of pine trees. The hard kernels containing the nuts are found inside the scales of the cone. When the cone is dry enough for the scales to open up fully, the kernels are shaken out and the hard shell cracked open to reveal a brown skinned nut. During our summer holidays in the mountains, we loved going to the woods to look for pine cones. After we gathered enough cones, we sat by a flat stone and with another small stone, we started cracking the hard kernels open. The secret was how to scale the strength of the hit so that we broke the shell without crushing the nut, a feat we occasionally achieved. They can also be eaten green. The fresh, ripe cone is cut with a knife in wedges and the soft, fleshy pine kernels are taken out, dipped in salt and eaten whole.

The Mediterranean pine nuts from *Pinus pinea*, which are the finest, are a long thin oval shape, whereas the rounder, shorter and less tasty ones are the produce of pine trees from North America *P. edulis*, *P. monophylla* and *P. cembroides* or from Korea or China *P. koraiensis*. The latter are more widely available and less expensive to buy. Pine nuts are very often used in our cuisine either raw or sautéed in butter or *samneh*. They have a tendency to burn very quickly after they have reached the desired golden brown color so make sure you remove them from the fat as soon as they are ready.

POMEGRANATE SYRUP
Rebb el-Rumman

A syrup made by boiling the juice of sour pomegranates until it is reduced to a thick dark brown liquid. Although widely used in the Near East, especially in Iran, it is relatively little known in western countries. It is worth experimenting with as it adds a subtle sweet and sour flavor to fried vegetables, sauces and stuffings.

PRESERVED MINCED MEAT
ʾAwarma

ʾAwarma is the Lebanese lamb equivalent of American corned beef. It was, until recently, the main winter meat reserve of mountain dwellers. Most families kept a fat-tail sheep that they force fed and fattened on vine and mulberry leaves during the summer to provide them with their ʾawarma for the winter. When the time came, the sheep was slaughtered, skinned and butchered. The fat was separated from the meat and both were chopped coarsely. The meat was salted, then two thirds fat were measured to one third meat. The fat was cooked in a large pan (*dist*) over a slow heat. It was stirred until melted, then left to boil until golden. The salted meat was added and cooked for about 10-15 minutes. The hot ʾawarma was then poured into tall earthenware jars and left to cool before being covered with a cloth, on top of which went a weighted lid. The jars were stored away in cool places.

In typical Lebanese fashion every bit of the rest of the lamb is used up. The men got busy preparing a *mezze* spread with the offal and the best part of the meat, which they saved for *kibbeh nayeh* (raw kibbé). The liver was served raw cut in small pieces, whilst the lungs, heart, kidneys and testicles were cut in chunks and either sautéed or barbecued. The spleen (*t'hal*) was stuffed with fresh coriander and crushed garlic and stewed in lemon juice then served cold, cut in slices. While the men were nibbling leisurely on their *mezze*, the women were hard at work scrubbing the intestines and stomach clean to stuff them with a mixture of rice, onion, chopped tomatoes, chick peas and minced meat. They cooked the *ghammeh* together with the head and feet for a meal the next day. This may sound rather off-putting but I can assure you that the various *mezzes* and the *ghammeh* were scrumptious and each dish was considered a great delicacy.

The bones were boiled with wheat in huge pans to make *h'reesseh* (see p. 165), an alms dish which was taken to the churchyard and distributed to the poor. Sometimes the whole cooking process of *h'reesseh* took place in the churchyard and the poor came to eat it there or take the food back home to their families.

Finally the sheep's skin was washed and treated to be used as a rug.

PRESERVED VINE LEAVES
Warak Enab Makboos

You can buy preserved vine leaves all year round from Middle Eastern or Greek groceries and from some supermarkets. There are two ways of preserving vine leaves, the first and best is a dry method, where the leaves are packed in liberally salted layers, in airtight jars. The other is with brine, where the leaves are layered in the jar then covered with salted water. To ensure that the water is salty enough use the floating egg trick described in the entry on olives (see p. 26). Whichever method you use, make sure you pick good tender leaves – from your own grapevine, if you are lucky enough to have one growing in your garden, or buy them when in season from specialty stores.

ROASTED GREEN WHEAT
Freekeh

Freekeh is a grain which is cooked like bulgur or rice. It is probably the least known Arab staple in the West and one of the most delectable, with its distinctive smoky taste. The green wheat stalks are harvested and gathered in bunches then roasted in the fields over an open wood or charcoal fire. When the roasted wheat is cool, it is shelled and either kept whole or cracked and then stored in canvas bags. My favorite type of *freekeh* is brownish green in color and very coarsely cracked. Available in Middle Eastern groceries.

ROSE PETAL JAM
Mrabbah al-Ward

A jam made with rose petals from which the lovely red, candied strips are taken to garnish creamy sweets.

ROSE WATER
Ma' el-Ward

Another fragrant water distilled from the petals of a local rose called *ward al-joori* in Arabic. Rose water is used more liberally than orange blossom water and both are often combined in the same sweet preparations.

SALEP
Sahlab

A fine powder extracted from a variety of dried orchid tubers which is used as a thickening agent in milk or nut ice-creams. Two different types are available in the Lebanon: a light gray powder labelled as Turkish, which is the one I prefer to use, and a white powder described as American, which is more difficult to dilute. *Sahlab* is also boiled with milk to make a thin sweet porridge which is served in soup plates and eaten together with French croissants or sesame biscuits. A similar drink seems to have been common in France in the seventeenth century.

SAUSAGES
Maqaneq wa suju^

We eat two types of sausages in the Lebanon. *Maqaneq* are thin, round sausages that are encased in lamb's intestines. They come in two different sizes, small or medium, and are made with minced lamb or beef which is seasoned with garlic and mixed spices. Some have pine nuts added to them. *Suju^* is a larger, flat sausage made only with beef. It is seasoned differently with a lot more garlic added to it and no pine nuts.

SEMOLINA
Smeet

Normal semolina (*smeet*) is used to make spongy cakes or fillings, whereas fine semolina (*firkha*) is used instead of flour to make Arabic biscuits. This gives them a lighter and crumblier texture.

SESAME SEEDS (RAW, ROASTED)
Semsum

The seeds of *Sesamum indicum* or *S. orientale* which are widely grown in hot countries. These are used to flavor breads, biscuits, *za'tar* and sometimes *falafels*. They are also prepared with sugar syrup to make a chewy sticky sweet called *simsmiyeh*.

TAHINI (SESAME SEED PASTE)
Tahineh

"Sesame is also widely cultivated in Syria, where, in preparing the oil, the grain is soaked in water for 24 hours, and then placed in an oblong pot, coated with cement, on which two men work with a hammer of 20-lb weight. Efforts are not made to mash the kernels. The skins are separated in a tub of water, salted to a degree sufficient to float an egg. The bran sinks, while the kernels remain on the surface. The sesame seeds are now broiled in an oven, and sent to the mill to be ground. From the millstone the oil drops into a jar, and is thick, of a dark yellow color, and sweet. It is used extensively by the poorer classes in place of cheese, syrup, honey, etc., and is popular on account of its saccharin properties.

"Confectionery is made by mixing sesame oil with syrup and other elements."

Law's Grocer's Manual, c 1892

You can buy two different types of *tahineh*, one dark and the other light, which personally I prefer. I suggest you buy imported tahini and halvah, as those available in supermarkets or health food stores do not compare with the Lebanese, Turkish or Greek brands. The quality differs from brand to brand. It might be a good idea to try out different small jars before you choose the one you prefer. Tahini separates when left for a long time and you simply need to stir the oil into the paste before using.

SEVEN PEPPER MIXTURE
Sabe^c B'harat Makhlootah

A classic ground spice mixture consisting of black and white pepper, allspice, cinnamon, cloves, nutmeg and coriander. The proportions vary according to regional and family variations. It is commercially available and is used in some savoury dishes, although purists reckon that it is only people who are not accomplished cooks who will buy the ready-made mixture.

SUMAC
*Summa^*

Sumac is made from the dried berries of the *Rhus coriaria* (Tanner's or elm leafed sumach, not to be confused with other poisonous plants of the same family). The purplish brown berries are harvested at the end of the summer and left on the branch to dry in the sun. Once dry, the berries are ground and sifted, to get rid of the stony seeds, to produce a coarse textured powder ranging in color from deep maroon to a brighter red. It has a pleasing lemony taste and is used to season salads, stuffings, fried eggs and grilled fish or meat.

TURMERIC
Kurkum

A yellow spice used to color and flavor the yellow cakes, see p. 239.

THYME MIXTURE
Za^ctar

A savoury mixture of dried thyme powder, sumac and toasted or raw sesame seeds. The proportions are two thirds thyme to one third sumac, to this you add raw or toasted sesame seeds, the type and amount of which varies according to taste, but rarely exceeds the equivalent of one quarter of the quantity of thyme and sumac mixture. The blend is then put in a pan, salted to taste and stirred over a low heat to warm it up; this increases its keeping quality.

VERJUICE
Aseer hosrum

Verjuice is the sour juice of unripe grapes (*hosrum*) which we use to vary on lemon juice in salad dressings and cooked dishes. The fresh juice is also boiled with a little salt and preserved to use throughout the year.

CHECKLIST OF USEFUL INGREDIENTS FOR THE LEBANESE LARDER:

SPICES, FLAVORINGS AND FATS
B'harat, wa Adhan

Anise (seeds and powder)
Cinnamon (sticks and powder)
Ground allspice
Mastic
Olive oil (extra virgin)
Orange blossom water

Pepper (finely ground black and white)
Rose water
Sumac
Tahini
Thyme mixture

GRAIN, LEGUMES AND NUTS
Al-huboob

Almonds
Beans (broad, cannellini and butter)
Bulgur (fine and coarse)
Chick peas
Flour (all-purpose and bread)
Lentils (brown and green)
Pine nuts

Pistachios
Rice (white short grain)
Roasted green wheat
Semolina (regular and fine pastina)
Walnuts

CANS
Al-ʿElab

Chick peas
Italian canned tomatoes (whole and chopped). These are the nearest in taste to the fresh, ripe Mediterranean ones.

FRESH INGREDIENTS
Al-khodar

Garlic
Lemons
Mint (fresh and dried)

Onions (regular and scallions)
Parsley
Coriander

Note about straying from tradition
In most recipes I have substituted butter for *samneh* (clarified butter), as it is lighter. I have also made a point of stressing the importance of thoroughly draining fried foods, which is not a usual practice amongst Lebanese cooks. I personally find that a maximum drainage of fried fats is essential for a healthier and more refined way of eating. It also improves the taste by keeping ingredients well defined. Whenever possible I have given time-saving variations, especially in the desserts section. These variations make for a somewhat less authentic product but are justifiable for most of us who work.

Note for vegetarians
Minced meat can be replaced with vegetarian dried mince substitute. If you use the vegetarian substitute you may need to increase the water quantities in the recipes as it absorbs more liquid.

SPECIAL UTENSILS

EGGPLANT, ZUCCHINI AND SQUASH CORER
Man^ara

A narrow vegetable scoop used to core eggplant, zucchini and squashes (vegetable marrows). It comes in two lengths, a short one for coring small eggplant and zucchini and a long one to hollow out squashes. A narrow apple corer makes an acceptable substitute.

FALAFEL SCOOP
^Aleb falafel

The falafel scoop is used both commercially and at home to shape the falafels and drop them straight into the frying oil. It is a brass implement that looks like a short candlestick without a base and with a round tray on top of which is a flat sheet of brass. The handle is round, about ¾ inch in diameter and the tray about 2¼ inches wide with a narrow straight rim ¼ inch high. The flat sheet is 2 inches wide and sits on a levered column that sinks, about ½ inch, into the handle when you press the lever down.

EASTER PASTRIES MOLDS
Tabe^c

Wooden molds of two basic shapes that are quite deeply carved on the inside and used to form and decorate Easter pastries. The domed one with a slightly pointed top is reserved for the pastries filled with nuts and the other, with a flat top, for those filled with date. The carvings vary slightly depending on where the molds are made but the size is more or less the same, about 2 inches in diameter at the base. They all have a thick handle and a flat rim above the cup where you tap the mold to drop the cake out.

DRINKS *and* FRUITS
Al-Mashroobat, Al-Fawakihah

ARAK
^cAraq

Arak is a clear alcoholic drink made from distilled grape juice and flavored with anise. The grapes used are white, sweet local grapes which are crushed on the stalk and left to macerate for about a week before the juice is strained and distilled in a still. It is then mixed with water and anise from Damascus (20 pounds anise to 100 quarts of distilled juice and 50 quarts water) and distilled again to produce three different batches of varying strength. These are blended together with again half their amount of water and more anise before another distillation, then the process is repeated a third time before a final distillation. The resulting alcohol is about 60 proof strong and left to age in earthenware jars for one to two years. Unlike wine, arak does not improve with age and after four or five years turns yellow and loses much of its taste.

Arak is served in small tumblers. First you pour arak into the bottom third of the glass (or more for hardier types) then you add water, which immediately turns the transparent liquid cloudy white. Then you slowly slide in one or two ice cubes depending on how full the glass is and always serve it with something to nibble on, either a few titbits or a full *mezze*. Arak should be drunk slowly and the glasses replenished as soon as they become empty.

LEBANESE WINES
Al-nabeedh al-lubnani

"When we arrived at the place where the Cedars grew, we saw but twenty four in all, growing after the manner of oak trees, but a great deal taller, straighter and greater and the branches grow so straight and interlocking, as though they were kept by art... Although that, in the days of Solomon, this mountain was overclad with forests of Cedars, yet now there are but only these, and nine miles westward thence, seventeen more... this mountain... is beautified with all the ornaments of nature, as herbages, tillage, pasturage, fructiferous trees, fine fountains, good corn, and absolutely the best wines produced upon the earth."
William Lithgow, *Rare adventures and painful peregrinations*, 1614/32

Wine has been made in the Lebanon since Phoenician times and is known for its excellence. French travellers referred to it as *vin d'or* (wine of gold). The most renowned vineyards are those of Château Musar in the Bekaa valley at an altitude of over 3000 feet. The reds are made from *Cabernet Sauvignon* and *Cinsault* grapes and are full-bodied mature wines. They are aged for two years in Nevers oak after which they are bottled and kept for another three years before being put on the market. The whites are made from *Obaideh* (a native *Chardonnay*) and *Merwah* grapes and are again full-bodied and very fine. They are aged for about six months in oak. The other lesser known wines are Kefraya and Ksara, the latter label being the oldest in production.

SOFT DRINKS
Al-Sharab

"I had never entered Beirut at such an undue hour, and I found myself like this man of the *one thousand and one nights* entering a city of Magi whose people had been turned into stone. All were still profoundly asleep; The guards underneath doorways, the donkey-men who were waiting on the square for their ladies, they too asleep in the high balconies of the bath; the sellers of dates and watermelons by the fountain, the *cafedji* in his shop as well as all his customers, the *hamal* or porter, his head resting on his load, the camel rider by his seated animal, and huge Albanian devils standing guard in front of the pasha's seraglio: everyone slept the sleep of innocence, leaving the city neglected."

Gerard de Nerval, *Voyage en Orient*, 1851

Fresh fruit and vegetable juices are very popular in the Lebanon and you find specialist juice stores and stalls at almost every street corner in downtown Beirut selling a large variety of freshly squeezed juices. The most famous of these was sited by the nineteenth century fountain (*birkeh*) mentioned by Gerard de Nerval above. The fountain stall was an essential detour for shoppers going through the souks of Beirut. There they served not only fresh juices, but also a scrumptious selection of creamy sweets and puddings, as well as an exciting range of fruit concentrates, ranging from mulberry (*sharab el-toot*) to rose water (*sharab el-ward*) to tamarind (*sharab tamer hindi*). All these delicious temptations were perched on the cool edges of the fountain to refresh a continuous flow of consumers. One of my regular orders there was *jellab*, a dark brown drink made from date and grape molasses that was diluted in water and packed with crushed ice, on which floated very white and tender pre-soaked pine nuts as well as pale raisins.

COFFEE
Al-Qahwah

"We found a little side valley for lunch, and made salad and cooked the coffee."

Freya Stark, Letters From Syria, 1942

Drinking coffee is as important to the Lebanese as drinking tea is to the English. It is the first sign of our legendary hospitality and is surrounded by a whole ritual.

We use very finely ground *Adani* (from Aden in the Yemen) or Brazilian coffee beans that are roasted until they become quite dark. The beans are bought, freshly ground, in small amounts and used up very quickly; or they are ground at home every time coffee is made. The coffee grinder is a fixture of every traditional Lebanese home.

It is a tall, cylindrical implement, about 12 inches long and 2 to 2½ inches in diameter, made in brass and decorated with intricate geometric engravings. The grinder part has a domed lid and a removable folding handle and the receptacle part, where the ground coffee falls, slots in and out of the top part.

We cook the coffee in a long-handled conical pot, called *rakweh*, that has a flat, rimmed spout. It varies in size from very small (1-2 cups) to quite large (10-12 cups), depending on the amount of cups needed and is made of brass, enamelware or stainless steel.

Turkish coffee is prepared to three different degrees of sweetness, *murrah* (bitter), *wassat* (medium) or *mazbootah* (correct), meaning the same, and *helweh* (sweet). It is cooked to taste except when there is a funeral or a sad or solemn occasion where only bitter coffee is served. To prepare a medium-sweet coffee measure 1 teaspoon of finely ground coffee and ½ teaspoon sugar for each coffee cup of water. If you want it sweet increase the quantity of sugar to 1 teaspoon.

Put the water in the *rakweh* first, place it over a medium heat and bring to the boil. Stir in the coffee and sugar, reduce the heat to low and wait until the coffee foams up. Take off the heat as soon as it starts rising, wait for the coffee to settle, then put it back over the heat. Remove as soon as the coffee foams up again and repeat, another two or three times, until there is no more foam (some people like their coffee quite foamy and take it off the heat after the first or second foaming).

The cups we serve the coffee in are small and narrow with a handle. They are slightly narrower and taller than the espresso cup. These are put on a tray before the coffee is poured into them and passed round the guests. Mountain people also use round cups with no handle in which they pour very little bitter coffee, this they call *shaffeh* (one sip). The coffee is served very hot.

After the coffee is drunk, more often than not one of the drinkers will ask if anyone present knows how to read the cup (*fee hadan b'yaᶜref yoˆra al-finjan?*). If so, the finished cups of coffee are turned over onto the saucer for the dregs to trickle down the sides. The resulting pattern is interpreted according to the images made by the black liquid against the white porcelain; for instance, two long uninterrupted trickles of coffee with a clean line between them mean you have an open road ahead of you (*ᶜendek tareeˆmaftoohah*). If the white line is interrupted by coffee trickles, then your road is marred by obstacles and if the cup is heavily covered with coffee, your heart is black (^albek aswad). Before the reading is over, the person whose cup it is, is asked to stamp the bottom of the cup with his/her finger and if the dried coffee gathers in a round smudge with tiny dots around it, it means he/she is about to have a meeting with a group of people (ʿendek jamʿah) and so on. The latter was a very successful interpretation as most people in the Lebanon lived 'en famille' or, if they lived alone, went to visit relatives on a regular basis. It was all great fun and I often posed as an expert coffee cup reader, especially with my non-Lebanese friends whom I could fool more easily, and loved inventing new symbols for predictable occurrences of daily life.

HERBAL TEAS
Shay al-Aʿshab

Herbal teas are very popular in the Lebanon, especially in the mountains where most people collect a yearly stock of wild herbs and flowers to dry for home-use. They are considered to have beneficial properties especially for minor ailments. One of the prettiest and most used is *z'hoorat*, a lovely mixture of dried herbs and flowers which consists of *baboonge* (camomile), *shoshat al-darrah* (corn 'silk'), *khatmiyah* (which is like hibiscus), *qossʿayn*, a herb similar to wild thyme and *ward* (roses). Measure 1 teaspoon of *z'hoorat* for a medium tea pot and leave the dried mixture to infuse in boiling water for about 10 minutes. We also make infusions with the individual herbs from *z'hoorat* as well as hyssop (*al-zoffa*), fresh mint (*naʿnaʿ akhdar*), sage (*maramiyeh*) or anise (*yansoon*). The individual herbs or seeds are boiled in water for 1-2 minutes, then left to infuse for about 5 minutes before serving.

FRUITS
Al-Fawakihah

"..., I took long walks in the beautiful gardens of Seyde[1]. When I passed through the lanes separating these, the owners invited me in; They offered me bananas, sugar cane, and white apricots: these latter fruits are in such abundance, and so beneficial, that the Arabs, who are usually very sober, make them almost their sole nourishment during the season. The inhabitants of Sidon have a habit of carrying their carpets near the sources or streams of their gardens, where they lay them at the foot of the apricot trees which provide them with this exquisite food; and thus they spend whole days in the shade, in the middle of their fields, between their food and their drink."

Marcellus, *Souvenirs de l'Orient*, 1839

Lebanese people usually finish their meals with fruit and coffee and fresh seasonal fruit is plentiful all year round in the Lebanon. During the autumn and winter there is a wide choice of citrus fruit. Oranges and lemons appear on the market from October onwards, when their skin is still green and are available through to the spring. Of the many different kinds of oranges there is an unusual yellow, smooth-skinned one with a sweet taste called *laymoon helo* (sweet orange). There are also tangerines (*Yussef Afandi*), clementines, grapefruits (*griffon*), Pomelos (*kabbad*) and bananas (*moz*).

Spring is the season of fresh almonds (*loz akhdar*), when the nut is eaten whole with its crunchy, furry skin, of fat, juicy medlars (*akke denya*) and a variety of apricots (*meshmosh*), amongst them the exceptionally sweet, white apricot (*Baalbaki*) mentioned by Marcellus above. There are also cherries (*karaz*), both red (*ahmar*) and white (*abyad*), greengages – plums (*janarek*), which we eat unripe, dipped in salt, and luscious red, and white mulberries (*toot*) that used to be peddled from house to house in large, white enamelware bowls.

During the summer the choice of fruit becomes overwhelming. There are red plums: *abu riha* (the father of smell), *Istanbooli* (the one from Istanbul), and a tiny dark plum, more like a cherry, known as *el-qarassia*, as well as white plums. Then there are grapes, which many Lebanese grow in their garden or on their terrace. The grapevines grow over a 'tonnelle' to provide shade as well as freshly picked fruit and leaves. Of the many varieties of grapes *maqassi*, a

[1] Sidon

small, golden grape, is the sweetest; *al-bayadi* (the white one) is a prettier grape but not as sweet, *ᶜenab zayni* has a long, firm white fruit and *ᶜenab helwani* is a deliciously refreshing, pale red, crunchy grape. Unripe grapes (*hosrum*) are also eaten, with a little salt and their juice is extracted to make a sour dressing for salads or fried vegetables.

Apples (*teffah*), pears (*n'jass*) and peaches (*derraˀ*) are bountiful in their different varieties. Prickly pears (*sobbayr*) are sold by the roadside in enamelware bowls and the seller will cut them open for you to eat there and then. Jujube (*ᶜennab*), a fruit not much known in the West, looks like a glossy, maroon olive with a melting, pistachio green flesh. *Henblass* (myrtle) is a pale green fruit that looks like a miniature pomegranate and tastes quite dry in the mouth. *Zaᶜroor* (Neapolitan medlar), a rather uncommon, sour-sweet, maroon fruit, is similar in shape to *henblass* but twice the size and is sold by specialty stall holders. From mid to late summer one can start feasting on sweet or sour pomegranates, custard apples (*ˆashtah*) and all kinds of different figs (*teen*): small bright green figs with a red flesh (*teen naᶜoossi*), very sweet pale green ones with a pale creamy flesh, lovely dark red ones, delicious big green figs with a crimson flesh (*al-bokrati*) and similar winter figs (*al-shatawi*) with an even redder flesh which start ripening in September. There are also melons (*batteekh asfar*), watermelons (*batteekh ahmar*) and quinces (*s'farjal*) from which we make a delicious pale pink jam (quince turns pink when cooked).

Hors d'Oeuvres
Mezze

VEGETARIAN
Bedoon Lahmeh
Eggplant Purée
Eggplant and Chick Peas in Tomato Sauce
Broad Beans with Fresh Coriander and Garlic
Dried Broad Beans and Chick Pea Rissoles
Chick Pea Purée   Zucchini in Tomato Sauce
Fried Eggplant   Fried Cauliflower
Fried Onion Wings   Green Beans in Tomato Sauce
Lentils and Rice   Okra in Tomato Sauce
Wild Endive in Olive Oil

NON-VEGETARIAN
Ma Lahmeh
Fried Chicken Livers
Lebanese Steak Tartare
Chicken Wings Marinated in Garlic

 One of the most vivid memories of my childhood in the Lebanon is that of long Sunday lunches at a waterside restaurant in Zahleh (a town famed for its food, north east of Beirut on the way to Baalbek). We went there whenever my father returned from a long business trip to celebrate the family being reunited. Once seated, at a table overlooking the river, my parents would order a gargantuan *mezze* spread consisting of at least twenty different dishes. These were not all served at the same time; first on the table were the indispensable platter with a heart of lettuce, a large tomato, a few cucumbers, scallions, peppers and sprigs of mint, a bowl of olives, another of peanuts and maybe a plate of salted *tormus* (lupine seeds, see Lebanese larder, p. 24). Then came the cold dishes, followed by the hot ones, after which we were served a large bowl of various seasonal fruits and some baklawa.

The colors on the table were quite wonderful. Many of the dishes were served in Lebanese slipware bowls decorated with lovely brown and cream glazes. Inside them the food ranged from delicate shades of beige, a light ivory *hommus* (chick pea purée) to a raw silk-like *baba ghannooge* (eggplant purée), each decorated with a sprinkling of red paprika interspersed with fresh green mint leaves. There were bright colors too, purple pickles, a glossy green *tabbooleh* (parsley salad) dappled with tiny red tomato cubes and light brown *bulgur* grains and pink *habrah nayeh* (pounded raw meat). Then there were the savoury pastries, mini black thyme breads, light brown meat pizzas dotted with roasted pine nuts, dainty golden triangles and so many other colorful dishes. We spent a long afternoon nibbling at this remarkable array of exquisite food. Sometimes we left our parents at table to take a break from eating. We went to play by the cool water or run around chasing each other. After this we went back to a new display of food.

This renowned Lebanese *mezze* has always been the realm of restaurant eating. If you found it in homes it was usually prepared by professional cooks or brought in by caterers. Even on special occasions, when a large number of relations or official guests were visiting, a home cook prepared and served no more than half a dozen *mezze* dishes, two or three main course dishes and followed with a home-made sweet and a bowl of fruits. In today's world, where more and more people work full time, the menu has dwindled down to two or three starters, one main course, fresh fruit and more often than not commercially bought sweets.

EGGPLANT PURÉE
Baba Ghannooge

This dish can be prepared a day in advance provided you reserve the blending of the lemon juice and garlic until just before serving. An interesting and low calorie variation is to replace the tahini with an equivalent amount of low fat yogurt (try goat's yogurt for a slightly sharper flavor) and prepare in the same way as above.

SERVES 4

3 large eggplants (about 10½ oz each)	garnish
	fresh mint or parsley leaves
3 tablespoons tahini (tahineh)	paprika or pomegranate
juice of 1 lemon, or to taste	seeds
2 garlic cloves, peeled and crushed	(the sour type)
	extra virgin olive oil
salt to taste	

Prick the eggplants in several places with a small knife or a fork – to stop them from bursting during cooking – and cook whole with stalks on under a hot grill for 25-30 minutes, turning them to expose all sides equally to the heat. When cooked the eggplants should have shrivelled to about half their original size, be very soft to the touch with blistered skin. If this is not possible, you can bake them in a preheated oven at 350°F for 45 minutes (or microwave them on HIGH for 5-6 minutes). However, if you use the oven or the microwave methods, you will sadly lose the charred taste of the open-fire cooking that is so typically Lebanese.

Cooling your fingers under cold running water, peel and discard the skin of the eggplants while they are still hot and put the flesh in a colander to drain for about 15 minutes.

Cut off and discard the stalks before putting the eggplants in a wide mixing bowl and mashing them with a masher or fork along the grain of the pulp.

If you prefer to use a blender or food processor, be careful not to liquidize the eggplants too much. Two or three turns should be enough to get the right consistency. Check and if necessary turn your machine on and immediately off once again. The purée made with the food processor will be creamier than the handmade one, but just as good.

When the eggplants are mashed, stir in the tahini and salt to taste and mix well. As you are blending the tahini you will notice that the color of the eggplant becomes lighter. Mix in the lemon juice and crushed garlic. Taste the purée and adjust seasoning if necessary.

Pour the purée into a shallow serving bowl and spread it across the dish raising it slightly over the sides. Arrange either the mint, parsley leaves or pomegranate seeds in a star shape in the middle and (unless you are using pomegranate seeds, in which case sprinkle the raised edges with paprika) dribble a thin strip of olive oil between the raised edge and the middle garnish. The pomegranate seed garnish is by far the prettiest and the most complementary of the three. The pearly pink or ruby red seeds (depending on the type of pomegranate) are set off against the raw silk-like purée like precious embroidery and their tangy and juicy bite is a delicious contrast to the creamy texture. Serve with Arabic bread.

EGGPLANTS and CHICK PEAS in TOMATO SAUCE
Moossakaᶜa

Although the Arabic name of this dish sounds the same as that of another Greek eggplant dish, the two are quite different. The Lebanese version is vegetarian and normally prepared with small whole eggplants and chick peas. You can use dried or canned cooked chick peas, the latter being the easiest option as it eliminates the soaking and skinning of the dried chick peas. Personally I do not like the slightly metallic taste of canned peas and I use the ready split dried peas, which are easier to prepare than whole ones. *Moosakaᶜa* is served at room temperature as its Arabic name indicates, *moosakaᶜa* meaning 'cooled down.' You can prepare this dish without the chick peas, in which case the tomato sauce takes a little longer to thicken.

SERVES 4

⅓ cup split or whole chick peas, soaked overnight, or ⅔ cup canned chick peas, drained and rinsed (optional)	¼ teaspoon baking soda (optional) 12 small eggplants or 2 large ones (about 1¼ lb)

45

vegetable oil for frying	1¾ lb ripe tomatoes,
3 tablespoons extra virgin olive oil	peeled and chopped, or same amount Italian canned
2 medium onions, thinly sliced	salt to taste
4 garlic cloves, peeled and thinly sliced	

The night before

Put the chick peas to soak in three times their volume of water as they will double in size. Stir in one quarter teaspoon baking soda; this should soften them and therefore help reduce their cooking time.

Preparation

If you are using uncooked split chick peas, rub them with your hands in their water to loosen the skins. Do that a few times, changing the water between each rubbing, so that the skins float to the surface, then either pour the floating skins out or skim them with your hands. If you are using whole chick peas, drain and spread on a kitchen towel, cover with another towel and press over them lightly with a rolling pin, this should split them as well as loosen their skin. Put them back in a bowl, run cold water over them and get rid of the skins as with split peas.

Rinse the chick peas under cold water, put them in a saucepan, cover them with water and place over a high heat. Bring to the boil, then reduce the heat, and boil gently for one hour or until tender. During that time prepare the eggplants. If the eggplants have long stalks, shorten them to approximately ½ inch and trim away the husk that caps their skin. Peel off a thin strip of skin, about ½ inch wide, the full length of the eggplant, leave an equal strip of skin unpeeled, peel another and continue until you have a striped eggplant. Do the rest of the eggplants the same way. If small eggplants are not available, use large ones. Peel these in wider strips and cut them in quarters, lengthways.

Fill a wide frying pan with enough vegetable oil to deep fry the eggplants and place it over a medium heat. When the oil is hot (to test the heat, dip in the bottom end of an eggplant, and if the oil bubbles around it, it is ready), fry the eggplants until golden on all sides, about 2-3 minutes on each side. Remove the fried eggplants with a slotted spoon and place on several layers of paper towels to soak up the surplus oil. A lighter alternative, though not as delicious, is to brush the eggplants with vegetable oil and place them in a medium hot oven to cook for about 30 minutes or until soft.

Put the 3 tablespoons of olive oil, sliced onion and garlic into a deep saucepan that is sufficiently wide for the eggplants to fit in one layer. Place the frying pan over a medium heat and fry the sliced onion and garlic until golden. Add the drained cooked chick peas and sauté for a couple of minutes. Stir in the chopped tomatoes, season with salt to taste, cover the pan and boil gently for 15 minutes. Then carefully arrange the eggplants in one layer in the tomato sauce, put the lid back on and boil gently for another 20 minutes or until the tomato sauce has thickened. If the sauce is still too runny, uncover the pan and boil for a few more minutes until any excess liquid has evaporated. Let the eggplants cool down before transferring them carefully onto a serving platter. Pour the sauce in between the eggplants so as to show the striped effect and serve at room temperature.

BROAD BEANS *with* FRESH CORIANDER *and* GARLIC
Fool Akhdar bil-Kizbrah

This dish can only be prepared when young tender broad beans are available in spring. When choosing these, make sure that the skins are soft and the beans inside the pods well developed. In the U.S., broad beans are often called fava beans.

SERVES 4

3 tablespoons extra virgin olive oil	1 bunch fresh coriander, (about 7 oz on the stalk), washed, dried, most of the stalks
1 medium onion, finely chopped	cut off, finely chopped

47

5 large garlic cloves, peeled and crushed	½ teaspoon ground cinnamon
salt	¼ teaspoon cayenne powder (optional)
1¾ lb broad beans (fava beans), topped, tailed, stringed and washed, then cut into pieces 2 inches long	¼ teaspoon finely ground black pepper

Put the olive oil and chopped onion in a large sauté pan, place over a medium heat and fry until golden. Stir in the chopped coriander, crushed garlic and a pinch of salt and sauté for one minute or until the coriander softens. Add the broad beans and season with cinnamon, cayenne pepper if desired, pepper and more salt to taste. Mix well together, cover the pan and cook over low heat for 25 minutes or until the beans are done to your liking and all liquid has evaporated. Uncover the pan slightly and let the beans cool before transferring them to a serving dish. Serve at room temperature.

DRIED BROAD BEANS
and CHICK PEA RISSOLES
Falafel

This is an import from Egypt, and like *m'lookhiyeh* (see p. 23), has become so much part of our repertoire that it is found in every sandwich shop and at many a *mezze* table. Falafels are very easy to make and once you have tried them at home you will probably never want to eat them outside.

MAKES ABOUT 16

½ lb dried, peeled and split broad beans (fava beans)	1 teaspoon baking soda
⅔ cup dried chick peas	5 large garlic cloves, peeled

1 medium onion, peeled and quartered	1 teaspoon ground cumin
	1 teaspoon ground allspice
1 small leek, washed, trimmed and cut into two or three pieces	¼ teaspoon finely ground black pepper
¼ bunch coriander or parsley, (about 2 oz on the stalk), trimmed, washed and dried	⅛ teaspoon cayenne pepper (optional)
	salt to taste
½ teaspoon baking soda	

The night before
Put the broad beans and chick peas to soak separately in three times their volume of water as they will double in size. Stir in ⅔ teaspoon baking soda in the bean water and ⅓ in the peas; this will soften them and therefore reduce their cooking time.

Finishing and serving
Skin the chick peas (see *moossaka^ca*, p. 45), then drain both peas and broad beans and rinse under cold water. Put the legumes in a blender (or food processor) together with the rest of the ingredients and process into a smooth paste. If your blender is too small to process all the ingredients together, divide in half and make the *falafels* in two batches. Transfer the *falafel* mixture into a mixing bowl, taste, adjust seasoning if necessary and leave to rest for 30 minutes.

Take a handful of the *falafel* paste mixture and shape between the palms of your hands into a fat round cake with tapering sides, about 2 to 2½ inches in diameter and place on a plate. Continue making the cakes until you have finished the mixture; you should end up with about 16 *falafels*, depending on how fat you make them.

Heat enough vegetable oil in a large pan to deep fry the *falafels*, and when the oil is very hot (test with the edge of one cake; if the oil bubbles around it, it is ready), drop in as many as you can fit comfortably and fry until golden on both sides. Remove with a slotted spoon and put to drain on several layers of paper towels. Continue frying and draining until all the *falafels* are cooked. Serve hot, tepid or at room temperature with pita bread, and an accompaniment of diced tomatoes, pickled cucumbers, sweet chili peppers and turnips (the cucumbers and chili peppers quartered lengthways and the turnips divided into slices) and a double portion of tahini (*tarator*) or dip (*ba'doones bi-tahineh*), pp. 67-8. Ideally you should make the dip with the same herb as that used in the *falafels*.

● You can also use a special brass *falafel* maker (see Lebanese larder, p. 34) to shape the cakes. If so, you will be dropping each cake into the oil as you make it. Heat the oil before starting to make the cakes and when the oil is hot, press down the special lever to make space for the cake, scoop out as much paste as you can and, with the help of a spatula, shape the top into a shallow pyramid. Drop directly into the hot oil by releasing the lever and carry on making, frying and draining the *falafels* until you finish the paste. Serve as above.

⌐ ⸲ ○ ⼂ 𝒫𝒫 ⩩ ⹋ ⼂ ⼂ 日 日 工 ∃⋎⼂

CHICK PEA PURÉE

Hommus bi-Tahineh

Hommus bi-tahineh is one of the staples of our *mezze* and is served with a variety of toppings that distinguish our *hommus* from that of other Middle Eastern countries. In order to get the required smooth ivory mixture, cook the chick peas until very tender and grind them very fine.

SERVES 4

1 cup dried chick peas	juice of 2 lemons, or to taste
1 teaspoon baking soda	3 garlic cloves, peeled and
Scant cup tahini	crushed
salt to taste	paprika and olive oil for garnish

The night before
Put the chick peas to soak in three times their volume of water as they will double in size. Stir in one teaspoon baking soda; this should soften them and therefore help reduce the cooking time.

Preparation
Rinse the chick peas under cold water, put them in a saucepan, cover well with cold water and place over a high heat. Bring to the boil, reduce the heat to medium, cover the pan and cook for 1½ hours or until very tender.

Drain the peas, keeping some of the cooking water in case you need it later to thin the purée. Put the peas in a blender or food processor, reserving a few whole peas for the garnish. Process to a smooth purée and transfer into a mixing bowl.

Stir in the tahini; as you are mixing it in, the color of the purée will become lighter. Add salt to taste and blend well together. Pour in half of the lemon juice. It is difficult to give exact amounts for lemon juice as sizes and tastes vary, so I suggest you add it gradually and decide for yourself how sour you like your *hommus*. Add the crushed garlic and mix again. If the purée is too thick use a little of the cooking water to thin it down – the purée should be soft and creamy but not runny. Taste, adjust seasoning if necessary, then pour into a shallow round or oval bowl and spread across the dish, raising the purée slightly over the sides. Arrange the reserved whole peas in a little mound in the middle, sprinkle the raised edges with paprika and trickle a little olive oil in the dip between the paprika and the mound of whole peas.

● You can vary on both taste and presentation with a choice of the following toppings:

1 – Pine nuts (⅓ cup) sautéed until golden brown in a little *samneh* (see Lebanese larder, p. 20), then poured together with the hot fat over the *hommus*. It is better to use *samneh*, as it does not burn like butter, making the presentation nicer.

2 – Pine nuts (⅛ cup/1 ounce) sautéed until golden brown in a little *samneh* to which you add coarsely minced lamb (2 ounces); cook until the meat has lost all traces of pink and pour with the hot fat over the *hommus*.

3 – One *suju^* sausage (see Lebanese larder, p. 30), sliced and fried in a little *samneh* until crisp and arranged over the *hommus* without the hot fat.

Serve the above variations immediately or else the fat will solidify and the taste and presentation will be spoiled.

51

ZUCCHINI *in* TOMATO SAUCE
Motabba^at Koossa

You can use either white or green zucchini for this dish or better still, although not very Lebanese, baby or dwarf, which you leave whole.

SERVES 4

1¼ lb small or dwarf zucchini	1¼ lb ripe tomatoes,
3 tablespoons extra virgin olive oil	peeled and chopped, or same amount Italian canned
2 medium onions, thinly sliced	salt to taste
3 garlic cloves, thinly sliced	1 tablespoon dry mint or fresh mint, finely chopped

Cut off and discard the stem ends of the zucchini and shave off the bottom brown skins. Rinse under cold water and slice the small zucchini, in circles, about ½ inch thick (or keep dwarf ones whole).

Put the olive oil, sliced onion and garlic into a saucepan, place over a medium heat and fry until golden. Stir in the zucchini, reduce the heat to low, cover the pan and simmer for 5 minutes, stirring occasionally.

Add the chopped tomatoes and salt to taste, put the lid back on, increase the heat to medium and boil gently for 15 minutes or until the zucchini have become soft – be careful not to overcook them to a mush. Carefully stir in the dry mint and cook uncovered for another 5 minutes or until the mint has softened and the sauce thickened. If you are using fresh mint, boil the zucchini for 20 minutes and only stir in the chopped mint after you have turned off the heat. Serve at room temperature.

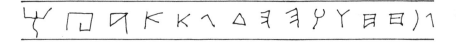

FRIED EGGPLANT
Batinjen Me'li

Fried eggplant is served either on its own or with a bowl of yogurt or with a dressing of pomegranate syrup, garlic and olive oil. The latter is the most interesting combination as the taste of the mellow velvety eggplant is deliciously set off by the blend of sweet and sour syrup, pungent garlic and olive oil.

SERVES 4

2 large eggplants (about 1¼ lb)	2 cups yogurt (16 oz) (optional)
salt	or
vegetable oil for frying	pomegranate sauce p. 66 (optional)

Cut off and discard the stem ends of the eggplants, peel most of the skin, lengthways, leaving thin strips of skin, about ½ inch wide, unpeeled. Cut the peeled eggplant in long slices, about ½ inch thick and arrange the slices in salted layers in a colander. Leave to sweat for about 30 minutes, then rinse under cold water and pat dry with paper towels.

Pour enough vegetable oil in a large frying pan to deep fry the eggplant and place over a high heat. When the oil is very hot (to test the heat, dip in the tip of an eggplant slice, and if the oil bubbles around it, it is hot enough), put as many slices as you can fit comfortably in the pan and fry until golden brown on both sides. Remove with a slotted spoon and put to drain on several layers of paper towels. Cover the fried slices with a double layer of paper towels and lightly press the paper down to soak up the excess oil from the top. Continue frying and draining the rest of the eggplant until finished.

Leave to cool before carefully transferring the fried eggplant slices onto a flat serving platter. If you are serving the eggplant with the pomegranate sauce, prepare it while the slices are left to cool, making sure you mix it well and trickle a little dressing over each slice. Serve at room temperature.

FRIED CAULIFLOWER
^Arnabeet Me'li

You can serve fried cauliflower simply with yogurt or with a pomegranate syrup sauce.

SERVES 4

2 small cauliflower or 1 large one, cut into medium-sized florets	salt
	vegetable oil for frying

Blanch the cauliflower florets for 3 minutes until half cooked, drain and spread to dry on a clean paper towel.

Heat enough vegetable oil in a frying pan to deep fry the cauliflower. When the oil is hot (to test heat, dip in the bottom end of a floret, and if the oil bubbles around it, it is ready), fry the florets until golden all over. Remove with a slotted spoon and put to drain onto several layers of paper towels. Serve tepid or at room temperature with either a side dish of yogurt or the pomegranate dressing described on p. 66.

FRIED ONION WINGS
Jawaneh Bassal Me'liyeh

These crispy onion slices are delicious and usually served as part of a selection of fried vegetables such as French fries and fried eggplant. They are also used to garnish *m'jaddarah* (see p. 56) or *m'dardarah* (see p. 185). To achieve maximum crispness, make sure you fry the onions in very hot oil, then spread them thinly on a thick layer of paper towels so that they drain well.

SERVES 4

4 medium onions, cut in slices, about ⅛ inch thick	vegetable oil for frying

Put enough vegetable oil in a frying pan to deep fry the onion slices and place it over medium heat. When the oil is very hot (test with the tip of one slice; if the oil bubbles around it, it is ready), fry the onion slices, stirring occasionally, until they become crisp and dark brown, without letting them burn. Remove with a slotted spoon and put to drain onto several layers of paper towels. Serve at room temperature.

GREEN BEANS *in* TOMATO SAUCE
Loobyeh bil-Zeyt

This is my favorite way of preparing beans and other green vegetables when in season. This dish can be prepared a day in advance and served either as a starter or as a light vegetarian main course, in which case double the quantities. Make sure you use very red tomatoes to produce a really tasty, thick sauce; if you can't get hold of any, use Italian canned ones.

SERVES 4

about 1¼ lb fresh green beans	5 tablespoons extra virgin olive oil
about 1¼ lb ripe tomatoes, peeled and chopped, or same amount Italian canned	1 medium onion, finely chopped
	8 unpeeled garlic cloves
	salt to taste

Top, tail and string the beans, then cut them in pieces about 2 inches long. Rinse under cold water and set aside. If you are feeling lazy, use frozen whole French beans, although neither the texture nor the taste will be as nice as that of fresh ones.

If you are using fresh tomatoes, put them in a bowl, cover them with boiling water and take them out after a few seconds; this way they will peel easily. Then chop them coarsely.

Put the olive oil, chopped onion and unpeeled garlic cloves in a large saucepan that will also accommodate the beans. (If you think this amount of garlic is excessive, use fewer cloves or discard them before serving). Place the saucepan over a medium heat and fry until the onion turns golden. Add the beans, sprinkle with a generous pinch of salt, and sauté for a few minutes, stirring regularly, until they become glossy and turn a brighter green. Pour in the chopped tomatoes, add salt to taste, mix well and cover the pan. Boil gently for about 40 minutes or until the tomato sauce has thickened and the beans are done to your liking. Serve hot, tepid or at room temperature with pita bread.

Serving and eating the village way

Take one pita bread, tear it open at the seams and lay one half, rough side up, on a plate. Spoon some beans and tomato sauce onto the bread, spreading the vegetables evenly across it, and serve hot with trimmed scallions, or peeled and quartered onions. Eat with your hands by using a torn piece of bread from the other half to scoop up a few beans and with each mouthful take a bite of onion and suck a garlic clove out of its skin. Once you finish eating the beans, arrange a few pieces of onion in a line in the middle of the tomato-soaked bread, roll it up and eat like a sandwich. Then lock yourself up for the next 24 hours as no one will want to be anywhere near your breath!

LENTILS and RICE
M'jaddarah

This dish is one of the Christians' staple meals during Lent. It is also a favorite weekend lunch in both mountains and towns where it is cooked slowly from early morning and left to cool while the women do the weekly spring cleaning of the house. M'jaddarah is served cold with a cabbage salad, trimmed onions and Arabic bread. The quantity given below will serve four as starters; if you want to serve it as a main course, double the quantity and either pour the mixture into one big serving dish or four individual soup plates.

You can prepare m'jaddarah with green or brown lentils. The difference between the two is quite noticeable, both in texture and taste, with the green ones mashing up more and making for a smoother texture.

SERVES 4

1 cup large green or brown lentils	½ teaspoon ground cinnamon or cumin
9 cups water	½ teaspoon ground allspice
7 tablespoons extra virgin olive oil	¼ teaspoon finely ground black pepper
2 medium onions, finely sliced	salt to taste
⅛ cup white short grain rice	

Spread the lentils on a tray and pick them clean of any impurities. Put them in a sieve and rinse them under cold water before putting them in a saucepan. Add the water and place over a high heat. Bring to the boil, then reduce the heat to medium – give the lentils a good stir in case some have stuck to the bottom of the pan – and boil gently for 1 hour or until the lentils are tender and the water has reduced by two-thirds.

In the meantime, put the olive oil in a frying pan, place over a medium heat and when hot, fry the sliced onions until they become soft and transparent; remove half with a slotted spoon and put onto a plate and continue frying the rest until they caramelize and turn a rich dark brown, without actually letting them burn (see p. 60).

Remove with a slotted spoon and put to drain onto several layers of paper towels, spreading them thinly so that they drain well and become crispy. Rinse the rice in a sieve under running cold water, drain and set aside.

When the lentils are cooked, add the soft onions and their frying oil, and the washed rice. Season with cinnamon or cumin, allspice, pepper and salt to taste and simmer uncovered for 20 minutes, stirring regularly, until the rice is done and the mixture has thickened, without letting it dry out. Taste, adjust seasoning if necessary, and pour immediately into a shallow serving bowl. Leave to cool before scattering over the caramelized onions. Serve at room temperature.

● A variation on the above which we call *m'jaddarah m'saffayeh* is to purée the lentils before adding the onions and rice. Drain the lentils while saving their cooking water, put them in a blender or food processor and process until they turn into a smooth paste. Put the puréed lentils back in the pan together with their cooking water and finish as above.

OKRA *in* TOMATO SAUCE
Bamya bil-Zeyt

Ideally you should use young okra for this recipe. The large ones, which are more generally available, are too tough and stringy and will be neither as good nor as attractive as the smaller type. You could also use dried okra (see Lebanese larder, p. 22), which you need to soak overnight in hot water before draining, drying and using as with fresh ones. Frozen okra, which you can find in specialty stores or some supermarkets, is a very good and easy alternative. All you have to do is defrost and dry it before using it like the fresh one.

SERVES 4

1¼ lb okra	¼ bunch fresh coriander,
7 tablespoons vegetable oil	(2 oz on the stalk), washed,
2 tablespoons extra virgin olive oil	dried, most of the stalks cut off, coarsely chopped
1 medium onion, thinly sliced	1¼ lb ripe tomatoes,
5 large garlic cloves, peeled and crushed	peeled and coarsely chopped, or same amount Italian canned
	salt to taste

Shave off the stem end of the okra, following the slant to end up with a smooth, unbroken and pointed peeled top. Immerse in cold water and dunk a few times to loosen any grit or other dirt. Drain the okra in a colander then spread on a kitchen towel, cover with another towel and pat dry.

Pour the vegetable oil into a medium-sized frying pan and place over a medium heat. When the oil is very hot (to test the heat dip in the tip of an okra; if the oil bubbles around it, it is ready), sauté the okra for about 2 minutes, in two or three batches, until bright green and crisp without letting them brown. This seals the okra and stops the release of the mucilaginous substance that is such a characteristic of this vegetable. When the okra are done, remove with a slotted spoon and put to drain on a double layer of paper towels.

Put the olive oil and sliced onion in a saucepan, place over a medium heat and fry until golden. Stir in the crushed garlic and chopped coriander and sauté for one minute, or until the coriander softens. Add the chopped tomatoes, bring to the boil, and leave to bubble for 5 minutes. Add the okra, cover the pan and boil gently for 20 minutes or until the okra is done and the tomato sauce thickened. Uncover the pan and leave to cool before transferring onto a serving dish. Serve at room temperature.

WILD ENDIVE *in* OLIVE OIL
Hindbeh bil-Zeyt

Wild endive is available from Lebanese shops in London during the winter months. The wild endive (a misnomer as it is actually cultivated in Lebanon or Cyprus and imported from there) comes in long bunched leaves that are wide with a curly edge and dark green in color. If you cannot find it in the U.S. use chicorée frisée (or frisée or culy endive as it is known in the States). The frisée leaves are paler in color and less strong in taste but still a delectable alternative. They are more tender, so reduce the cooking time by half.

SERVES 4

About 2 lb wild endive (or frisée)	4 medium onions, thinly sliced
	salt to taste
7 tablespoons extra virgin olive oil	lemon wedges for garnish

Wash and drain the wild endive (or frisée) and cut into pieces, about 2½ inches long. Put in a large saucepan, cover with boiling water, add salt to taste and place over a high heat. Bring back to the boil and cook for 3 or 6 minutes, depending on the vegetable that you are using (frisée takes less time). Drain the cooked endive and leave to cool.

Put the olive oil in a large frying pan and place over a medium heat. When the oil is hot, add the onion slices and fry, stirring occasionally, until they become a rich brown, without letting them burn. Take off the heat, remove three quarters of the onion with a slotted spoon and put to drain onto several layers of paper towels and leave the rest in the pan.

Squeeze out as much water as you can between the palm of your hands, then separate the pressed leaves and put them in the pan with the fried onion and place over a medium heat. Sauté for a few minutes, stirring regularly until the endive is well blended with the oil and onion slices, then transfer to a flat serving platter. Leave to cool before scattering the crispy onions on top and arranging the lemon wedges all around the cooked endive. Serve at room temperature and eat with a little lemon squeezed over the greens.

● An interesting variation, although difficult to get here in the West, is to use dried green beans (*loobyeh mo`addadeh*; see Lebanese larder, p. 22). Boil the dried beans for 1 hour, drain and squeeze out as much water as you can, and prepare as above.

FRIED CHICKEN LIVERS
^Asbett D'jej Me'liyeh

SERVES 4

3 tablespoons extra virgin olive oil	salt to taste
About 1 lb chicken livers	3 garlic cloves, peeled and crushed
1 medium onion, peeled and spiked with 5 cloves	juice of 1 lemon, or to taste
½ teaspoon ground allspice	1 tablespoon of finely chopped fresh coriander
¼ teaspoon finely ground black pepper	

Put the olive oil in a large frying pan and arrange the chicken livers in an even layer in the pan with the cloved onion in the middle. Fry over a medium heat for 3 minutes, turn them over and cook for another 2 minutes. Season with allspice, pepper and salt to taste, then stir in the crushed garlic and lemon juice and take off the heat. Leave to cool slightly, then sprinkle with chopped coriander and serve lukewarm.

Variation

● You can also cook lamb's kidneys (about 1 lb) in the same way but without the spiked onion and cook until done to your taste.

● You can replace the chicken liver with lamb's liver (ˆasbeh sawdah meˈliyeh). Use butter (4 tablespoons) instead of olive oil and either cut the liver in medium chunks or in slices, about ½ inch thick. Melt the butter over a medium heat, add the liver and fry for 1 to 1½ minutes on each side. Take off the heat, season with allspice, pepper and salt to taste, then stir in the garlic and lemon and serve as above.

Lamb's liver is also served raw (ˆasbeh sawdah nayeh), which in the Lebanon is considered a great delicacy. This practice would horrify most people in the West. Worse still, it is eaten for breakfast, warm out of a freshly slaughtered lamb. If you are served it, you should feel honored; your host or hostess will have had a lamb killed especially for the occasion of your visit or else placed a special order with their butcher.

The liver is cut into bite-sized pieces and served with small pieces of raw fat from the sheep's tail (liyeh) together with a little plate filled with a mixture of seven spices (see Lebanese larder, p. 32) and another in which there is salt. Each piece of liver is dipped in the salt then the spice mixture before being wrapped in a piece of pita bread together with a piece of fat.

LEBANESE STEAK TARTARE
Habrah Nayeh

Our steak tartare is a simpler and smoother version than the French one. Only herbs and onion are added, so the taste of the meat comes through very clearly. If you do not have a meat grinder, a food processor, or a blender that is strong enough to mince the meat, get your butcher to prepare the meat by boning it and cutting off all the fat, white tendons and other chewy bits before putting the meat through the fine mincer. *Habrah nayeh* is best prepared just before serving, or else the raw meat will quickly change from an appetizing pink to a rather off-putting gray.

SERVES 4

1 medium onion, peeled and quartered	salt to taste
	a bowl of lightly salted water
About 1 lb boneless lean lamb from the top of the leg, minced (ground)	*garnish*
	1 tablespoon extra virgin olive oil
a handful of fresh basil or sprigs of mint	1 tablespoon pine nuts
1 teaspoon ground cinnamon	a bunch of spring onions (scallions), trimmed
1 teaspoon ground allspice	sprigs of fresh mint
¼ teaspoon finely ground black pepper	

Put the quartered onion in a blender or food processor and process until very finely chopped. Add the minced meat, basil (or mint, leaves only), cinnamon, allspice, pepper and salt to taste and grind until the texture of the meat is very smooth. Transfer to a mixing bowl and drag a serrated knife through the meat. The knife's teeth will catch the last chewy bits that you want to remove from the ground meat. Wipe the blade clean and repeat a few times, cutting in different directions until you have taken most of the chewy bits out.

Prepare a bowl of lightly salted water and dip your hand to moisten it before kneading the meat well. Taste and adjust seasoning if necessary, then transfer to an oval or round serving dish. Flatten the meat into a shallow cake and use your index finger or the tip of a small spoon to make little curved dips in a straight line down the middle and again either side of it. Trickle a little olive oil into the dips, scatter a few raw pine nuts over the surface and serve immediately with trimmed spring onions and sprigs of fresh mint.

CHICKEN WINGS
MARINATED *in* GARLIC
Jawaneh D'jej Bil-Toom

Chicken wings are often left unused and here is a simple way to prepare them as a tasty starter or as part of a barbecue meal.

SERVES 4

8 big chicken wings or 12 small ones	juice of 1 lemon, or to taste
marinade	⅛ teaspoon ground cinnamon
8 large garlic cloves, peeled and crushed	½ teaspoon ground allspice
	¼ teaspoon finely ground black pepper
2 tablespoons extra virgin olive oil	pinch cayenne pepper (optional)
	salt to taste

Rinse the chicken wings in cold water and pat them dry with paper towels.

Put the crushed garlic in a large mixing bowl and stir in the olive oil, lemon juice and seasonings. Add the chicken wings, coat them well with the marinade and leave for an hour, turning them over occasionally.

Grill or barbecue the wings, for about 10 minutes on each side, or until they are nearly charcoaled and crispy. Alternatively you can bake them for about 30 minutes in a hot oven, turning them over halfway through, so that they are crisp on both sides. Serve hot with a garlic dip, p. 158.

Salads
Al-Salatat

DRESSINGS AND DIPS
Al-Salsat
Lemon and Garlic Dressing
Pomegranate Syrup Sauce
Tahini and Parsley Dip   Tahini Sauce

RAW AND SEASONAL SALADS
Salatat Al-Fassel
Fresh Thyme Salad
Mixed Herb and Toasted Bread Salad – 1
Mixed Herb and Toasted Bread Salad – 2
Parsley, Tomato and Bulgur Salad
Purslane, Tomato and Wild Cucumber Salad
Arugula Salad   White Cabbage Salad
Yogurt and Cucumber Salad

COOKED VEGETABLE SALADS
Al-Salatat Al-Matbookhah
Fresh Broad Bean Salad   Butter Bean Salad
Carrot and Zucchini Salad   Grilled Eggplant Salad
Swiss Chard Stalks in Tahini
Wild Endive Salad

 The planning of most meals in the Lebanon is based on seasonal supply and daily freshness and menus are devised accordingly. This applies particularly to a whole range of delectable salads which are eaten in abundance. Having to procure a daily supply of fresh ingredients never seemed much of a problem in pre-war Beirut. Every morning we were alerted to the approach of travelling vegetable and fruit sellers by the sound of their voices shouting the names of their produce. They walked the streets of residential Beirut pushing wooden carts piled high with either fresh fruit or vegetables. The choice of the day's salads and other dishes depended largely on what was announced – when we were young my sisters and I could guess what was for lunch after hearing the cries of these hawkers – and home cooks would wait for their ritual arrival before deciding on their meals. They would then go out onto their balconies or to their windows and deal with the vegetable or fruit seller. Most home cooks went down to pick their own selection unless they knew the seller well and therefore trusted him to give them the best he had.

Because we always chose our own fruit and vegetables, I have yet to get used to not being allowed to select my own ingredients in western street markets and shops. Fortunately not all greengrocers insist on serving you and I tend to favor those who let you pick your own vegetables and fruit and large supermarkets with their huge variety of exotic produce. This way I can make sure I have a perfect selection.

LEMON *and* GARLIC DRESSING
Zeyt bil-Toom

This is quite a pungent dressing. If you are not too keen on having (or being subjected to) a strong smell, use less or no garlic and the dressing will be equally good. You can also add crushed fresh herbs, such as mint or basil. The mint lends itself particularly well to grilled eggplant or fresh broad bean salad, see pp. 79 and 76. For a perfect taste use a mortar and pestle to crush the garlic and herb of your choice, always adding a generous pinch of salt to absorb the juices released from the crushed ingredients. It is also best to prepare the dressing at the last minute and mix it in with the salad just before serving.

SERVES 4

3 garlic cloves, peeled and crushed	4 tablespoons extra virgin olive oil
salt	⅓ oz fresh mint, basil or coriander leaves, washed, dried and crushed (optional)
juice of 1 lemon, or to taste	

Chop the garlic coarsely (with the herb of your choice, if any) and put it into a mortar, add a pinch of salt and pound with a pestle until you have a smooth paste. Stir in the lemon juice and then the olive oil. Taste, adjust seasoning if necessary, mix in with the salad of your choice and serve immediately.

● You can substitute fresh sour pomegranate juice or verjuice (the juice of unripe grapes, see Lebanese larder, p. 33) for the lemon juice.

ㄥ ⟩ ○ ⟨ φφ w ₮ ㄥ ㄥ 日 日 工 ⟨ Y ㄥ

POMEGRANATE SYRUP SAUCE
Rebb el-Rumman bil-Zeyt wa Toom

A rather unexpected combination that adds another dimension to fried vegetables. Pomegranate syrup is available in Middle Eastern markets.

SERVES 4

2 tablespoons pomegranate syrup	6 tablespoons extra virgin olive oil
1 large garlic clove, peeled and crushed	salt to taste

Put the pomegranate syrup in a small mixing bowl, stir in the crushed garlic and olive oil, add salt to taste, and serve with fried eggplant or fried cauliflower, see pp. 53 and 54.

TAHINI *and* PARSLEY DIP
Ba´doones bil-Tahineh

A delectable and addictive dip (watch the calories, though) which also doubles up as a salad dressing. If you are using it as a dressing, you may want to dilute it with a little more water or lemon juice, depending on your preference.

SERVES 4

½ cup plus 2 tablespoons tahini	¼ bunch parsley (2 oz on
juice of 1½ lemons, or to taste	the stalk), washed, dried, most of
7 tablespoons water	the stalk cut off, finely chopped
2 garlic cloves, peeled and crushed	salt to taste

Put the tahini in a mixing bowl and gradually stir in the lemon juice and water alternately, always turning the spoon in the same direction. The sesame paste will first thicken into a purée-like consistency before it starts to dilute again – taste the dip before you finish pouring in the lemon juice so that you can adjust the tartness of the dip according to your preference. If you use less lemon juice, make up for the loss of liquid by adding more water, or vice versa. Keep stirring until the sauce has the consistency of creamy yogurt. If the tahini is too thick to start with – this usually happens by the time you reach the bottom of the jar – or has not diluted properly, stir with a whisk at the end to incorporate the lumpy bits.

Stir in the crushed garlic and chopped parsley, add salt to taste and mix well together. Taste, adjust seasoning if necessary, and serve with either pita bread or a selection of crûdités. You can substitute fresh coriander for parsley whenever you feel that the taste would be more appropriate.

TAHINI SAUCE
Tarator

SERVES 4

Use the same ingredients as for the dip, leaving out the parsley and making the sauce a little more runny.

FRESH THYME SALAD
Salatet Za'tar Akhdar

The thyme used here is the type with long narrow leaves a bit like rosemary but softer. You can buy it in specialty stores and some supermarkets and fresh produce markets. Although this salad is quite delicious, it has a strong taste and is best served in small quantities as part of a *mezze*, maybe with *hommus* (see p. 50), and a fried vegetable (see pp. 53-54). If you find the taste of thyme too strong, replace it with purslane, if available.

SERVES 4

2 bunches thyme (about 7 oz on the stalk)	2 teaspoons sumac, or more to taste
1 medium onion, very finely chopped	salt to taste
	4 tablespoons extra virgin olive oil

Strip the thyme leaves off their stalks, wash them in cold water and dry them. Put the thyme in a salad bowl, add the chopped onion, sprinkle with sumac and salt to taste, pour in the oil and toss together. Taste, adjust seasoning if necessary, and serve immediately.

● This salad is also a perfect accompaniment to roast lamb.

MIXED HERB *and* TOASTED BREAD SALAD – 1

Fattoosh – 1

This is one of the most popular and adaptable of Lebanese salads. You can make it with whatever salad ingredients you have available as long as you use sumac (see Lebanese larder, p. 32) to give it its special lemony flavor. Here are two basic recipes; *fattoosh*-1, where the herb leaves are used whole with the rest of the salad ingredients, and *fattoosh*-2, where these are coarsely chopped and mixed with shredded lettuce. Whichever variation you chose, it is important you select the herbs young and fresh, as the overgrown ones are too tough and have less taste. Purslane can often be found in Greek, Turkish or Lebanese shops in spring and summer; if it is not available, use an equivalent amount of parsley.

This salad works pretty well without toasted bread for those who are on a restricted diet, although technically it is no longer considered *fattoosh*.

SERVES 4

2 medium round pita bread	8 medium red radishes, thinly sliced in half circles
1 bunch flat-leafed parsley (7 oz on the stalk), washed, dried and leaves picked off stalks	6 small tomatoes (about ¾ lb), quartered
½ bunch mint (3½ oz on the stalk), leaves picked off stalks	***Dressing***
	3 tablespoons sumac
½ bunch purslane (3½ oz on the stalk), leaves picked off stalks	5 tablespoons extra virgin oil
	1 tablespoon chili oil (optional)
	salt to taste
1 bunch spring onions (scallions), trimmed and thinly sliced	juice of ½ lemon, or to taste
3 small cucumbers or ½ long one, thinly sliced in half circles	

Tear the pita bread open and toast it under a hot grill or in an oven until golden brown. Place on a rack to cool.

In the meantime prepare all the other ingredients – if the mint and purslane leaves are dirty, gently rub any grit off with your fingers as I find them too delicate to wash.

Break the toasted bread into bite-sized pieces and put them in a salad bowl. Sprinkle with sumac, add the oil and mix until the bread is thoroughly coated. Add the raw ingredients, salt to taste and lemon juice and mix well together. Taste, adjust seasoning if necessary, and serve immediately.

Coating the bread with the oil and sumac is one way of sealing it and stopping it from going soggy; another is to mix in the bread last after having seasoned and tossed the salad. In either case serve immediately as it is important that the bread remains crunchy for a perfect *fattoosh*.

MIXED HERB *and*
TOASTED BREAD SALAD – 2
Fattoosh – 2

This is a slight variation on no. 1, both in taste and presentation and is my favorite of the two.

SERVES 4

4 small Bibb lettuces or 1 large Romaine lettuce	3 firm red medium tomatoes (about ¾ lb), chopped into bite-sized pieces
1 bunch spring onions, (scallions), trimmed and thinly sliced	1 bunch flat-leafed parsley (7 oz on the stalk), washed, dried, most of the stalks cut off, coarsely chopped
3 small cucumbers, sliced in medium-thin half circles	

½ bunch mint, (3½ oz on the stalk), leaves only, coarsely chopped	salt to taste
	6 tablespoons extra virgin olive oil
½ bunch purslane (3½ oz on the stalk), leaves only	*bread garnish*
dressing	1 medium pita bread, opened up, toasted and broken into
3 tablespoons sumac	bite-sized pieces

Strip and discard any outer damaged leaves of the lettuce, wash and dry the rest, then cut across in ½-inch strips. Put the shredded lettuce in a salad bowl and add the rest of the salad ingredients. Sprinkle with sumac and salt to taste, pour in the olive oil and toss lightly together. Taste, adjust seasoning if necessary, and mix in the toasted bread. Serve immediately before the bread goes soggy.

PARSLEY, TOMATO *and* BULGAR SALAD
Tabbooleh

The secret of a truly refined *tabbooleh* lies in the way you chop the ingredients. In order to produce the required thin, crisp slivers of parsley and mint, you should chop the leaves with a minimum of bruising. Some cooks advocate the use of a food processor as a great time saver and an acceptable alternative. Personally I do not agree, as the herbs end up bruised and mushy because of the powerful rotating action of the chopping blade. Sadly you still have to resort to the old-fashioned and time-consuming hand chopping technique to produce an excellent *tabbooleh*. The amount of bulgur used varies according to regional or family tradition. I learned from my mother to use very little, but you can adjust the amount to your liking, bearing in mind that tomato and parsley are the predominant ingredients.

Tabbooleh is normally eaten with either lettuce, fresh vine or white cabbage leaves. Use the leaf of your choice to scoop up the salad, as if it were bread. The measures given below are for four Lebanese portions, which might appear too generous by western standards; if so reduce the quantities according to your appetite and that of your friends or family.

SERVES 4

⅛ cup fine bulgur	¼ teaspoon ground cinnamon
About 1¼ lb firm ripe tomatoes, diced into small cubes, ¼ inch square	½ teaspoon ground allspice
	¼ teaspoon finely ground black pepper
½ bunch spring onions (scallions), trimmed and very thinly sliced	salt to taste
	juice of 1 lemon, or to taste
2 bunches flat-leafed parsley, very finely chopped	½ cup plus 2 tablespoons extra virgin olive oil
⅓ bunch mint (2½ oz), leaves only, very finely chopped	4 Bibb lettuces or 1 Romaine lettuce, washed and quartered (or fresh tender vine leaves or white cabbage leaves, washed and dried)

Rinse the bulgur in several changes of cold water, drain well and put in a salad bowl large enough to mix the *tabbooleh* in.

The most efficient way to dice the tomatoes into small cubes is to cut them in thin slices, about ¼ inch thick, place these – in a pile of two or three – on your chopping board and cut them in strips of the same thickness, then cut across the strips to produce cubes about ¼ inch square. Spread the diced tomatoes and their juice over the bulgur, then add the sliced onions.

Wash and dry the parsley. Here is a very effective way of drying so much parsley, provided you have a garden or terrace. Trim off the messy stalk ends without undoing the tied bunch. Plunge the bunched parsley in cold water, dunk it a few times to loosen the grit. Allow the grit to sink before lifting the parsley out of the water. Shake off the excess water, wrap one bunch into a clean kitchen towel and take it outside. Hold the bunch by the stalk end and with swift, wide movements swing the wrapped parsley back and forth to shake off as much water as you can. An alternative way of spraying plants. Put the nearly dry bunch into a glass, fluff up the leaves and let them dry completely. Wash and dry the second bunch in the same way.

Undo the tie and gather a handful of parsley sprigs in a neat bunch – aligning them so that where the lower leaves join the stalks they are all at the same level – and lay them on your chopping board. Hold the bunch, with the leaves under your palm and cut off and discard most of the stalks, leaving a length of about ¾ inch. Take a razor-sharp knife and start chopping the parsley, from the stalk end, as if you were slicing it, as thinly as possible, in pieces ⅒ inch wide. In order to achieve this, maintain a tight grip on the parsley as you are cutting it. Put the chopped parsley over the spring onions, looking out for big pieces; if there are any, take them out and chop them finely.

After you finish the parsley, prepare the mint – I do not usually wash it, preferring to wipe any earth off gently with my fingers – strip the leaves off the stalks, bunch them together and chop them as thinly as the parsley. Add the chopped mint to the parsley, cover with a clean paper towel and leave for about half an hour for the bulgur to absorb the tomato juices and soften.

Season the *tabbooleh* with cinnamon, allspice, pepper and salt to taste, pour in the lemon juice and olive oil and mix well together – traditionally this is done by hand but you can mix it just as well with salad servers. Taste, adjust seasoning if necessary, and serve with either lettuce, fresh vine leaves or white cabbage leaves.

PURSLANE, TOMATO and WILD CUCUMBER SALAD

Salatet Ba'leh ma Banadoorah wa Me'teh

Purslane and wild cucumber are generally available during the summer months from Greek, Turkish or Lebanese shops in London; check out local sources in the U.S. Purslane has an intriguing earthy taste and is an interesting variation on the more common herbs. The succulent leaves bruise easily though and should be handled with care. As with mint leaves, I prefer to rub off any grit gently with my fingers instead of washing them.

Wild cucumber is quite different from normal cucumber. The skin is more ridged and slightly furry, the color much paler and the shape longer and thinner, whilst the taste is crunchier and less watery.

SERVES 4

2 bunches purslane (about 1 lb on the stalk)	8 very small tomatoes (about ½ lb), quartered
2 medium wild cucumbers (7 oz), washed, dried and thinly sliced	*dressing*
	1 tablespoon sumac
	salt to taste
1 bunch spring onions (scallions), trimmed and thinly sliced	3 tablespoons extra virgin olive oil

Strip the purslane leaves off the stalks, gently rub off any dirt with your fingers and put in a salad bowl. Add the sliced wild cucumbers, spring onions and quartered tomatoes. Sprinkle with sumac and salt to taste, pour in the olive oil and toss lightly together. Taste, adjust seasoning if necessary, and serve immediately.

You can vary the taste by dressing the salad with a crushed garlic and mint dressing, p. 65.

$$日\ 日\ \mathcal{l}\ \mathcal{l}\ \mp\ O\ \mathcal{P}\ \mathcal{P}\ w\ x\ \mathcal{1}\ \mathcal{1}\ \mp\ \triangleleft\mathcal{1}\mathcal{1}$$

ARUGULA SALAD

Salatet Roccah

I always buy arugula in Greek, Turkish or Lebanese stores, where it is sold in wonderful generous bunches. In the U.S., buy arugula from a good greengrocer or fine supermarket produce counter.

SERVES 4

3 bunches arugula (about 1¼ lb)	juice of ½ lemon, or to taste
2 firm plum tomatoes, chopped into bite-sized pieces	6 tablespoons extra virgin olive oil
	salt to taste

Cut off and discard the thick bottom stalks of the arugula, then plunge the leaves in cold water and dunk a few times to loosen the

74

grit. Lift out of the water and dry in a salad dryer. Chop the arugula into strips, about ½ inch wide and put in a salad bowl. Add the chopped tomatoes, pour in the lemon juice and olive oil and season with salt to taste. Toss lightly, taste, adjust seasoning if necessary and serve immediately.

● You can also serve the arugula without the tomatoes for a sharper taste.

WHITE CABBAGE SALAD
Salatet Malfoof Abyad

A quick and tasty salad which is an ideal accompaniment to roast game or Lenten dishes such as *m'jaddarah*, p. 56, or *m'dardarah*, p. 185. The most suitable type of cabbage is the tender flat-topped one. Unfortunately, it is not only difficult to find in Europe and the U.S., but expensive to buy from the specialty shops which import it. A good alternative is an organically grown, young white cabbage.

SERVES 4

1 white cabbage, (about 1¼ lb)	lemon and garlic dressing, p. 65
2 medium firm tomatoes diced into cubes, about ½ inch square (optional)	

Quarter the cabbage, cut off and discard the core and shred the leaves very finely, using a very sharp knife or the fine slicer attachment of a food-processor. Prepare the garlic and lemon dressing, p. 66, and mix in with the shredded cabbage. Add the tomatoes (if you are using them) and toss lightly. Taste, adjust seasoning if necessary, and serve.

YOGURT *and* CUCUMBER SALAD
Laban ma Khyar

This salad is more like a dip and is a perfect accompaniment to *kibbeh bil-saniyeh* (see p. 117).

SERVES 4

1 pint (2 cups) yogurt	about ¾ lb small cucumbers,
1 tablespoon dried mint, finely	quartered and thinly sliced
crumbled	1 garlic clove, peeled and
salt to taste	crushed

If you cannot find small cucumbers and are using large ones, sprinkle the slices with salt, leave to sweat for 30 minutes, then rinse under cold water and pat dry with paper towels before folding into the yogurt.

Put the yogurt in a salad bowl, stir in the dried mint and salt to taste and leave for 15 minutes or until the dried mint has softened. Fold in the sliced cucumber and crushed garlic. Taste, adjust seasoning if necessary, and serve at room temperature with *kibbeh bil-saniyeh*, or as part of a mezze.

FRESH BROAD BEAN SALAD
Salatet fool Akhdar

A summer salad which is only possible when broad beans are young and fresh and their skins tender. If you cannot find young enough whole broad beans, strip the skins, weigh an equivalent amount of beans only and prepare as below (when fresh broad beans are not available use frozen fava or broad beans).

SERVES 4

about 2 lb young tender	salt to taste
fresh broad beans in the pod	lemon and garlic dressing, p. 65

76

Rinse the broad beans whole under cold water, put into a saucepan, cover with water and add salt to taste. Place over a high heat and bring to the boil. Reduce the heat to medium and boil gently for 20-30 minutes or until the beans are tender.

Drain in a colander, run cold water over the beans to stop them cooking and spread on a clean paper towel to dry. Top, tail and string the cooled pods, cut into medium pieces, about 2 inches long and put in a salad bowl.

Prepare the garlic and lemon dressing, pp. 65-6, pour over the beans and toss lightly together. Serve tepid or at room temperature.

● You can also use the tahini sauce, p. 68, to vary on the dressing.

BUTTER BEAN SALAD
Salatet Fassolyah

This is a hearty mountain salad that is delightful when prepared with fresh butter beans (also called lima beans in the U.S.). These are available in London in Lebanese shops during the summer months. Dried lima beans are readily available in the U.S.; sometimes fresh ones, too.

SERVES 4

1¼ cups dried butter or lima beans, soaked overnight, or about 1 lb fresh beans	lemon and garlic dressing, p. 65
	2 sprigs parsley
	8 spring onions (scallions),
1 teaspoon baking soda	cleaned and trimmed
salt to taste	

The night before
Put the dried butter beans to soak in three times their volume of water as they will double in size. Stir in a teaspoon of baking soda; this should soften them and therefore reduce their cooking time.

Preparation
Rinse the soaked beans under cold water, put them in a saucepan, cover with cold water, add salt to taste and place over a high heat.

Bring to the boil, then reduce the heat to medium and simmer for 1 hour or until the beans are tender. If you are using fresh butter beans there is no need to soak them, simply put them to boil for 20-25 minutes or until tender.

Drain the cooked beans and leave them to cool. Prepare the lemon and garlic dressing, pp. 65-6. Put the beans in a salad bowl and stir in the dressing. Taste, adjust seasoning if necessary, then garnish with parsley leaves, either whole or finely chopped, and serve tepid or at room temperature with trimmed spring onions.

● You can vary on the above by using dried chick peas, in which case the salad is called *balilah* in Arabic or dried broad or lima beans (*fool mudammas*). Follow the same instructions as for the dried butter beans and crush the legumes lightly when you are mixing them with the dressing. Serve as above.

CARROT *and* ZUCCHINI SALAD

Salatet Jazar wa Koossa

Whenever my mother prepared this salad in Beirut, I complained at being given hospital food even though no one in the family was ill. I have changed my mind since and am quite keen on it now, especially its presentation with the lovely mixture of orange carrot and two-toned green zucchini slices, glistening with oil and speckled with crushed garlic.

SERVES 4

3 carrots, peeled and cut into thin circles	salt to taste
4 small zucchini, cut into thin circles	lemon and garlic dressing, p. 65

Peel the carrots, rinse under cold water and slice into roundels ¼ inch thick. Wash the zucchini, cut off and discard both tops and bottoms and slice in roundels the same thickness as the carrots. Put the carrots in a steamer and steam for 10 minutes, add the zucchini and steam for 5 more minutes or until the vegetables are cooked *al dente*; allow a few minutes longer if you prefer them more tender.

You can also boil them separately, in which case keep them whole, put them in separate pans, cover with water, add salt to taste and place over a high heat. Bring to the boil, reduce the heat to medium and boil the carrots gently for 10-15 minutes and the zucchini for 5 minutes or until tender. Drain and leave to cool then cut into roundels the same thickness as above.

Prepare the garlic and lemon dressing, pp. 65-6 and mix it in carefully so that you do not damage the tender slices. Serve tepid or at room temperature.

GRILLED EGGPLANT SALAD
Batinjen M'tabbal

This is quite a wonderful way of preparing eggplant that takes very little time to prepare.

SERVES 4

4 large eggplants, (about 10½ oz each)	a bunch of spring onions (scallions), trimmed and thinly sliced (optional)
3 firm medium tomatoes, (about ½ to ¾ lb), seeded and diced into ½-inch cubes	lemon and garlic with mint dressing, pp. 65-6
	fresh mint leaves for garnish

Prick the eggplants in several places with a small knife or a fork – to stop them from bursting during cooking – and cook whole with the stalks on under a hot grill for 25-35 minutes, turning them to expose all sides equally to the heat. When cooked the eggplants should have shrivelled to about half their original size, be very soft to the touch and their skin blistered. Alternatively you can bake them in a 350°F preheated oven for 45 minutes (or microwave them for 5-6 minutes), in which case you will lose the charred taste of the open-fire cooking that is so typically Lebanese. Cooling your fingers under running cold water, peel and discard the skin of the eggplants while hot and put the flesh in a colander to drain for about 15 minutes.

After the excess juices have run out, pat the eggplants dry with paper towels, cut them, lengthways, in strips, about ½ inch wide, then cut across to the same width. Arrange the eggplant pieces in a neat layer on a flat serving platter, scatter the diced tomatoes over them and the sliced spring onions over the tomatoes. Garnish the center with a few mint leaves; then prepare the mint, garlic and lemon dressing variations p. 66, and put in a sauce boat. It is best to let diners mix the salad on their plates as it is difficult to achieve a pretty pre-mixed presentation with the soft eggplant. Serve at room temperature.

SWISS CHARD STALKS *in* TAHINI
Dloo⁶ el-Sille^ bi-Tahineh

Swiss chard (Silver beet) look like succulent giant spinach, although they are not related botanically. As this dish makes use of the stalks only, save the unused leaves to prepare "Stuffed Swiss Chard Leaves", p. 152 or "Swiss Chard Triangles", p. 95. Alternatively you can serve all three dishes together as a Swiss Chard *dégustation*. The colors on the table will be very pretty and the tastes interestingly different. The lime green stalks showing through the pale cream sauce will contrast nicely with the dark green rolled leaves and the golden pastry triangles. The only drawback of such a feast is the time it will take to prepare – four or five hours at least.

SERVES 4

about 2 lb Swiss chard	tahini sauce (*tarator*), see p. 68
salt to taste	a few leaves of parsley or mint for garnish

Cut the stalks off the leaves, trim the dirty bottom ends and pull the strings out if the stalks are stringy. Wash and cut the stalks in pieces about 1 inch long. Put them in a saucepan, cover with water, add salt to taste and bring to the boil. Reduce the heat to medium and boil gently for 5-10 minutes, or until done to your liking, less time for *al dente*, or longer for a softer bite.

During that time prepare the tahini sauce, p. 68, then drain the stalks in a colander and leave to cool before delicately folding them into the tahini sauce until they are thoroughly coated. Transfer to a serving dish, garnish with parsley or mint leaves and serve tepid or at room temperature.

● You can vary on this salad by using any of the following:

Cauliflower (one large or two small ones) cut into medium-sized florets and boiled for 5 minutes or until cooked *al dente*; if you prefer a softer bite, cook longer. Drain and pat dry with paper towels before dressing and serving as above.

Beetroot or potatoes (about 1¾ pounds), boiled or baked until done. (Beetroots take 1 hour, or a little longer in a hot oven and the potatoes about half an hour to boil or 45 minutes to bake, in a hot oven.) Peel and cut the cooked vegetables into medium thin slices and serve tepid or at room temperature with tahini and parsley dip, p. 67 on the side.

Dried broad or lima beans, soaked overnight and cooked as in the recipe on pp. 76-78. Drain and dress with tahini and parsley dip, p. 67. Serve tepid or at room temperature.

WILD ENDIVE SALAD
Salatet Hindbeh

SERVES 4

about 2 lb wild endive, or frisée or curly endive	salt
	lemon and garlic dressing p. 65

Prepare the wild endive as in the recipe on p. 59. While it is draining, prepare the lemon and garlic dressing, pp. 65-6. Squeeze the cooked endive very dry with your hands and separate the pressed leaves before tossing with the dressing. Serve tepid or at room temperature.

Soups
Al-Shorbat

NON-VEGETARIAN
Ma Lahmeh
Chicken and Rice Soup   Kishk Soup
Vegetable and Lamb Soup with Rice

VEGETARIAN
Bedoon Lahmeh
Lentil and Onion Soup
Lentil and Swiss Chard Soup with Lemon Juice
Lentil, Chick Pea and Bean Soup

 Soups are served routinely as main meals and are normally considered to be curative foods. They are prepared to provide warmth on cold winter days, coolness during the summer heat or regenerative power in case of illness.

CHICKEN *and* RICE SOUP
Shorbah Bayda

Bayda means white in Arabic and this soup is so-called because of the pale color of its ingredients.

SERVES 4

1 chicken, free-range if available (about 2¾ lb)	6¾ quarts water
	3 cinnamon sticks

82

½ tablespoon coarse sea salt	⅓ cup white short grain rice
1 medium onion, peeled and spiked with 5 cloves	½ teaspoon finely ground white pepper

Rinse the chicken under cold water and put it in a medium saucepan. Pour in the water and place over a high heat. As the water is about to boil skim the surface clean – it is important you do this before the water boils, if not the scum will break down and sink back into the water. Add the cinnamon sticks, salt and spiked onion, reduce the heat to medium, cover the pan and boil gently for 45 minutes.

Wash the rice in several changes of cold water. Drain, add to the chicken and boil for another 15 minutes or until both chicken and rice are cooked. Taste, adjust seasoning if necessary, and take off the heat. Remove the chicken onto a chopping board, pick the flesh off the bone, discarding the skin, and cut it into strips about ¾ inch wide. Remove the spiked onion and cinnamon sticks from the broth. Discard the cinnamon and cloves, cut the onion into thin slices and stir back into the soup.

Pour the soup into a tureen, scatter the chicken pieces into the soup, saving the breast pieces till last to achieve maximum whiteness, and serve hot.

● You can also purée the soup, though not too much; you want the chicken meat to be reduced to thin filaments and not to disappear into the liquid. Serve as above.

KISHK SOUP
Shorbet Kishk

This thick soup has an unusual sour taste due to the fermentation process during the making of kishk. It is served blistering hot for breakfast and people use torn pieces of pita bread to scoop it up. The main ingredients, kishk and ˆawarma, were winter staples of Lebanese mountain dwellers in the days before easy transport. Both ingredients were prepared in large quantities at the end of the summer and kept in store for the cold winter months. ˆAwarma is not easily available in the West (I know of only one Lebanese butcher in

London who will make it to order, and none in the U.S.), so I am giving a minced meat alternative in the recipe below. You can also omit the meat altogether and make the soup with butter and garlic.

SERVES 4

2 oz ʿawarma (see Lebanese larder, p. 28) (2 tablespoons butter and 1 oz minced lamb or beef)	4 large garlic cloves, peeled
	5 oz (about ¾ cup) kishk (see Lebanese larder, p. 23)
	4 cups water
	salt to taste

Put the ʿawarma and garlic in a saucepan, place over a medium heat and cook until the fat has melted and the garlic softened. If you are using minced meat, melt the butter over a medium heat, add the garlic and sauté until soft, then brown the minced meat and follow the recipe as with ʿawarma.

Stir in the kishk and add the water gradually, stirring in one cup at a time, so that the mixture does not become lumpy. Depending on the brand of kishk you may need a little more or less water to achieve the right consistency. Bring to the boil, stirring constantly, then reduce the heat to low, taste before adding salt as the kishk is already salted and simmer for 3 minutes. The soup should be thick – not too thick though, like thin porridge. Serve very hot with pita bread.

VEGETABLE and LAMB SOUP with RICE
Shorbet Mowzat ma Khodrah

This is the classic soup for minor ailments. My mother would set about preparing a big pot of this soup as soon as any one of us went down with a cold.

SERVES 4

about 2 lb lamb meat from the shank, on the bone	12 green beans, topped, tailed, stringed and cut into small pieces
6¾ cups water	2 medium ripe tomatoes,
1 tablespoon sea salt	(about 7 oz) peeled and finely
3 cinnamon sticks	chopped, or same amount Italian
1 medium onion, peeled and spiked with 5 cloves	canned
3 medium carrots, peeled and diced into	scant ¼ cup white short grain rice or vermicelli
½-inch-small cubes	⅛ teaspoon finely ground black pepper
3 small zucchini, diced into small cubes	3 tablespoons finely chopped parsley

Put the lamb shanks in a saucepan, pour in the water and place over a high heat. When the water is about to boil, skim the surface clean, add the sea salt, cinnamon sticks and spiked onion. Reduce the heat to medium, cover the pan and cook for 40 minutes.

Add the diced and cut vegetables along with the chopped tomatoes. Season with pepper and more salt to taste and boil for 15 minutes, or until the vegetables are done to your liking. Taste, adjust seasoning if necessary, and serve hot, garnished with chopped parsley.

● For a less cloudy and more refined version, make the soup in two stages. After you have boiled the meat, plunge the pan in iced water until the stock has cooled and the fat has solidified. Skim the fat off and lift the meat out of the stock. Take it off the bone, discard the bones and return the meat to the pan. Bring back to the boil and finish as above.

LENTIL and ONION SOUP
Shorbet Adass

This is a delectable and simple soup in which you can change the taste noticeably by substituting cumin for cinnamon, both spices being ideal complements to lentils.

SERVES 4

2¼ cups large green or brown lentils	1 teaspoon ground cinnamon or cumin
about 13½ cups water	½ teaspoon finely ground black pepper
4 tablespoons extra virgin olive oil	
2 medium onions, finely chopped	salt to taste

Spread the lentils on a platter and pick them clean of any impurities. Put them in a large saucepan, add the water and place over a high heat. Bring to the boil, then reduce the heat to medium. Stir the lentils in case some have stuck to the bottom of the pan and boil gently for 45 minutes or until tender. Brown lentils take longer to cook, so allow for an extra half hour cooking time and add more water (about 1¼ cups).

In the meantime put the olive oil and chopped onion in a frying pan and fry over medium heat until the onions become golden.

Take the lentils off the heat and leave to cool for about 10 minutes before liquidizing in a blender. Return the puréed lentils to the pan, stir in the fried onions and their oil, season with cinnamon (or cumin), pepper and salt to taste. If the soup becomes more like a purée than a thick soup, add a little water to achieve a runnier consistency, though not too runny as the soup is meant to be thick, and simmer for 10 minutes. Taste, adjust seasoning if necessary, and serve hot or cold with toasted pita bread (or pieces of pita bread fried in olive oil; but this is rather heavy).

LENTIL *and* SWISS CHARD SOUP *with* LEMON JUICE
Adass bil-Hamod

This cold summer soup can be served as a light vegetarian lunch or as a nourishing starter.

SERVES 4

1 cup large green lentils	¼ teaspoon salt
14 oz Swiss chard	juice of 2 lemons, or to taste
6¾ cups water	¼ cup plus 2 tablespoons extra
10 garlic cloves, peeled and crushed	virgin olive oil

Spread the lentils on a platter and pick them clean of any impurities. Wash the Swiss chard, trim the dirty bottom ends of the stalks, if any, and chop into thin strips about 1 cm (½ inch) wide. Put the lentils and water in a large saucepan and place over a high heat. Bring to the boil, add the chopped chard, reduce the heat to medium, cover the pan and boil gently for 15 minutes. Mix the softened chard and the lentils well and cook covered for another 45 minutes or until the lentils are tender.

In the meantime peel the garlic cloves, chop them coarsely and put them in a mortar. Add a generous pinch of salt to absorb the juices released from the crushed garlic and pound with a pestle until you have a smooth paste. You could squeeze the garlic with a garlic crusher but I prefer using a mortar and pestle as the texture and taste of pounded garlic is finer.

Slowly incorporate the lemon juice into the garlic paste, then the olive oil. When the lentils and chard are done, stir the garlic mixture into the soup. Season with salt to taste and simmer uncovered for 5 minutes. Taste, adjust seasoning if necessary, and serve at room temperature.

◁ ◁ ∃ У Ƴ ⊟ ⁄ ⁊ ∨ ○ ○ ∓) ⁊⁊ ∨ ○

LENTIL, CHICK PEA
and BEAN SOUP
Shorbah Makhlootah

SERVES 4 TO 6

⅓ cup cannellini beans	½ cup plus 2 tablespoons extra virgin olive oil
½ cup whole dried chick peas	
½ teaspoon baking soda	2 medium onions, finely chopped
¾ cup brown lentils	2 teaspoons ground cinnamon or cumin
10¾ cups water	
about ⅛ cup coarse bulgur	2 teaspoons ground allspice
about ⅛ cup white short grain rice	½ teaspoon finely ground black pepper
	salt to taste

The night before
Put the beans and chick peas to soak in three times their volume of water. Stir in half a teaspoon of baking soda. This should soften them and therefore help reduce their cooking time.

Preparation
Spread the lentils on a tray, pick them clean of any impurities and put them in a large saucepan. Rinse the soaked beans and chick peas under cold water and add to the lentils. Pour in the water, cover the pan and place over a high heat. Bring to the boil, then reduce the heat to medium and boil gently, covered, for one hour or until the legumes are tender.

In the meantime put the olive oil and chopped onion in a frying pan, place over a medium heat and fry until golden. Wash the bulgur and rice separately in several changes of cold water, drain and set aside. When the legumes are ready, add the bulgur, rice and fried onions with their oil. Season with cinnamon (or cumin), allspice, pepper and salt to taste and simmer for 15 minutes. Adjust the soup consistency to your taste. If it is too liquid, boil for a little longer and if too thick, add a little boiling water. Boil for a couple of minutes and take off the heat. Taste, adjust seasoning if necessary, and serve hot, tepid or cold.

Savoury Pastries

Al-Mu'ajjanat

THE PASTRIES

Al-Ma'joonat

Bread Dough   Crescent and Triangle Pastry

TOPPINGS AND FILLINGS

VEGETARIAN

Bedoon Lahmeh

Curd Cheese Crescents   Spinach Triangles
Strained Yogurt Triangles   Thyme Bread

NON-VEGETARIAN

Ma Lahmeh

Minced Meat Crescents
Minced Meat, Tomato and Onion Bread

Savoury pastries are an integral part of our cuisine which we serve as part of buffets or *mezze* spreads. In the days when home cooks still prepared their own bread, they made enough dough for a weekly supply of bread and for a number of large savoury pastries to give their family on baking day. The old-fashioned large shapes are now replaced by small dainty triangles, crescents or mini breads to cater to an increasingly sophisticated local and international clientele. The luscious range of fillings and toppings remains the same with the sad loss of an exciting variety of wild herbs that are not easily found anymore.

89

BREAD DOUGH
ᶜAjeenet al-Khobz

This is the basic bread dough which we use to make plain bread or breads garnished with a variety of toppings, see pp. 94-99.

MAKES ABOUT 20 SMALL BREADS OR 4 MEDIUM ONES

9 oz (2½ cups) "hard" white bread flour	2 tablespoons vegetable oil
1 teaspoon salt	½ cup plus 1 tablespoon lukewarm water (not hot)
½ teaspoon Quick Rise or other rapid-rise dry yeast	

Sift the flour and salt onto a pastry board, mix in the yeast and make a well in the center. (Rapid-rise dry yeast differs from active dried yeast in that it can be added to the flour without the need to activate it with sugar and water. The same goes for easy blend or easy bake yeast. Whichever you decide to use, make sure you follow the manufacturer's instructions.)

Pour in the oil and work together with the tops of your fingers until the oil is completely absorbed. Add the water in two or three goes – it is difficult to measure the exact amount of water as it depends on the brand of flour you are using. Knead the dough with your hands until it is smooth and elastic. Form into a ball, cover with a damp cloth and leave in a warm place for one hour or until the dough has doubled in size.

In the meantime grease a large baking sheet with a little vegetable oil and preheat the oven to 450°F.

To make small breads

Divide the dough into two balls. Slightly flatten one, dip both surfaces in flour, shake the excess off and roll out, into a large circle, turning over the dough regularly, about ⅛ inch thick. Use a round pastry cutter 3 inches in diameter to cut the flattened dough into as many circles as you can. Start from the very edge and work your way around the outside, then the inside. If you do not have pastry cutters use a thin-edged glass or cup. Pick up any excess dough, knead it into a smooth ball and let it rest. (If you want to make plain bread simply finish making the dough circles and put them on the oiled baking sheet. Bake in the preheated oven for 10-15 minutes or until they have puffed up and are lightly golden. If you want to prepare garnished breads proceed as follows.)

Turn the circles over and raise the edge of each one by pinching it between your fingers. Make a few dimples across the flat dough, pressing hard with the tips of your fingers. This is done to stop the oil or juice of the topping running out during cooking. Transfer onto the oiled baking sheet. Prepare the second ball of dough in the same way, then do the cut outs. It is important you let the cut outs rest a little before you roll them out so that they regain their elasticity. Garnish with the topping of your choice (see pp. 94-99).

To make four medium breads
Divide the dough into four equal balls, roll out each one into a medium-sized circle, the same thickness as the small ones, and prepare as above.

CRESCENT *and* TRIANGLE PASTRY
ʿAjeenet al-Fatayer wa al-Samboosak

Before you start making this pastry you need to choose and prepare one of the fillings on pp. 94-99. The filled crescents are fried in vegetable oil, whereas the filled triangles are baked in the oven. It is important you make and fry the crescents in batches, as the dough will become too dry if you wait to finish making all the crescents before frying them. You can freeze these pastries very well. For best results half fry the crescents before you freeze them so that you can cook them afresh after they have defrosted. Whereas you can freeze the triangles after they have been fully baked and only reheat them before serving.

MAKES ABOUT 30 PIECES

5 oz (1½ cups) all-purpose flour	2 tablespoons vegetable oil
¼ teaspoon salt	5 tablespoons water

Sift the flour and salt onto a pastry board and make a well in the center. Pour in the oil and work together with the tip of your fingers until the oil is completely absorbed. Add the water in two or three goes – it is difficult to measure the exact amount of water as it depends on the brand of flour you are using – and knead with your hands until the dough is smooth and elastic. Form into a ball, cover with a damp cloth and leave for 5 to 10 minutes.

To make crescents (samboosak)
Divide the dough into two balls. Flatten the first slightly, dip both surfaces into flour, shake off the excess and roll out, into a large circle, about ⅒ inch thick, turning over the pastry regularly. Use a round pastry cutter, 3 inches in diameter to cut the flattened pastry into as many circles as you can. Start from the edge and work your way around the outside, then the inside. If you do not have pastry cutters, use a thin-edged glass or cup. (This size will make medium crescents. You can also make smaller ones, 2 inches in diameter, to pass round as tidbits with drinks, but you will have to practice a little before you succeed in producing nicely formed ones.) Pick up any excess pastry, knead it together and let it rest.

Turn the circles over, then take one and lay it on the fingers of one hand. Put a teaspoon, or less depending on the size of the pastry, of the stuffing of your choice (see following pages) in the middle and fold the dough over the filling, aligning the edges together to form a half circle. With your free thumb and index finger pinch the edges together into a thin flat hem, starting at one end of the half circle. Slide the filled pastry onto the tips of your fingers so that the flat edge is on the outside. Pinch the end that is furthest from you, to flatten the edge even more and fold it towards you in a little diagonal pleat. Continue pinching and pleating the hem until you form a fluted edge (or until you form a border resembling a twisted cord). This is done to decorate as well as seal the pastry tightly together so that it does not open during frying. Continue making the crescents, putting the finished ones onto a floured surface, until you finish the first lot of circles.

Fill a medium-sized frying pan with enough vegetable oil to deep fry the pastries. Place the pan over a high heat and when the oil is very hot (to test the heat, dip in the corner of one pastry; if the oil bubbles around it, it is ready) slide the crescents in and fry until golden all over. Remove with a slotted spoon onto several layers of paper towels and leave to drain. Take the oil off the heat and roll out the second half of the pastry, knead the cut outs together, leave to rest, then make more crescents and fry them. Roll out the leftover dough and finish making the crescents. You should end up with about 30 pieces. Serve tepid or cold.

To make triangles (fatayer)
Preheat the oven to 450°F and grease a baking sheet with a little vegetable oil.

Prepare and cut the pastry as above. (As with the crescents you can make smaller triangles – the smaller and thinner, the more refined they are.) Put a teaspoon of stuffing, or less depending on the size of the pastry, in the middle of each circle then lift two sides, each one third of the circle, and with your thumb and index finger pinch them together, half way down, making a thin raised joint. Lift the open side and pinch it equally to both loose ends in order to form a triangle with rounded sides and a thin raised inverted y in the middle. Make sure you pinch the pastry tightly together so that it does not open during baking. Transfer the filled pastry carefully onto a greased baking sheet and continue until you have finished both

dough and filling. You should end up with about 30 pieces.

Bake in the preheated oven for about 10 minutes, or until golden, and serve hot, tepid or at room temperature. These will freeze as well as the crescents, but unlike the crescents you can bake the triangles completely before freezing and only warm them after defrosting.

To make large triangles
Divide the dough into 4 balls and follow the same instructions for making the small triangles.

CURD CHEESE CRESCENTS
Samboosak bil-'Areesh

This filling is traditionally made with a local cheese called 'areesh (see Lebanese larder, p. 18), which is not available in the West. Curd cheese makes an excellent substitute. If not available you can also use ricotta or farmer cheese, although they seem too soft and fresh to my taste. Feta cheese is another possible substitute.

MAKES ABOUT 30

2 tablespoon butter	2 spring onions (scallions), trimmed and very thinly sliced
1 egg, organic if possible	
7 oz 'areesh or curd cheese (or ricotta, etc.)	¼ teaspoon ground cinnamon
	½ teaspoon ground allspice
a handful of sprigs of parsley (1 oz on the stalk), washed, dried and most of the stalks cut off, very finely chopped	½ teaspoon finely ground black pepper
	salt to taste
	crescent pastry, p. 91
a few sprigs of mint (1 oz on the stalk), leaves only, very finely chopped	

Melt the butter in a small frying pan over a medium heat, add the egg and scramble it, leaving it quite soft.

Put the scrambled egg in a mixing bowl, add the cheese, chopped parsley, mint and spring onions. Season with cinnamon, allspice, pepper and salt to taste and mix well together. Taste, adjust seasoning if necessary, and set aside.

Prepare the triangle and crescent pastry (see pp. 91-94) and follow the instructions to make the crescents.

SPINACH TRIANGLES
Fatayer bil-S'banegh

You can use your choice of tasty tender green leaves for this filling. The traditional variations are purslane (leaves only), sorrel or Swiss chard, as well as dandelion, wild chicory and other edible wild herbs. Whichever you choice is, follow the instructions in this master recipe.

MAKES ABOUT 30 SMALL TRIANGLES OR 4 LARGE ONES

about ½ lb spinach, chopped in thin strips, about ¼ inch wide	1 tablespoon sumac
	1 tablespoon pine nuts (optional)
salt	juice of ½ lemon, or to taste
1 small onion, very finely chopped	1 tablespoon extra virgin olive oil
¼ teaspoon finely ground black pepper	triangle pastry, p. 91

Put the chopped spinach in a mixing bowl, sprinkle on a little salt and rub the salt in with your fingers until the spinach wilts. Season the chopped onion with a little salt and pepper and again rub the seasonings in with your fingers to soften it before adding it to the spinach. Add the sumac and pine nuts, pour in the lemon juice and olive oil and mix well together. Taste, and adjust seasoning if necessary. The filling should be quite strongly flavored to offset the rather bland pastry, then cover with a clean paper towel and set aside.

Prepare the crescent and triangle pastry (see pp. 91-94) and follow the instructions to make the triangles.

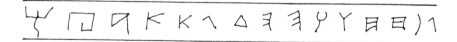

STRAINED YOGURT TRIANGLES
Fatayer bil-Labneh

This filling is particularly luscious. There is a perfect moment as you take the first bite, when the pastry breaks open to release the hot tangy juice of the melting *labneh* into your mouth. A taste that conjures up memories like Proust's *madeleine*.

MAKES ABOUT 30

1 small onion, very finely chopped	salt to taste
¼ teaspoon ground cinnamon	1 small tomato, diced into very small cubes
¼ teaspoon ground allspice	5 oz (about ¾ cup) strained
⅛ teaspoon finely ground black pepper	yogurt (see Lebanese larder, p. 19)
	½ teaspoon butter, softened
	triangle pastry, p. 91

A few hours ahead of time
Put the strained yogurt in a cheese cloth and hang it over the sink or place it in a colander to drain its excess water.

Preparation
Put the chopped onion in a mixing bowl, add the cinnamon, allspice, pepper and salt to taste and rub the seasonings into the onion with your fingers to soften it. Add the diced tomato, strained yogurt and butter and mix well together. Taste, adjust seasoning if necessary, cover with a clean paper towel and set aside.

Prepare the crescent and triangle pastry on p. 91 and follow the instructions to make either the crescents or triangles.

● A variation which is much stronger in taste is to replace the *labneh* with a fermented cheese known as *shankleesh* (see Lebanese larder, p. 18). Depending on how mature the cheese is, you may have to remove the crust then prepare as above.

THYME BREAD
Mana‸eesh bil-Zaᶜtar

This is a bread spread with *zaᶜtar*, a savoury powdered mixture made with dried thyme, sumac and raw or toasted sesame seeds. You can make your own *zaᶜtar* (see Lebanese larder p. 32) or buy it ready-made from Middle Eastern stores.

Thyme bread is a typical breakfast food. In today's Lebanon, the dough is rarely made or baked at home. Home cooks simply prepare their own thyme mixture, which they send out to the nearest public bakery to be cooked on the baker's dough in a long, tunnel-shaped, earth oven fuelled by a strong wood fire at the bottom. Although home-made Thyme bread is delicious, it never tastes quite as good as when it is baked in a tunnel oven. The wood flavor and heat distribution can never be reproduced in a domestic oven.

An interesting and quick variation (which I have developed here in the West) is to spread the *zaᶜtar* onto toasted slices of good brown bread. Put these under the grill for a couple of minutes, then cut them up in bite-sized squares, garnish them with thin slivers of cucumbers or spring onions and serve either hot or cold.

SERVES 4

bread dough (full recipe, p. 90) 2 oz thyme mixture (*zaᶜtar*)	7 tablespoons extra virgin olive oil 1 small onion, finely chopped (optional)

One hour in advance
Prepare the bread dough as in the recipe on p. 90.

Finishing and serving
Put the thyme mixture and olive oil in a bowl and stir well together; you can also add a finely chopped onion to sweeten the taste of the topping. Make the breads following the instructions on p. 90. Stir the thyme mixture again, to reblend the oil and thyme, and spread a teaspoon over each small bread, or a quarter of the mixture over each of the medium ones. Bake in the preheated 450°F oven for 10 minutes or until the breads are cooked. Serve hot or tepid, either alone or with a bowl of strained yogurt (*labneh*) and another of olives.

MINCED MEAT CRESCENTS
Samboosak bil-Lahmeh

You can vary the taste of this meat filling by replacing the lemon juice with either vinegar, verjuice or pomegranate syrup (see Lebanese larder, pp. 28 and 33). Each time you make them you can introduce a subtle change in flavor.

MAKES ABOUT 30

4 tablespoons unsalted butter	2 teaspoons lemon juice (or your
⅛ cup pine nuts	choice of above-named
¼ lb or bit more lean	variations)
minced (ground) lamb	salt to taste
¼ teaspoon ground cinnamon	triangle and crescent pastry,
½ teaspoon ground allspice	p. 91
⅛ teaspoon finely ground black	vegetable oil for frying
pepper	

Melt the butter in a frying pan over a medium heat, add the pine nuts and sauté, stirring regularly, until golden brown. Remove with a slotted spoon and put to drain onto a double layer of paper towels. Cook the minced meat in the same butter until it loses all traces of pink. Keep stirring and mashing the meat with a wooden spoon or fork so that it separates well and does not form lumps. Season with cinnamon, allspice, pepper and salt to taste, stir in the lemon juice (or vinegar, verjuice or pomegranate syrup) and the sautéed pine nuts. Cook for another minute or so, then taste, adjust seasoning if necessary and set aside.

Prepare the crescent and triangle pastry (see pp. 91-94) and follow the instructions to make the crescents (*samboosak*).

MINCED MEAT, TOMATO
and ONION BREAD
Lahem bil-Ajeen

MAKES ABOUT 20 SMALL BREADS OR 4 MEDIUM ONES

bread dough (full recipe, p. 90)	1 teaspoon lemon juice, or to taste
1 medium onion, very finely chopped	¼ teaspoon ground cinnamon
1 medium tomato, peeled and diced into ¼-inch-square cubes	½ teaspoon ground allspice
salt to taste	⅛ teaspoon finely ground black pepper
5 oz lean minced (ground) lamb	¼ teaspoon cayenne powder (optional)
	1 tablespoon pine nuts (optional)

One hour in advance
Prepare the bread dough on p. 90.

Finishing and serving
Put the chopped onions and tomatoes in a mixing bowl. Season with salt and rub firmly with your fingers to soften the onions and tomatoes. Drain any juices before adding the minced meat, lemon juice, cinnamon, allspice, pepper, cayenne powder and more salt if necessary. Mix together with your hands until all the ingredients are well blended. Taste, adjust seasoning if necessary, then cover with a clean paper towel and set aside.

Make the breads following the instructions on pp. 90-91. Spread half a teaspoon of meat topping, flatly and thinly over the small breads or a quarter of the topping over each of the 4 medium ones. Scatter a few pine nuts over the meat (if you are using them) and bake in the preheated oven for 10-12 minutes or until the breads and nuts are golden brown. Serve hot or tepid.

● You can vary on the above topping by mixing 3 tablespoons yogurt or tahini sauce, p. 68, into the meat mixture and bake as above.

Eggs
Al-Beyd

VEGETARIAN
Bedoon Lahmeh
Zucchini Omelette   Fried Eggs with Sumac
Fried Eggs with Pomegranate Syrup
Scrambled Eggs with Spring Onions
Scrambled Eggs with Potatoes and Onions
Scrambled Eggs with Tomatoes

 Eggs are a regular part of the Lebanese diet, especially in the mountains where villagers keep their own chickens. Lebanese omelettes are like flat pancakes and very often prepared with leftover ingredients from other dishes.

ZUCCHINI OMELETTE
'Ejjet Koossa

This omelette is a perfect example of the ingeniousness of the Lebanese cook, who is loath to waste any edible food. It should be planned together with stuffed zucchini as it makes use of the pulp from the cored zucchini.

MAKES ABOUT 14 SMALL OMELETTES OR 4 LARGE ONES

the pulp from about 1 lb young zucchini, (about 6 oz pulp), very finely chopped	1 teaspoon salt
	3 eggs, organic if available

½ bunch spring onions (scallions), trimmed and thinly sliced (about ¼ cup)	¼ teaspoon ground cinnamon
	¼ teaspoon ground allspice
	⅛ teaspoon finely ground black pepper
¼ bunch flat-leafed parsley, washed, dried, most of the stalk cut off, finely chopped (about ¼ cup)	1 tablespoon all-purpose flour
	2 tablespoons water
	vegetable oil for frying
2 garlic cloves, peeled and crushed	

Sprinkle the chopped zucchini pulp with a teaspoon of salt and rub firmly with your hands until soft and mushy. Squeeze the watery pulp very dry between the palm of your hands and set aside. Break the eggs into a large mixing bowl and beat well before stirring in the chopped onion, parsley and crushed garlic. Add the zucchini pulp, flour, water, cinnamon, allspice, pepper and salt to taste and blend well together.

Put enough vegetable oil in a large frying pan to shallow fry the omelettes and place over a medium heat. When the oil is hot, drop in 2 tablespoons of egg mixture and spread into a medium-thin circle, about 3 inches in diameter. You should be able to fit 5 or 6 small omelettes per batch. Fry until golden on both sides, remove with a slotted spatula and put to drain onto several layers of paper towels. Continue cooking – you might have to add some oil after every other batch – until you finish the egg mixture, ending up with 14 small omelettes.

Alternatively you can drop in more egg mixture at a time to make 4 large omelettes. Serve tepid or at room temperature.

● You can make this omelette with eggplant pulp, see p. 136, instead of zucchini, or make a parsley omelette (ʿejjet baʿdoones) by leaving out both the zucchini pulp and the garlic. Follow the same instructions as above for either variation.

● You can make delicious sandwiches with these omelettes. Take a medium round pita bread and tear it open at the seams to end up with two similar round disks. Arrange the small omelettes in a row down the middle or lay one big one over the rough side of the bread. Roll the bread in a cigar shape and serve.

FRIED EGGS *with* SUMAC

*Beyd Me'li bil-Summa^*

SERVES 4

4 tablespoons extra virgin olive oil	1 tablespoon sumac
8 eggs, organic if available	salt to taste
	¼ cup spring onions (scallions), finely chopped

Pour the olive oil into a frying pan which is large enough to take all 8 eggs and place over a medium heat.

Break the eggs into a shallow bowl, making sure they stay whole, and when the oil is hot, carefully slide them into the pan. This way the eggs go in all at once and will cook evenly. Gently shake the pan from side to side to spread the eggs across it. Sprinkle with sumac and salt to taste and cook until the whites are done and the yolks are still soft. Serve immediately with the chopped scallions.

FRIED EGGS *with* POMEGRANATE SYRUP

Beyd Me'li bi Rebb el-Rumman

SERVES 4

4 tablespoons extra virgin olive oil	2 tablespoons water
8 eggs, organic if available	salt to taste
1 tablespoon pomegranate syrup (see Lebanese larder, p. 28)	

Follow the recipe for fried eggs with sumac (above), and replace the sumac with 1 tablespoon pomegranate syrup diluted with 2 tablespoons water and salted to taste. Pour the sauce over the nearly cooked eggs and let it bubble before taking it off the heat. Serve hot.

SCRAMBLED EGGS *with* SPRING ONIONS

M'farraket Bassal Akhdar

SERVES 4

6 tablespoons extra virgin olive oil	8 eggs, organic if available
2 bunches spring onions (scallions), trimmed and thinly sliced	¼ teaspoon finely ground black pepper
	salt to taste

Put the olive oil and sliced onions into a large frying pan and place over a medium heat. Fry, stirring regularly, until the onions are soft.

Break the eggs into a shallow bowl and whisk them lightly. When the onions are ready, pour the beaten eggs into the pan. Season with pepper and salt to taste and scramble them until done to your liking. Serve hot.

● You can vary on the above by using chives instead of spring onions.

ᛯᛯᛯ w + ⊕ ᚻ ᚻ ᚕ ᚃ ᛞ ᛚᛚᛱ ᛋ ᛉ ᛏ

SCRAMBLED EGGS *with* POTATOES *and* ONIONS

M'farraket Batatah wa Bassal

SERVES 4

6 tablespoons vegetable oil	6 eggs, organic if available
4 medium potatoes, peeled, washed and diced into ½-inch cubes	¼ teaspoon finely ground black pepper
2 medium onions, finely chopped	salt to taste

103

Put the vegetable oil in a large frying pan and place over a medium heat. When the oil is hot (to test the heat drop in a cube of potato, and if the oil bubbles around it, it is ready) put in the diced potatoes and sauté until lightly golden. Add the onions and cook until both potatoes and onions are golden brown. In the meantime break the eggs into a mixing bowl and whisk them lightly before pouring over the potatoes and onion. Season with pepper and salt to taste and scramble until the eggs are done to your taste.

● You can also prepare this dish with either potatoes or onions on their own.

SCRAMBLED EGGS *with* TOMATOES
Beyd bil-Banadoorah

This dish is particularly delicious when prepared with duck or goose eggs.

SERVES 4

3 tablespoons extra virgin olive oil	¼ teaspoon finely ground black pepper
1 medium onion, finely sliced	salt to taste
about 14 oz ripe tomatoes, peeled and coarsely chopped, or same amount Italian canned	4 eggs, organic if possible, preferably duck or goose (if the latter, only 2)

Put the olive oil and sliced onions in a deep frying pan, place over a medium heat and fry until golden. Add the chopped tomatoes, season with pepper and salt to taste and boil for 20 minutes or until the tomatoes have lost most of their liquid.

During this time break the eggs into a mixing bowl and beat them well. Pour the beaten eggs into the thickened tomato sauce and scramble until they are done to your liking. Serve hot, tepid or at room temperature with pita bread.

Fish
Al-Samak

Baked Fish with Tahini
Fried Fish with Rice and Caramelized Onions
Baked Fish with a Coriander and Nut Stuffing
Fish Stewed in Spicy Coriander   Fish Kibbé

 Although the Mediterranean coastline of the Lebanon stretches over 100 miles and provides an ample supply of fresh fish, its people have a limited repertoire for elaborate fish dishes. Traditionally those who have cooked and eaten fish have been the prosperous coastal dwellers and they have only accounted for a small percentage of the Lebanese population. Most people have not been able to enjoy fish because of its high cost. Those who could afford it but who lived in the mountains were not able to get a fresh supply until recently when refrigerated transport became available. So it was left to the few Sunni families (the main Muslim sect in the Lebanon), who have been the undisputed lords of the coast for centuries, to devise the few fancy fish dishes in our cuisine.

Because of the ready supply of fresh fish, we usually cook fish plainly. We either grill or fry it and serve it with pita bread that has been fried in olive oil, tahini sauce (*tarator*) (see p. 68) and French fries, a favoured legacy of the French protectorate. Before grilling, the fish is scaled and cleaned, then rubbed with salt and olive oil. It is grilled over an open charcoal fire or under a hot grill until the skin is blistered and the flesh tender. The Lebanese have an unfortunate tendency sometimes to overcook food, a waste of good material, especially in the case of fresh fish, so make sure you do not leave it too long or else the meat will dry up. When we fry fish we normally serve it covered with small triangular pieces of single layers of pita bread which have been fried in olive oil.

The few elaborate dishes given in this section are served on special occasions such as big family gatherings or formal parties.

K K △ ∃ ∃ 𝑃 Y ⊟ ⊟ ⊕ ⸝ ⸝ ⤳ ⊤ o

BAKED FISH *with* TAHINI
Samak bil-Tahineh

In Lebanon this dish is prepared with a whole fish, as there is no tradition of filleting or cutting fish; also because of our habit of using every bit of food we are preparing. The fish head, skin and bones make the sauce tastier, but the time spent picking the fish debris out of the sauce rather spoils the pleasure of savouring it. I therefore suggest using fish fillets or steaks for this recipe.

SERVES 4

about 2 lb white fish fillets or steaks or 1 whole fish weighing about 2 lb	juice of 2½ lemons, or to taste
	vegetable oil for frying
salt	3 large onions, thinly sliced
¾ cup plus 2 tablespoons tahini	1 tablespoon pomegranate seeds for garnish (optional)
1½ cups water	

Rinse the fish pieces (or whole fish) in cold water, pat dry with paper towels and rub lightly with salt. Set aside for half an hour to soak up the salt.

In the meantime pour the tahini into a mixing bowl and gradually stir in the water and lemon juice, alternately, until you have a pale creamy liquid. The tahini will first thicken to a purée-like consistency before it starts to dilute again. If you use less lemon juice, make up for the reduction in liquid by adding more water. The sauce should be quite runny, like a thin, creamy soup.

Preheat the oven to 425°F.

Take a large non-stick frying pan, pour in vegetable oil to a depth of ½ inch and place over a medium heat. When the oil is hot (to test the heat dip in one end of a fish piece, and if the oil bubbles around it, it is ready), fry the fish pieces or whole fish for 1 minute on each side to seal. Remove fish with a slotted spoon and put on a plate for later use.

Fry the sliced onion in the same oil as the fish until golden. Remove with a slotted spoon and drop the onion into the tahini sauce. Add salt to taste, mix well together and pour into a deep baking dish. Arrange the fish in the tahini and onion sauce, turning it to coat evenly, and bake in the preheated oven for 30 minutes or until the sauce has thickened and is bubbling all over. Serve tepid or at room temperature, garnished with a few pomegranate seeds (if you are using them).

FRIED FISH *with* RICE
and CARAMELIZED ONIONS
Sayadiyeh

The rice in this dish has the most lovely golden brown color due to the fact that it is cooked in caramelized onion and fish stock. You will need to order the fish heads from your fishmonger so that you can make the stock.

SERVES 4

2¼ cups (14 oz) white short grain rice	salt
about 1 lb white fish heads	vegetable oil for frying
4 cups water	4 medium onions, sliced
2 to 2¼ lb white fish fillets or steaks	½ teaspoon ground cumin
	½ finely ground black pepper
	1 lemon, quartered

Wash the rice in several changes of cold water and leave it to soak in boiling water for half an hour. Put the fish heads in a saucepan, add the water, and place over a medium heat. Just as the water is about to boil, skim the surface clean and boil gently for 15 minutes.

Rinse the fish pieces in cold water, pat them dry with paper towels and rub them lightly with salt. Fill a large non-stick frying pan with vegetable oil to a depth of ½ inch and place over a medium heat. When the oil is hot (to test the heat dip in a piece of fish and if the oil bubbles around it, it is ready), fry the fish pieces for 1 minute on each side to seal them. Remove with a slotted spoon and put them to drain on a double layer of paper towels.

Add more oil to the pan to deep fry the onion and wait until it is extremely hot before inserting the onion slices. Fry them until they caramelize and turn a rich dark brown, without letting them burn and blacken. Remove with a slotted spoon and spread them thinly on several layers of paper towels for them to drain well and become crispy.

Lift the fish heads out of the stock and drop in three-quarters of the fried onion (reserve the rest for the garnish). Bring back to the boil and simmer for 10 minutes or until the stock takes the color of the onion. Strain the onion over a clean saucepan to collect the brown stock. Liquidize it and stir the onion purée back into the stock.

Place the pan over a medium heat, drain the rice and add to the stock together with any loose fish flakes from the fried pieces, season with cumin, pepper and salt to taste and bring to the boil. Reduce the heat, cover the pan and simmer for 15 minutes or until the rice is done and the liquid absorbed. Place the fish pieces on top of the rice, wrap the lid of the pan with a clean paper towel, put it back on and leave to steam for a few minutes or until the fish is done. Transfer delicately onto a serving dish, making sure the fish sits over the rice. Scatter the reserved crispy onion slices on top and serve hot or at room temperature with the lemon quarters.

● You can vary on the above by adding pine nuts (⅓ cup). Sauté the nuts in a little butter (2 tablespoons) until golden brown and stir into the rice just before serving. This variation is called *sayadiyeh royale*, because of the added luxury of the pine nuts.

BAKED FISH *with a* CORIANDER *and* NUT STUFFING

Samkeh Harrah

Samkeh harrah is a speciality of Tripoli, a large coastal town north of Beirut. It is a particularly delectable way of preparing fish and it is served cold, which makes it an ideal dish for a cold buffet or summer meal. I like to keep the presentation simple and just slide a few sprigs of fresh coriander in the opening between the head and the body, leaving the rest of the fish unadorned. You can use one whole fish, two medium ones or four individual ones. Any one of the following is suitable: sea bass, sea bream, grey mullet, cod, grouper, John Dory, even pike, which, although it is a freshwater fish, has a delicate and firm white flesh that is ideally suited for the stuffing.

SERVES 4

3 lb white fish, scaled and gutted	1 medium onion, finely chopped
Stuffing	1 medium tomato, diced into ¼-inch cubes
⅓ cup pine nuts, ground medium fine	½ cup plus 2 tablespoons extra virgin olive oil
⅓ cup walnuts, ground medium fine	juice of 2 lemons, or to taste
20 garlic cloves, peeled and crushed, or less to taste	1 teaspoon ground cumin
1 teaspoon ground coriander	¼ teaspoon finely ground black pepper
salt	½ teaspoon cayenne powder
2 bunches fresh coriander (about 14 oz on the stalk), washed, dried, most of the stalk cut off, finely chopped	8 small firm tomatoes, topped, seeded and drained (to fill with leftover stuffing)

Pull the gills out of the fish without damaging the head. Rinse the fish under cold water, pat dry with paper towels and rub with a little salt, both inside and outside.

Put the nuts in a blender or food mill or processor and grind until medium fine – do not pulverize into a fine powder as the stuffing should retain a nice crunch. Transfer the ground nuts to a large mixing bowl and put the garlic cloves in the blender or food processor, together with the ground coriander and a pinch of salt. Process into a smooth paste and add to the nuts. Add the chopped coriander, onion, tomato, olive oil and lemon juice. Season with cumin, pepper, cayenne powder and salt to taste and mix well together. Taste, adjust seasoning if necessary, and cover with a paper towel.

Preheat the oven to 350°F.

Sew up about 2 inches of the fish opening, starting from the tail end, to begin forming a pocket for the stuffing. Use a thick thread and prick the needle well inside the flesh so that it does not come apart during cooking. Put as much stuffing as you can inside the fish and into its mouth and finish sewing up the sides. (You can use toothpicks or mini metal skewers to close the fish, but the presentation will not be as nice as with the sides sewn.)

Take a large baking dish, grease it with a little olive oil and lay the fish onto it. Wrap any leftover stuffing in aluminium foil and place next to the fish or onto another tray. Bake in the preheated oven for 40 minutes or until the fish is just done. Take it out of the oven and leave to cool before filling the prepared tomato halves with the cooled extra stuffing. Arrange the filled tomatoes around the fish and serve at room temperature.

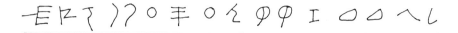

FISH STEWED *in* SPICY CORIANDER
Samkeh Harrah Matbookhah

SERVES 4

2 to 2¼ lb white fish fillets or steaks	2 bunches fresh coriander (about 14 oz on the stalk),
salt	washed, dried, most of the stalks
4 medium onions, finely chopped	cut off, finely chopped

10 large garlic cloves, peeled and finely chopped	1 teaspoon ground cumin
	½ teaspoon ground coriander
vegetable oil for frying	½ teaspoon cayenne powder
½ cup plus 2 tablespoons extra virgin olive oil	about 1¼ cups lemon juice, or to taste

Rinse the fish pieces in cold water, pat dry with paper towels and rub slightly with salt. Set aside for half an hour to soak up the salt, during which time set about preparing the chopped ingredients.

Put enough vegetable oil in a large non-stick frying pan to deep fry the fish and place over a medium heat. When the oil is hot (to test the heat dip in one tip of a fish piece, and if the oil bubbles around it, it is ready), put as many fish pieces as you can fit comfortably and fry for 1 minute on each side to seal them. Remove with a slotted spoon and put to drain onto a double layer of paper towels.

Put the olive oil and chopped onion in a wide saucepan and place over medium heat. Fry until golden, then add the chopped garlic and sauté for 1 minute. Add the fresh coriander, cumin, coriander powder and cayenne pepper and stir for a minute or until the coriander softens. Pour in the lemon juice, add pepper and salt to taste and bring to the boil and keep boiling for 5 minutes. Reduce the heat and arrange the fish in the coriander sauce. You can put in the fish as it is or flake it in small pieces. Cover the pan and simmer for another 5 minutes or until the fish is done and the sauce has thickened. Serve tepid or at room temperature with or without rice.

FISH KIBBÉ
Kibbet Samak

This is a northern speciality and rarely prepared in the capital or south of it.

SERVES 4

1 tablespoon of olive oil	salt to taste
½ bunch fresh coriander (about 3½ oz on the stalk), washed, dried and most of the stalk cut off	¾ cup bulgur, washed and drained
	stuffing
about 1 lb boneless and skinless white fish	about ½ lb onions, finely sliced or chopped (about 1¼ cups)
1 medium onion, peeled and quartered	¼ teaspoon finely ground white pepper
grated zest of ½ orange or lemon	salt to taste
½ teaspoon ground cinnamon	5 tablespoons extra virgin olive oil
¼ teaspoon finely ground white pepper	⅓ cup pine nuts

The fish kibbé

Put the coriander in a blender or food processor together with the fish, quartered onion, orange or lemon zest, cinnamon, pepper and salt to taste. Process the ingredients together, then wash and drain the bulgur and add to the fish mixture. Blend again until you have a smooth mixture; do not overprocess or the fish will lose its texture. If your blender or processor is too small to take all the ingredients in one go, divide them in two and process in two batches.

The stuffing

Put the sliced (or chopped) onion, pine nuts and olive oil in a mixing bowl, season with pepper and salt to taste and mix well together.

Finishing and serving

Preheat the oven to 350°F and grease a medium baking dish with a little olive oil.

Divide the fish mixture into two equal parts then make and decorate the kibbé following the same instructions as for *kibbeh bil-saniyeh* on pp. 118-119. Dribble a little olive oil over the top and bake

in the preheated oven for 30 minutes or until cooked. Serve hot or tepid.

Kibbé
Kibbeh

Raw Kibbé   Baked Kibbé   Kibbé Balls
Kibbé Balls Stewed in Yogurt
Kibbé and Chick Peas Cooked in Tahini Sauce
Potato Pie

VEGETARIAN KIBBÉ
Kibbeh Bedoon Lahmeh
Pumpkin Kibbé
Vegetarian Kibbé Cooked in Kishk Sauce

 Kibbeh is a highly seasoned mixture of finely minced lamb, bulgur and chopped onion. When it is served raw (*nayeh*), the mixture is made with less bulgur and a handful of crushed basil or mint leaves are added to give the meat a fresh and fragrant taste. In the Lebanon a little *liyeh* (fat from the sheep's tail) is also added to make it more velvety. It is one of our great national dishes and until the arrival of the food processor, the meat was pounded by hand in a marble or stone mortar (*jorn*) with a wooden pestle (*m'daʾah*). Because of the time and effort involved in its preparation, *kibbeh* was – and still is – a festive dish served either to honour guests or as a special family treat.

I can still remember the excitement of *kibbeh* being made by hand at our home in Beirut and, after so many years, can still see my mother and grandmother taking turns to pound the meat. They sat on low stools, either side of a beautiful white marble mortar in which were pieces of tender pink lamb. The rhythmic sound of pounding swelled from a slow dull beat to a faster, louder one as the meat was pounded into a smooth paste. It was only broken by the time it took

113

to pass over the pestle and lasted for what seemed like hours – in fact merely one. My sisters and I darted in and out of the kitchen, repeatedly asking the same question "Is it ready yet?" and unfailingly getting the same answer "Not yet, we will call you when it is." We lingered outside the kitchen waiting for the smell of pounded basil (*haba^*), the final addition, hence our cue to rush back into the kitchen before the *kibbeh* was even finished.

We each grabbed a plate and waited like ravenous urchins, our eyes fixed on my mother's long white fingers – as the mistress of the house she mixed the *kibbeh* – blending the bulgur, onion, basil and seasonings into the meat. Finally it was done and we held out our plates for my mother to give each of us a little *kibbeh nayeh* (raw), which we ate with relish before carelessly abandoning my mother and grandmother to prepare the second batch of *kibbeh* that was to be cooked.

Cooked *kibbeh* is prepared in two different ways. It is either shaped into balls (*kibbeh ^rass*) or made into a pie (*kibbeh bil-saniyeh*) with a minced meat, onion and nut stuffing. The latter is an essentially Lebanese dish, whilst the former is shared with other neighboring countries.

Kibbeh ^rass is made in three shapes: a small ovoid ball with slightly pointed ends; an elongated version of the ball where the shape is stretched to at least twice the length and with narrower ends; and a medium disc, about 4 inches in diameter, with a slightly raised middle top under which is a little stuffing or a piece of sheep's fat from the tail (*liyeh*). The disc-like shape is more typical of mountain and Syrian cooking.

The small ovoid balls vary slightly in shape depending on the dexterity of the cook. To make perfect balls you need to produce a mixture with the right proportion of bulgur to meat and other trimmings. You must not overdo the grinding and kneading to achieve the right consistency. Finally you have to perfect the skill of making well-formed balls. This said you can easily make utterly delicious balls without fussing too much about achieving perfection to compete with mothers and sisters in-law as they do in the Lebanon. The size of the balls changes according to whether they are offered as nibbles (very small and rather difficult to make), cooked in a sauce or served as a starter (medium and still requiring a special knack to produce attractive ones).

Kibbeh balls are cooked in a variety of sauces: a cooked yogurt sauce flavored with fresh coriander and garlic with sometimes meat dumplings (*sheesh barak*) added to it; one made with cooked tahini, fried onion and lemon juice; and another made with kishk (see Lebanese larder, p. 23).

Kibbeh discs and the elongated balls are a speciality of the North and Syria. They are grilled or fried and eaten as a main course.

Kibbeh bil-saniyeh is traditionally cooked in round tin baking dishes. Each family has their own variation, whether it is in the choice of ingredients or in the way of decorating and cooking it, to make theirs better than that of others. Some layer it very thinly with a generous spread of stuffing in between. Others make the layers thicker and the stuffing less predominant. The variations on the stuffing are numerous. The pine nuts can be sautéed or left raw, a dash of pomegranate syrup or a squeeze of lemon or a secret mixture of spices can be added, or not, and so on. The decoration ranges from a bold uniform geometric design to an intricately incised one, with each triangle decorated differently.

It is almost impossible to serve *kibbeh* to a Lebanese person without provoking – after much praise for your own – a comment on how they or an expert member of their family makes *kibbeh* another way, with an extra ingredient that makes the taste that much more delicate, the implication being that theirs is superior to the one you are serving them.

In the following pages I give my mother's recipes for *kibbeh*. I will avoid the clichéd comment that hers are the best, but they are the ones I know best and have made successfully many, many times. I am also including some vegetarian recipes for those readers who do not eat meat.

RAW KIBBÉ
Kibbeh Nayeh

When preparing *kibbeh nayeh* you have to make sure that the meat you use is very fresh, lean and cleaned of all ligaments and other chewy bits. The leg fillet is the cut you want to use and you can either ask your butcher to prepare and mince (grind) it for you or you can bone, defat and clean it yourself before processing it in a electric meat grinder or food processor.

SERVES 4 TO 6

1 small onion, peeled and quartered	½ teaspoon finely ground black pepper
a handful of fresh basil or mint leaves	salt to taste
1 to 1¼ lb lamb from the top of the leg, boned, skinned and defatted and put through the meat grinder or food processor	1 cup fine bulgur
	small bowl of lightly salted water
	pine nuts for garnish
2 teaspoons ground cinnamon	chopped spring onions (scallions), and fresh mint sprigs for garnish
2 teaspoons ground allspice	

Put the onion in the blender or food processor and process until finely chopped. Add the basil (or mint) and process until you have a smooth paste.

Add the minced meat, cinnamon, allspice, pepper and salt to taste and blend together until smooth. If your machine is not big enough to take the onion, meat and spices in one go, process them in two equal batches. Make sure you do not over-process the meat, as it will lose its fresh pink color.

Prepare a bowl of lightly salted water and have it at hand, before transferring the meat into a mixing bowl.

Put the bulgur in a bowl and add two or three changes of cold water. Drain well and add to the meat. Mix all together with your hand, dipping your hand every now and then in the salted water to moisten both it and the *kibbeh* and knead until you have a smooth meat paste, about 3 minutes. Taste, adjust seasoning if necessary and then drag a serrated knife through the processed meat to catch the last bits of ligaments, wiping these off the blade between each dragging until you stop picking up any pieces of ligament.

Transfer the meat to an oval or round serving dish and flatten it into a shallow cake. Use your index finger or the tip of a small spoon to make little curved dips in a straight line down the middle and again either side of it. Trickle a little olive oil into the dips, scatter a few raw pine nuts over the surface and serve immediately with chopped spring onions and sprigs of fresh mint.

BAKED KIBBÉ
Kibbeh bil-Saniyeh

My London butcher is used now to my eccentric request for a leg of lamb, which he has to bone, skin, defat and, the ultimate crime, put through a fine mincer. If there are other customers waiting, I have to first apologize for monopolising the butcher's time, then I feel compelled to explain that the meat is not being misused but, on the contrary, prepared for one of our most renowned national dishes, *kibbeh bil-saniyeh*.

Kibbeh bil-saniyeh freezes very well (the same goes for kibbé balls, p. 119). I freeze it before cooking so that I can serve kibbé at very short notice and if there are any leftovers, I can freeze them again.

SERVES 4 TO 6

stuffing	1 medium onion, peeled and quartered
6 tablespoons unsalted butter	
⅓ cup pine nuts	about 1 lb lamb from the leg, boned, skinned, defatted and minced (ground)
about 1 lb large onions, finely chopped	
about ½ lb lean minced (ground) lamb	1 cup fine bulgur
	2 teaspoons ground cinnamon
2 teaspoons ground cinnamon	2 teaspoons ground allspice
2 teaspoons ground allspice	½ teaspoon finely ground black pepper
½ teaspoon finely ground black pepper	
	salt to taste
salt to taste	small bowl of lightly salted water
kibbé	6 knobs (pieces) of butter

To prepare the stuffing
This stuffing has a number of variations. You can slightly sour the taste by adding 1 teaspoon of pomegranate syrup or lemon juice or make it more bland by adding the pine nuts uncooked.

Melt the butter in a deep frying pan over a medium heat and sauté the pine nuts, stirring regularly, until they turn golden brown. Make sure they don't burn – they can blacken very fast. Remove with a slotted spoon and put to drain onto a double layer of paper towels.

Fry the chopped onion, in the same butter, until soft and transparent. Stir in the minced meat and cook until it loses all traces of pink, mashing and stirring it with a wooden spoon or fork, so that it separates well and does not form lumps. Take off the heat and season with the cinnamon, allspice, pepper and salt to taste. Stir in the pine nuts. Taste and adjust seasoning if necessary.

To prepare the kibbé

Put the quartered onion in a blender or food processor and process until it is very finely chopped.

Add the minced lamb along with the cinnamon, allspice, pepper and salt to taste. Blend together until smooth. If your machine is not big enough to take the onion, meat and spices in one go, process them in two equal batches.

Prepare a bowl of lightly salted water and have it at hand before transferring the meat mixture to a large mixing bowl.

Put the bulgur in a bowl and add two or three changes of cold water. Drain the bulgur well and add to the meat mixture. Mix together with your hand, dipping your hand every now and then in the salted water to moisten both it and the *kibbeh*. Knead the mixture until you have a smooth meat paste, which takes about 3 minutes. Taste and adjust seasoning if necessary.

Finishing and serving

Grease a deep baking dish about 12 x 8 x 2 inches with a knob of butter.

Divide the *kibbeh* into two equal parts. Moisten your hands in the salted water and pinch off a handful of *kibbeh* from one piece. Flatten it between your palms, to a thickness of about ½ inch and place it on the bottom of the baking dish starting from one corner. Smooth it down evenly with your fingers, pinch off another handful from the same piece, flatten and lay next to the first piece, slightly overlapping it. Dip your fingers in water and smooth the pieces together until the joint disappears – make sure you connect the *kibbeh*, pieces well together so that they do not come apart during cooking. Continue the above process until you finish the first half of *kibbeh*, and you have covered the bottom of the pan. Then go over the whole layer with moistened fingers to even it out.

Spread the stuffing evenly over the lining layer of *kibbeh* and lay the other half of *kibbeh* over the stuffing in the same way as above.

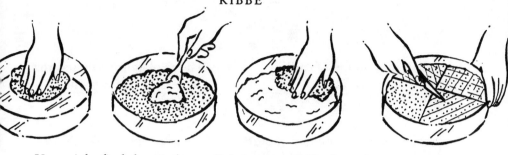

You might find the top layer slightly more difficult to do as you will be laying the meat over the loose stuffing instead of the smooth surface of the baking dish, but you will soon get the hang of it.

Preheat the oven to 350°F.

Cut the *kibbeh* into quarters, then with a knife make shallow incisions to draw a geometric pattern across the top of each quarter (see diagram or make up your own design). The decoration work is time-consuming and can be omitted without affecting the taste, although the presentation will lose its attractive traditional look. After you finish decorating the pie make a hole in the middle with your finger, put a piece of butter over the hole and one over each quarter. Insert a round pointed knife between the edge of the pie and the side of the pan and slide it all along the pie to detach the meat from the sides.

Bake in a preheated oven for 15 to 20 minutes or until the pie has shrunk slightly and the meat is just done. Take out of the oven and leave to sit for a few minutes, then cut into medium-sized rectangular pieces (if you have baked the *kibbeh* in a round dish cut it into triangles) and transfer carefully onto a serving dish. Serve hot or tepid with a yogurt and cucumber salad, p. 76, or with *hommus*, p. 50, and an arugula salad, p. 74.

KIBBÉ BALLS

Kibbeh ˆRass

Kibbé balls are fried to serve as a starter or left raw and cooked in a sauce made from yogurt (*bil-labniyeh*), or tahini (*ˆarnabiyeh*) or kishk (*bil-kishk*).

MAKES 20

half the amount of stuffing, p. 117	small bowl of lightly salted water
half the amount of *kibbeh*, p. 117	vegetable oil for frying

Prepare half the amount of stuffing and *kibbeh*, pp. 117-118, then divide the *kibbeh* into 20 balls, each the size of a walnut.

Lightly moisten your hands in the salted water and placing one meat ball in your hand, with the index finger of your other hand burrow a hole into the meat ball while rotating it to make the hollowing out easier and more even. You should produce a meat shell resembling a topless egg, with sides about ¼ inch thick. Be careful not to pierce the bottom or sides of the meat. If you do, mend the break with your moistened finger or press the meat into a ball and start again.

Put approximately two teaspoons of stuffing inside the meat shell and pinch the open edges together with your fingers. Cup your free fingers over the filled ball and gently shape it into an ovoid ball with slightly pointed ends. Put the finished ball on a freezer-proof plate and continue making the balls until you have finished both meat and stuffing. Put these in the freezer so that they stiffen a little and do not lose their shape in the handling before frying.

Heat enough vegetable oil in a frying pan to deep fry the balls. Test to see when the oil is hot by inserting the tip of one ball; if the oil bubbles around it, it is ready. Once the temperature is correct, delicately drop in as many balls as will fit comfortably and fry them until browned all over, for about 3 minutes. Remove with a slotted spoon and put to drain onto several layers of paper towels. Serve hot, tepid or at room temperature.

KIBBÉ BALLS STEWED *in* YOGURT
Kibbeh bi-Labniyeh

SERVES 4

kibbé balls, p. 120	1 cup water
yogurt sauce, p. 172	salt to taste

Prepare the kibbé balls as in the recipe on p. 120 and put them uncooked in the freezer while you make the yogurt sauce.

Prepare the yogurt sauce, p. 172, adding the water to the yogurt and egg before bringing to the boil and keep the coriander (or mint) and garlic mixture on the side.

Once the yogurt has boiled, drop in the barely frozen kibbé balls, reduce the heat to low, and simmer for 5 minutes, stirring occasionally – do this gently so that you do not break the kibbé balls. Stir in the coriander (or mint) and garlic mixture and simmer for another 3 minutes.

Serve hot, preferably as soon as it is ready. You can reheat it, but as with all dishes cooked in yogurt you have to be careful not to let the yogurt separate during the re-heating process. First shake the pan from side to side to reblend the water that might have seeped out of the yogurt. Place the pan, uncovered so that no steam drops back into the yogurt, over a low heat and simmer until hot, gently stirring regularly. *Kibbeh bil-labniyeh* is served in soup plates and eaten with a spoon.

KIBBÉ *and* CHICK PEAS COOKED *in* TAHINI SAUCE
Kibbeh ˆArnabiyeh

SERVES 4

¾ cup dried chick peas, soaked overnight	kibbé balls, p. 120 (without stuffing)
½ teaspoon baking soda	12 baby onions
7 oz lamb meat from the shank, cut into medium chunks	(about ¾ lb), peeled
2 or 3 lamb bones (optional)	*sauce*
3 cinnamon sticks	2 cups tahini
	juice of 3 lemons (or to taste)
	2 cups lamb stock
	salt to taste

The night before
Put the chick peas to soak in three times their volume of water. Stir in half a teaspoon of baking soda; this should soften them and therefore help reduce their cooking time.

Preparation
Prepare the kibbé balls as in the recipe on p. 120, omitting the stuffing. When it comes to shaping the balls, close the empty, hollowed shells and shape as if you had filled them, a more difficult operation but easily managed after the first two or three attempts. Put the uncooked kibbé balls on a plate and pop them in the freezer.

Rinse the meat, the bones (if you are using them) and the drained chick peas under cold water and put them in a large saucepan. Cover with water, place the pan over a high heat and bring to the boil. As the water is about to boil, skim the surface clean and add the cinnamon sticks. Reduce the heat to medium, cover the pan and boil gently for 45 minutes.

Meanwhile peel the baby onions. When the 45 minutes are up, add the onions and cook for another 15 minutes, then remove and discard the bones. Strain the meat, chick peas and onions, collecting the broth in a bowl for later use and keep them warm. Measure 2 cups of lamb stock and keep it at hand for the tahini sauce.

Pour the tahini into a mixing bowl and gradually add the lemon juice and stock alternately, stirring in the same direction. The mixture will thicken into a purée-like consistency before it starts to dilute again. Taste the sauce two-thirds of the way through so that you can adjust the amount of lemon juice to taste. If you decide to use less lemon juice, add a little more stock to make up for the lost liquid. You should end up with a runny sauce that has the consistency of a thin creamy soup.

Pour the tahini sauce into a large clean saucepan or casserole, add salt to taste and place over a medium heat. Bring it to the boil, stirring constantly in the same direction (or else the sauce will curdle) and boil for 2 minutes.

Remove the kibbé balls from the freezer and gently drop them into the tahini sauce. Add the chick peas, meat and onions, bring back to the boil and simmer for 3 minutes. Stir occasionally, very carefully so that you do not break the kibbé balls. Taste, adjust seasoning if necessary, and transfer delicately to a deep serving dish. Serve hot with vermicelli rice, or at room temperature with Arabic bread.

● You can produce several variations of this dish:
1 Make the *kibbé* balls with the stuffing, p. 119, and prepare as above.
2 Omit the lamb meat and prepare as above.
3 Use sliced onions instead of whole ones. Weigh up an equivalent amount of medium onions, slice thinly and shallow fry them in vegetable oil until golden before adding to the tahini sauce and prepare as above. Some people think that the melting onion slices blend better with the meat and the sauce than the individual baby ones.
4 Make a vegetarian version by replacing the meat and kibbé balls with about 1 pound colocasia or taro (see Lebanese larder, p. 21). Peel the colocasia and rinse under cold water. Pat dry with paper towels, cut into medium chunks and shallow fry in vegetable oil until golden all over. Drop in the boiling tahini sauce as with the meat and cook for 10 minutes or until tender.

POTATO PIE
Kibbet Batatah

This potato pie is quite similar to the English shepherd's pie and is probably a vestige from colonial days. Still it is very much part of our daily diet and the taste is made exotic by the inclusion of pine nuts and the cinnamon and allspice seasoning. Another difference is that the stuffing is quite dry, without onions or tomatoes. The pie should be served with a refreshing salad such as arugula, p. 74.

SERVES 4

about 3 lb potatoes	½ teaspoon ground allspice
salt	¼ teaspoon finely ground black
4 tablespoons butter	pepper
½ cup pine nuts	½ cup plus 2 tablespoons crème
1 lb lean minced	fraîche, or sour cream if
(ground) lamb	unavailable
½ teaspoon ground cinnamon	1 egg yolk

Wash the potatoes and put them in a large saucepan. Cover with water, add a generous pinch of salt, put the lid over the pan and place over a high heat. Bring to the boil, then reduce the heat to medium and boil gently for 30 minutes or until the potatoes are done.

Preheat the oven to 400°F and grease a deep baking dish, about 12 inches x 8 inches, with a little butter.

Melt the butter in a frying pan over a medium heat and sauté the pine nuts, stirring regularly, until they become golden brown. Remove with a slotted spoon onto a plate. Sauté the minced meat in the butter until it loses all traces of pink. Keep mashing and stirring it with a wooden spoon or fork so that it separates well and does not form lumps. Remove from the heat and season with cinnamon, allspice, pepper and salt to taste. Stir in the pine nuts, taste, adjust seasoning if necessary and set aside.

Drain the cooked potatoes. Peel and purée them. Stir in the cream and egg yolk and season with pepper and salt to taste. Spread half of the purée in an even layer over the bottom of the baking dish. Spread the stuffing over the potatoes and cover with a layer of the remaining purée. Bake for 30 minutes or until the top becomes golden and the pie is hot throughout. Serve hot.

● To make a vegetarian version, replace the minced meat with ¾ pound onions, finely chopped and fried until golden in the same butter as the nuts.

PUMPKIN KIBBÉ
Kibbet La'teen

Pumpkin kibbé is a rather uncommon dish which has a lovely orangey-brown color and a very nutty and quite delicious taste.

SERVES 4

⅛ cup dried split chick peas, soaked overnight, or ⅓ cup canned peas, coarsely chopped	1 tablespoon all-purpose flour
	a bowl of slightly salted water
¼ teaspoon baking soda	*stuffing*
pumpkin kibbé	5 tablespoons extra virgin olive oil
about 2 lb fresh pumpkin	3 medium onions, thinly sliced
1 medium onion, peeled and quartered	⅓ cup walnuts, coarsely chopped
1 teaspoon ground allspice	1 teaspoon ground allspice
½ teaspoon ground cinnamon	½ teaspoon ground cinnamon
⅛ teaspoon finely ground black pepper	⅛ teaspoon finely ground black pepper
salt to taste	1 tablespoon pomegranate syrup
1¾ cups fine bulgur	(see Lebanese larder, p. 28)

The night before
Put the chick peas to soak in three times their volume of water. Stir in half a teaspoon of baking soda, this should soften them and therefore help reduce their cooking time.

To prepare the kibbé
Peel the pumpkin and cut it in medium-sized pieces. Put the pumpkin pieces in a large saucepan, cover them with water and place over a high heat. Bring to the boil, then reduce the heat to medium and boil gently for 15-20 minutes or until very soft.

Drain the pumpkin in a colander and press a plate over it to extract all the excess liquid. The pumpkin has to be squeezed very dry so that it blends well with the bulgur for you to be able to shape the mixture without any trouble. Transfer to a large mixing bowl, mash the pumpkin with a masher or a fork and set aside.

Prepare a bowl of slightly salted water and have at hand for when you mix the kibbé.

Put the quartered onion and the allspice, cinnamon, pepper and salt in a blender or food processor and process until very finely chopped. Add the chopped onion and spices to the mashed pumpkin. Add the bulgur and the tablespoon of flour and mix with your hand until you have a smooth paste. Taste, adjust seasoning if necessary, then cover with a clean kitchen towel and set aside.

To prepare the stuffing
Put the olive oil in a frying pan and place over a medium heat. When the oil is hot, add the sliced onion and fry until golden.

Meanwhile drain the soaked split chick peas (or canned ones) and rinse under cold water. Chop them coarsely before adding to the olive oil and onion and cook for another 3-4 minutes, stirring occasionally.

Add the chopped walnuts and season with the allspice, cinnamon, pepper and salt to taste. Stir in the pomegranate syrup and mix well together. Take off the heat, taste, adjust seasoning if necessary and leave to cool.

To prepare the kibbé
Pumpkin kibbé is made in the same way as meat kibbé. If you want to bake it, follow the same instructions as in the recipe for *kibbeh bil-saniyeh* on pp. 118-119, or make fried balls by following the instructions in the recipe for *kibbeh ´rass* on p. 120. Serve hot, luke-warm or at room temperature with plain yogurt and/or a salad.

⊿⊿ ∃ 𝑌 𝚈 日 𝓍 𝟐 ∨ ○ ○ ¥)?? ↓○

VEGETARIAN KIBBÉ
COOKED *in* KISHK SAUCE
Kibbet el-Heeleh bil-Kishk

In Arabic *heeleh* means stratagem and *kibbet el-heeleh* or 'kibbé of stratagem' is called thus because it pretends to be a meat kibbé without the meat. It is made with bulgur, all-purpose flour and onion, and apart from the slightly paler color, it looks very much like meat kibbé. I assume it was devised by the Christian Lebanese who still wanted to enjoy kibbé during the periods of Lent and had to find a meatless solution.

SERVES 4

Vegetarian kibbé	1 medium onion, finely chopped
1 small onion, peeled and quartered	⅓ cup walnuts, coarsely chopped
½ teaspoon ground allspice	½ teaspoon ground allspice
¼ teaspoon ground cinnamon	¼ teaspoon cinnamon
⅛ teaspoon finely ground black pepper	⅛ teaspoon finely ground black pepper
1 cup fine bulgur	1 teaspoon pomegranate syrup
8 tablespoons all-purpose white flour	(see Lebanese larder, p. 28)
salt to taste	*kishk sauce*
a bowl of lightly salted water	2 tablespoons unsalted butter
stuffing	9 oz (1½ cups) kishk
4 tablespoons unsalted butter	(see Lebanese larder, p. 23)
⅛ cup pine nuts	8 cups water

To prepare the kibbé
Put the quartered onion in the blender or food processor, add the allspice, cinnamon and pepper and process until very finely chopped. Transfer to a large mixing bowl.

Put the bulgur in a bowl and add two or three changes of cold water. Drain well and add the bulgur to the seasoned onion. Prepare a bowl of lightly salted water to have at hand before mixing the kibbé.

Add the flour to the bulgur and onion, add salt to taste and mix well with your hand, dipping your hand every now and then in the bowl of water to moisten both it and the bulgur mixture, until you have a smooth paste. Cover with a clean paper towel and set aside.

To prepare the stuffing
Melt the butter in a frying pan over a medium heat and sauté the pine nuts, stirring regularly, until they turn golden brown. Make sure they don't burn – they can blacken very fast. Remove with a slotted spoon and put to drain onto a double layer of paper towels.

Fry the chopped onion, in the same butter, until golden. Stir in the chopped walnuts and cook for 3-4 minutes, stirring occasionally. Season with the allspice, cinnamon, pepper and salt to taste. Stir in pomegranate syrup and the pine nuts, cook for another minute, then take off the heat. Taste, adjust seasoning if necessary and set aside.

To make the kibbé balls

Kibbet el-heeleh is made in the same way as meat kibbé. Follow the instructions to make kibbeh 'rass in the recipe on p. 120, using the above bulgur mixture and stuffing and put the balls in the freezer.

To prepare the kishk sauce

Melt the butter in a large saucepan over a medium heat. Stir in the kishk and gradually add the water, stirring in one cup at a time, so that the mixture does not become lumpy. Bring to the boil, stirring constantly, then reduce the heat to low. Taste before adding any salt, as the powdered kishk is already salted; add salt to taste and simmer for 3 minutes. The sauce should be like a thin porridge, and, depending on the brand of kishk, you might need a little more or less water to achieve the right consistency.

Finishing and serving

Take the kibbé balls out of the freezer and drop them into the kishk sauce. Bring back to the boil and simmer for 5 minutes, gently stirring occasionally. Kibbet el-heeleh is served very hot in soup plates and eaten with a spoon.

● You can also deep fry the kibbé balls and serve them lukewarm or at room temperature.

● If you want to bake kibbet el-heeleh follow the same instructions as for kibbeh bil-saniyeh, on pp. 118-119 and serve hot, lukewarm or at room temperature.

In the foreground: Eggplants and Chick Peas in Tomato Sauce, left (pp. 45-47) and Wild Endive in Olive Oil, right (pp. 59-60). In the background: Eggplant Purée (pp. 43-45).

Spinach Triangles (p. 95) and Minced Meat Crescents (p. 98).

In the foreground: Baked Kibbé, right (pp. 117-119), and Yogurt and Cucumber Salad, left (p. 76); in the background: Kibbé Balls (pp. 119-120).

In the foreground: Chicken with Roasted Green Wheat (pp. 168-170); in the background: Lentil and Swiss Chard Soup with Lemon Juice (pp. 86-87).

Eggplant, Rice and Nut Cake (pp. 180-182).

Okra and Meat Stew (pp. 193-194) and Plain Rice (p. 187).

Walnut Triangles (pp. 230-231).

Date and Walnut Pastries (pp. 231-233 and 236-238).

Kafta and Kebabs
Kaftah wa Lahem Meshwi

Kafta   Baked Kafta with Potatoes and Tomatoes
Kafta Grilled on Skewers   Meat Grilled on Skewers

 The Lebanese always serve their kebabs wrapped in pita bread. They tear the bread open along the seam, leaving a short section unbroken and place it on a plate by the heat before they start cooking the meat. While grilling, they regularly remove the kebabs from the heat and rest them on one open side of the bread. They flap the other side over the meat and press lightly for the bread to soak up the cooking juices.

During the meal the host or hostess will always offer the juiciest piece of bread to an honored guest or favored relative. The recipient of this delicious morsel is more often than not a man, our society being a male-dominated one. In my family it was my father or brother to whom my mother turned with this offering, leaving us girls forever wondering when our turn would come. I suppose we should consider ourselves lucky not to have been given away as unwanted progeny like the girl who was offered by her despairing mother to Freya Stark as described in the extract from one of her letters below.

"Brumana. 26.1.28

Yesterday as I came from a walk through a little group of houses, I was invited in (they always do this). I was glad of the rest too. The rooms were beautifully clean; stone floors and straw mats. In one corner a new yellow and white quilt and a head all wrapped in bandages (I thought). The lady of the house went up and shook the protesting head from its sleep. I couldn't tell whether it was a man or a woman, but asked whether it was wounded.

129

"'Oh no,' said the lady, much surprised, 'she is the mother of the baby,' and there in the cradle, so covered that not a breath of air could touch her, was a two-day-old baby girl. 'Another one here' said the grandmother lifting a far corner of the quilt and rolling out a child. 'And another here,' turning over what seemed to be a small bolster. I sat contemplating from the divan, feeling as one does in the presence of the conjurer who manufactures rabbits, and not knowing what to say. Three girls one on top of another is a real calamity to a young wife. 'You must be happy with your "bint[1],"' says I inadequately at last. 'You can take one away with you,' says the mother, suddenly arousing herself to animation."

Freya Stark, Letters from Syria, 1942

[1] Daughter

KAFTA
Kaftah

In Lebanon it is the butcher who normally prepares *kaftah*, a mixture of minced meat, chopped parsley and onion. I remember always wanting to go and buy it as I was fascinated by the butcher's expert handling of his large chopping knife as he made it. He deftly chopped the onion and parsley and then used the blade to blend these and the seasonings into the meat. Here in the West I prepare kafta in an electric meat grinder or blender and it is never as good as that prepared by hand because of the slight liquidizing of the parsley and onion caused by the mechanical blade. This gives the mixture a somewhat less agreeable texture, especially when it is eaten raw, although the difference is hardly noticeable when the meat is cooked.

SERVES 4

2 medium onions, peeled and quartered	½ bunch parsley (7 oz on the stalk), washed, dried and most of the stalk cut off
about 1¼ lb lean minced (ground) lamb (use leg)	¼ teaspoon finely ground black pepper
½ teaspoon ground cinnamon	salt to taste
½ teaspoon ground allspice	

Put the quartered onions and parsley in the blender or food processor and process until finely chopped. Transfer to a mixing bowl and process the minced meat with the seasonings until you have a smooth paste.

Mix the meat with the parsley and onion with your hand until well blended together. Taste, adjust seasoning if necessary, and serve it raw (*kaftah nayeh*) with your choice of Arabic bread or use it in one of the following recipes.

BAKED KAFTA *with* POTATOES *and* TOMATOES
Kaftah bil-Saniyeh

SERVES 4

a piece of butter	about 1¾ lb (about 5 or 6 small)
kaftah, p. 130	red tomatoes, thinly sliced
about 1 lb potatoes, peeled and very thinly sliced, about ¼ inch thick	salt to taste
	3 tablespoons water

Preheat the oven to 400°F and grease the bottom and sides of a medium deep baking dish with a little butter.

Pinch off a handful of meat, flatten it between your palms to a thickness of about ¾ inch and lay on the baking dish, starting from the edge. Take another handful of meat, flatten and lay next to the first piece, smooth together with your fingers and continue lining the baking dish with the *kaftah* until you finish it.

Spread the raw potato slices over the meat, sprinkle with salt to taste, cover with the tomato slices, sprinkle with more salt to taste, add the water and bake in the preheated oven for 45 minutes or until the potatoes are done. Serve hot.

KAFTA GRILLED *on* SKEWERS
Kaftah Meshwiyeh

I find the making of *kaftah meshwiyeh* a rather tiresome operation. The meat mixture is quite soft and it is difficult to bind it to the skewers. Worse still the meat has the habit of dropping off the skewers during cooking and I have to keep turning the skewers to try and get the meat back onto them. I always end up with crooked shapes instead of the perfectly straight and elongated grilled kafta fingers that I eat in restaurants. I wonder whether you will be more successful than I am at achieving good results.

SERVES 4

kafta, p. 130	2 large round pita bread or more

Prepare the kafta mixture on p. 130 and divide it into 12 pieces. Roll the meat pieces into balls. Put a meat ball in the palm of your hand. Take one skewer in the other hand and start wrapping the meat around the skewer. Squeeze the kafta upwards and then downwards to bind the meat around the skewer in a long sausage-like shape. Taper the edges and place on a rack ready to go under the grill or on a charcoal (or gas) barbecue. Do the rest of the meat in the same way.

Prepare a charcoal barbecue fire if you can or turn your grill on to maximum heat.

Open up one large pita bread and place it on a plate by the heat to use for when the kafta is ready. Put the meat skewers under a hot grill (or over a hot charcoal barbecue) and cook for 2-3 minutes on each side or until the meat is done to your liking. Once you have finished cooking the meat, wrap the bread round the skewers and pull the skewers out of the meat. Serve the kafta hot with extra supplies of fresh bread.

MEAT GRILLED *on* SKEWERS
Lahem Meshwi

This dish is commonly called Shish Kebab in the United States.

SERVES 4

1¾ lb lamb meat from the leg or shoulder, defatted and cut in bite-sized pieces	garlic marinade, p. 63
	10 baby onions, peeled and cut in half
	2 large round pita bread or more

2 hours in advance
Prepare the garlic marinade on p. 63 and put in the pieces of meat to marinate for 2 hours at room temperature, turning them over regularly. You can also leave them to marinate overnight in the refrigerator.

Preparation
Prepare a charcoal barbecue fire if you can or turn the grill on to maximum heat.

Open up one large pita bread and place it on a plate by the heat to use for soaking up the juices of the grilled kebabs during cooking (see p. 129). Thread 8 pieces of meat onto each of the eight long metal skewers, threading half a baby onion between each and leaving a little space between the pieces to allow them to cook evenly. Grill for 3 minutes on each side or until the meat is done to your liking. Take a few skewers at a time to press inside the bread, do that two or three times during cooking, to soak up the cooking juices.

Once you have finished cooking the meat, wrap the bread round the skewers and pull the skewers out of the meat and onions. Serve the kebabs hot with extra supplies of fresh bread.

● You can also grill the meat without marinating it first. Just season it with a little seven-spice mixture (see Lebanese larder, p. 32) and salt to taste. Cook and serve as above.

Stuffed Vegetables
Al-Mahashi

THE VEGETABLES AND HOW TO PREPARE THEM
Eggplants   Cabbage Leaves   Zucchini
Squash (Marrows)   Peppers   Swiss Chard Leaves

STUFFINGS
Al-Hashwat
Meat and Rice Stuffing
Meat, Rice and Tomato Stuffing
Meat and Pine Nut Stuffing   Vegetarian Stuffing

STUFFING AND COOKING THE VEGETABLES
Eggplants Stuffed with Minced Meat and Pine Nuts
Eggplants Stuffed with Meat, Rice and Tomatoes
Cabbage Stuffed with Meat, Rice and Tomatoes
Vegetarian Stuffed Zucchini
Marrows Stuffed with Meat, Rice and Tomatoes
Vegetarian Stuffed Peppers
Stuffed Swiss Chard Leaves
Stuffed Vine Leaves with Lamb Chops
Vegetarian Stuffed Vine Leaves

 Stuffed vegetables are usually served at large family gatherings and a variety of different vegetables are stuffed for the same meal. My mother's assortment was a beautiful selection of small pale green zucchini and dark purple eggplant on one serving dish and a very neat display of stuffed vine leaves on another. Alternatively we had a selection of squash and cabbage leaves, the taste of which she pepped up by adding, in the last 15 minutes of cooking, a mixture of crushed garlic, fresh or dried mint and lemon juice.

There are three types of stuffing in the Lebanon: a vegetarian one, another with meat and rice, and a third with meat and pine nuts. All these stuffings have numerous regional and family variations which can only be hinted at in the following recipes. The non-vegetarian stuffed vegetables are cooked with bones to produce a richer broth. Because it is no longer habitual to cook with bones in the West I have made this optional, but, if your butcher will supply them, do use them for a better result. Stuffed vegetables are always served with a bowl of yogurt.

Make sure the vegetables that you choose for stuffing are in perfect condition and of a similar size. In the following pages I am giving recipes for stuffed eggplants, zucchini, cabbage leaves, a type of squash called ʿaraʿ in Arabic, peppers, Swiss chard and vine leaves.

Both vegetables and stuffings take some time to prepare and I do not recommend you launch into making any of the following dishes unless you have time on your hands. The stuffing that takes longest to prepare is the vegetarian one, about 30 to 45 minutes, depending on how quick you are at chopping. As for the vegetables, the stuffed leaves take about 1 hour or more to fill and roll. The eggplants and zucchini take approximately the same time to core and another 20-30 minutes to fill. The marrows, on the other hand, take about half that time to prepare and the winners on the time-saving front are the peppers. Whichever dish you chose to make, allow from 1½ to 3 hours from beginning to end for the quantities given in the recipes. I am giving a time-saving variation for cabbage leaves, which I have not applied to Swiss chard or vine leaves as it does not work as well for them.

EGGPLANTS

Batinjen

Cut off and discard the stem ends of the eggplants and remove any husks capping the skin.

There are two ways of coring eggplants. One allows you to extract most of the pulp in one piece, to cook with the stuffed vegetable and serve on the side. The other is to core them as you do the zucchini (see p. 137), in which case the pulp will break up and be too messy to cook with the stuffed eggplants. In either case, use a narrow apple corer or a special one (see Lebanese larder, p. 34).

To extract the pulp in one piece

Take one eggplant and pinch the skin of the fat, bulging part between your thumb and index fingers. Gently squeeze it away from the pulp and continue pinching the skin away from the pulp, moving upwards to about ½ to 1 inch short of the top, then as far down as you can. Push the loose skin round to the firm side and continue pinching until it is loose all around.

Insert the corer into the cut top as close to the edge as possible, about ⅛ inch inside the skin, and gently push in until it meets no resistance. Take out, insert again next to the first incision and repeat until you cut a rosette all around the inside.

Squeeze the bottom end of the eggplant with your fingers to detach the skin from the pulp and slowly squeeze out the pulp. Do this gently; if not, the top of the eggplant will split open. Put the pulp on a plate and scrape the inside and bottom of the eggplant with the corer, being careful not to pierce the skin, to remove the last bits of pulp, leaving a shell with walls about ⅛ inch thick.

Plunge the emptied hull in a bowl of cold water and fill the inside with water. Core the rest of the eggplants and leave them to soak in the water.

To extract the pulp in pieces

Follow the same instructions as for coring zucchini, p. 137, and use the pulp as a variation for the zucchini pulp omelette, p. 100.

Use with the recipes on p. 146.

CABBAGE LEAVES
Wara^ Malfoof

You have to be particularly meticulous while preparing cabbage leaves as they are quite fragile, prone to break while raw and easy to tear after they are blanched. If possible, use organically grown flat-topped cabbage, as the leaves are more tender and it will make a difference to both the look and taste of the stuffed leaves.

Cut off the cabbage leaves, one by one, cutting as close to the core as you can. Gently remove each, making sure you do not break them in the process and discard any damaged outer ones. Divide the leaves into several piles and set aside.

Fill a large saucepan with boiling water, place over a high heat and bring back to the boil. Plunge the first pile of leaves and boil for 2-3 minutes or until the leaves have softened. Remove with a slotted spoon to a colander, still being careful not to damage the leaves, then put the next lot in the pan. Add more boiling water if necessary, cook and drain as with the first batch and continue until you have blanched all the leaves.

Take one softened leaf at a time and, depending on its size, keep it whole or cut across in two, taking where the spine becomes thin and pliable as a dividing line. Slice the thick spine off without breaking the leaf and lay on your working surface with the glossy side down. Do the rest of the leaves in the same way and arrange in neat layers, keeping the spines to one side.

Use with the recipe on p. 147.

ZUCCHINI
Koossa

Cut off and discard the stem ends of the zucchini, shave off the bottom brown skins and dip the cut tops in salt to soften the pulp and make coring easier.

Place one zucchini in the palm of your hand with the cut top facing you. Cup your fingers around it and hold firmly. Insert a narrow apple corer or a special one (see Lebanese larder, p. 34) into

the cut top as close to the edge as possible, about ⅛ inch inside the skin, and push half way down the zucchini. Take out, insert again next to the first incision and repeat until you cut a rosette all around the inside. Twirl the corer inside the zucchini to loosen the pulp and pull out the first piece. Slide it off the corer into a bowl (save the pulp to make zucchini pulp omelettes, p. 100), then insert again and, with a circular motion, scrape the sides and bottom to remove as much pulp as possible, leaving walls about ⅛ inch thick. Do this gently and carefully, gradually extracting the pulp, or else you will split the top or pierce the sides or bottom of the zucchini.

Plunge the cored zucchini in a bowl of cold water, filling the inside with water. Finish coring the zucchini and leave to soak while you prepare the stuffing.

Use with the recipe on p. 149.

SQUASH (MARROWS)
ˆAraᶜ

ˆAraᶜ is a type of marrow (*Cucurbito pepo* or *C. lagenaria*) and can grow very large. The ones you need for this dish are the small ones, about 8 inches long and with a lovely pale green color. It is unlikely you will find them outside Greek, Turkish, Lebanese or other Middle Eastern shops. They are not cheap, but utterly delectable and well worth taking the trouble to find and prepare. (In the event you cannot find vegetable marrows, you can substitute small zucchini, though I prefer the marrows myself.)

Cut off and discard the stem ends and bottoms of the marrows, leaving most of the narrow top end on. Peel the skin off and core the marrow from the wide bottom end, leaving walls about ⅛ inch thick (see coring zucchini, above). You need to use a long corer, which you should find in a well stocked kitchen shop or in a Middle Eastern store. Rinse the cored marrows in cold water, making sure

you wash out all the inner bitter seeds, and leave to drain.
Use with the recipe on p. 150.

PEPPERS
Fleyfleh

The nicest combination of colors for stuffed peppers is red and
yellow. The green ones turn a rather dull color after cooking and
do not look as appetising as the other two. There is a slight variation
in taste and texture between the different colors. Stuffed peppers
are much easier and quicker to prepare than other vegetables.

Take a small pointed knife and insert just outside where you guess
the edge of the seed core is. Cut all around and pull out, holding by
the stem. Slice off and discard the seed core, clean out any loose seeds
from inside the pepper and fit back the stem top. Do the rest of the
peppers in the same way and set aside.
Use with the recipe on p. 151.

SWISS CHARD LEAVES
*Sille^*

Cut off the stalks of the Swiss chard leaves and divide each leaf in
three pieces. First cut across the top third of the leaf, taking where
the spine becomes thin and pliable as a dividing line; after which
slice off and remove the thick spine leaving two more pieces of chard
leaf. The cut pieces should make rolls of about 3 to 4¾ inches long.
Some leaves are too small to cut in three, in which case divide each
in two, again taking the place where the spine becomes thin as a
dividing line. Shave off the backs of any particularly thick parts of
spine without breaking the leaf. Reserve both the stalks and the stems

to cook on the bottom of the casserole. (If the stalks are in good condition, they can be used to make a salad, see p. 80.)

Wash the cut leaves in cold water and arrange them, smooth side down, in neat layers inside a colander. Carefully run boiling water over them to soften them.

Use with the recipe on p. 152.

MEAT and RICE STUFFING
Hashwet Lahmeh wa Rezz

This stuffing is normally used with vine and cabbage leaves. The minced (ground) meat should ideally come from the shoulder of lamb, as it needs to be quite fatty to provide the rice with moisture during cooking.

SERVES 4

about ¾ cup white short grain rice	¼ teaspoon ground cinnamon
about ½ lb minced (ground) fatty lamb	½ teaspoon ground allspice
2 tablespoons water (or meat stock)	¼ teaspoon finely ground black pepper
	salt to taste

Wash the rice in two or three changes of cold water, drain and put in a mixing bowl. Add the minced meat, water (or stock) and season with cinnamon, allspice, pepper and salt to taste. Mix with your hands to blend well. Taste, adjust seasoning if necessary, and use to stuff the vegetable of your choice.

MEAT, RICE *and* TOMATO STUFFING

Hashwet Lahmeh wa Rezz ma Banadoorah

A variation on the previous stuffing which is used with zucchini, marrows, eggplants and peppers, as well as with vine and cabbage leaves.

SERVES 4

about ½ cup (3½ oz) white short grain rice	¼ teaspoon ground cinnamon
about 5 oz minced (ground) lamb	½ teaspoon ground allspice
2 medium ripe tomatoes, topped but whole, or same amount (8 oz) Italian canned	½ teaspoon finely ground black pepper
	salt to taste

Wash the rice in two or three changes of cold water, drain and put in a mixing bowl. Add the minced meat and squeeze the fresh tomatoes with your hands over the meat and rice, extracting as much juice and pulp as you can, then place the skins at the bottom of the pan in which you will cook the stuffed vegetables. If you are using canned tomatoes, use chopped ones and pour them straight over the meat and rice. Season with cinnamon, allspice, pepper and salt to taste and mix together with your hands to blend well. Taste, adjust seasoning if necessary, and use with the vegetable of your choice.

MEAT *and* PINE NUT STUFFING

Hashweh bil-Lahmeh ma S'noobar

This stuffing is used with eggplants and zucchini. I have devised my own vegetarian version for my many vegetarian friends.

SERVES 4

4 tablespoons unsalted butter	½ teaspoon ground allspice
⅓ cup pine nuts	¼ teaspoon finely ground black
about 5 oz minced (ground)	pepper
lean lamb	salt to taste
¼ teaspoon ground cinnamon	

Melt the butter in a frying pan over a medium heat and sauté the pine nuts in it, stirring regularly, until they become golden brown. Remove with a slotted spoon and put to drain onto a double layer of paper towels. Cook the minced meat in the same butter until it loses all traces of pink. Keep mashing and stirring it with a wooden spoon or fork so that it separates well and does not form lumps. Take off the heat and season with cinnamon, allspice, pepper and salt to taste. Mix in the pine nuts, taste, adjust seasoning if necessary, and use with the vegetable of your choice.

● You can also add one medium onion, finely chopped. In this case do the nuts as above and then fry the onion until golden, add the meat and finish as before.

● For a vegetarian version, leave out the meat, increase the amount of pine nuts to 1 cup and include a large onion, finely chopped. After you have browned and removed the nuts from the pan, fry the chopped onion in the same butter until golden, add the nuts and season as in the meat recipe.

$$999 w + ⊕ 日 日 \gtrless \lor \{))o\varphi\Upsilon I+$$

VEGETARIAN STUFFING
Hashweh bil-Zeyt

Bil-Zeyt means "in oil" and is the Lebanese term for vegetarian cooking. This stuffing is used with vine and Swiss chard leaves as well as with eggplant, zucchini and peppers. Some people omit the sumac and only use lemon juice to sour the stuffing. I prefer to add it, as it gives the dish an especially delicious and tangy taste.

SERVES 4

about ¾ cup (5 oz) white short grain rice	¼ bunch mint (about 2 oz on the stalk), leaves only, chopped medium-fine
2 medium (about 10½ oz) firm red tomatoes, diced into ¼-inch-square cubes	2 heaped tablespoons sumac
	¼ teaspoon ground cinnamon
½ bunch spring onions (scallions), trimmed and thinly sliced	½ teaspoon ground allspice
	¼ teaspoon finely ground black pepper
½ bunch flat-leafed parsley (about 3½ oz on the stalk), washed, dried, most of the stalks cut off, chopped medium-fine	salt to taste
	juice of 1 large lemon, or to taste
	½ cup plus 2 tablespoons extra virgin olive oil

Wash the rice in two or three changes of cold water, drain thoroughly and put in a mixing bowl. Add the diced tomatoes, sliced onions, chopped parsley and mint. Season with sumac, cinnamon, allspice, pepper and salt to taste. Pour in the lemon juice and olive oil and mix well together – the stuffing should look like a salad. Taste, adjust seasoning if necessary, and use with the vegetable of your choice.

● You can vary on this stuffing by adding split chick peas (⅓ cup), soaked overnight and skinned (see p. 46). Personally, I find their crunchy bite an unpleasant contrast to the melting rice. A variation from the south is to leave out the lemon juice and olive oil and increase the amount of sumac to 3 tablespoons.

EGGPLANTS STUFFED *with* MINCED MEAT *and* PINE NUTS
Sheikh el-Mehshi

This dish is considered the most elegant of stuffed vegetables as its Arabic name indicates 'the lord of stuffed vegetables.' It is particularly attractive when prepared with small eggplants and it is well worth going out of your way to find these. You must make sure you handle them with care at all stages of the preparation so that they retain their shape.

SERVES 4

12 small, thin eggplants, each about 4 inches long with stalks on (about 1½ lb), or 3 large ones (about ½ lb each)	1¾ lb ripe tomatoes, peeled and coarsely chopped, or same amount Italian canned
vegetable oil for frying	¼ teaspoon ground cinnamon
meat and pine nut stuffing, p. 41	¼ teaspoon ground allspice
	⅛ teaspoon finely ground black pepper
	salt to taste

If you are using small eggplants

Cut the stalks of the eggplants to an approximate length of ½ inch and trim away the husks that cap the skin. Peel off a strip of skin, ½ inch wide, the full length of the eggplant, leave ½ inch of skin unpeeled, and peel another as above; continue until you end up with a striped eggplant. Repeat the process with the rest of the eggplants.

Fill a large frying pan with enough oil to shallow fry the eggplants and place over a medium heat. When the oil is hot (test with the tip of one eggplant; if the oil bubbles around it, it is ready), fry the eggplants until golden all over. Remove with a slotted spoon (do not lift by the stalk as it might come off) and put to drain on several sheets of paper towels. You can also steam, bake or microwave the eggplants, but their taste and color will be quite different and I think not as nice.

While the eggplants are left to cool, prepare the meat and pine nut stuffing on p. 141 and preheat the oven to 350°F.

Take one eggplant and, with a small knife, slit it down the middle (the peeled section will cut more easily), lengthways, and no more than half way into the flesh. Prise the eggplant open and press the flesh inside to form a pocket in which you will put a tablespoon of meat stuffing. Place in a deep bake-and-serve dish and repeat the process until you have filled all the eggplants. Place any leftover filling on the bottom of the dish between the eggplants.

Season the chopped tomatoes with cinnamon, allspice, pepper and salt to taste and spread evenly over the eggplants. Place in the preheated oven and bake for 40 minutes or until the tomatoes have cooked and most of their juice evaporated. If you have not baked the eggplants in a bake-and-serve dish, be careful when you transfer them onto a serving dish, as their lovely presentation will easily spoil with casual handling. Serve hot with plain rice (p. 187).

● You can also cook this dish in a covered braising pan over a medium heat for 30 minutes or until the tomato sauce has reduced.

If you are using large eggplants

In this variation you need not worry so much about the presentation of the eggplants as they are not used whole.

Peel the eggplants and slice them lengthways or across to a thickness of about ½ inch. Arrange the slices in salted layers in a colander and leave to sweat for about 30 minutes.

In the meantime prepare double quantities of the meat and pine nut stuffing on p. 141 and preheat the oven to 350°F.

Rinse the salted eggplant slices under cold water, pat dry and fry until golden on both sides. Season the chopped tomatoes with cinnamon, allspice, pepper and salt to taste, then line the bottom of a deep baking dish with a layer of fried eggplant slices. Spread the meat stuffing evenly over them and cover with a layer of the remaining eggplants. Pour the seasoned tomatoes over the egg-plants. Bake in the preheated oven for 30 minutes or until the tomato sauce has thickened and serve hot with plain rice.

● A northern variation is to cook this dish in yogurt instead of tomatoes. Prepare the cooked yogurt sauce, p. 172, using mint instead of coriander. Mix the mint and garlic into the cooked yogurt before pouring it over the eggplants and simmer on the stove for 10-15 minutes instead of baking, as the yogurt might separate if cooked in the oven.

EGGPLANTS STUFFED *with* MEAT, RICE *and* TOMATOES

Mehshi Batinjen bil-Lahmeh

SERVES 4

about 2 lb small eggplants, approximately 20	2 small ripe tomatoes (about 7 oz), peeled and sliced, or same amount Italian canned
meat, rice and tomato stuffing, p. 141	salt to taste
3 or 4 lamb bones (optional)	2 cups (1 pint) plain yogurt

Core the eggplants following the instructions on p. 135.

Prepare the meat, rice and tomato stuffing on p. 141, then line the bottom of a casserole, large enough to take the stuffed eggplants half-standing comfortably, with the bones (rinsed under cold water), the sliced or canned tomatoes and the whole pulps (if any) spread on top.

Drain and rinse the eggplants under cold water. Take one and hold it upright, cupping your hand around it. Pick up a little filling with the other hand and gently push it into the eggplant, using your finger to force it inside. Every now and then shake the eggplant in a downward gesture to make sure the filling is well inside it (or push the filling in with your little finger). Only fill three-quarters of the eggplant, to leave enough room for the rice to expand, and put it in the casserole with the open end slightly raised – use the bones or pulp to prop it up.

Continue filling and arranging the eggplants, first around the side of the pan then on the inside – they should all fit comfortably in one half-standing layer – until you have finished both eggplants, and stuffing (if you have a little stuffing left, cook it separately in double its volume of water and serve on the side).

Pour a little water in the empty stuffing bowl, swirl it around to extract the last bits of flavoring and pour over the eggplants to barely cover them, about ¾ inch short from the open tops. Add salt to taste, bearing in mind that the stuffing is already seasoned, cover the pan and place over a high heat. Bring to the boil then reduce the heat to medium and boil gently for 45 minutes or until

146

the stuffing is done. Two thirds of the way through, taste the broth and add more salt if necessary.

Once done, leave the eggplants to sit covered for about 10 minutes before transferring to a serving dish. The best way to remove the soft, cooked eggplants intact is to use both your hand and a spoon. Cool the fingers of one hand with cold water and use to pull away one eggplant at a time and make space to gently slide a spoon underneath it. Lift holding it against the spoon with your fingers and arrange on a serving platter. Ladle some juice and eggplant pulp (if any) into a sauce boat and serve hot with pita bread, the sauce and a bowl of yogurt.

● You can also prepare small white or young green zucchini in the same way (*koossa mehshi bil-lahmeh*). Use about 2½ pounds zucchini (approximately 20; they weigh more than eggplants), and follow the recipe as above. (See p. 137 for instructions about coring the zucchini.)

⊲⊲ ∃ 𝑦 𝖸 ⊟ 𝘻 𝘭 ↓ ○ ○ ∓)⁊⁊ ↓○

CABBAGE STUFFED *with* MEAT, RICE *and* TOMATOES
Mehshi Malfoof

SERVES 4

1 white cabbage (about 3 lb)	7 large garlic cloves, peeled and crushed
meat, rice and tomato stuffing, p. 141	⅓ oz fresh mint leaves, crushed (or 1 tablespoon crushed dried mint)
3 or 4 lamb bones (optional)	
2 small ripe tomatoes (about 7 oz), peeled and sliced, or same amount Italian canned	2 tablespoons lemon juice, or to taste
salt to taste	2 cups (1 pint) plain yogurt

Prepare the cabbage leaves following the instructions on p. 137 or those given in the variation note at the end of this recipe.

Prepare the meat, rice and tomato stuffing, p. 141, and line the bottom of a large casserole with the bones (rinsed under cold water), tomatoes and cabbage spines.

Lay one cabbage leaf on your chopping board, with the cut or core side nearest to you and glossy side down. Spread ½ to 1½ teaspoons of stuffing depending on leaf size in a thin raised line across the leaf, about ½ inch inside the edge nearest to you and the same distance short of the side edges. Roll flatly and quite loosely to leave enough room for the rice to expand during cooking. Lift and place onto the bones and tomatoes, with the loose end of the stuffed leaf down.

Continue filling, rolling and arranging the leaves, side by side, doing one layer at a time until you have finished both leaves and stuffing. If you have any stuffing left over, put in a small pan, add double its volume of water, cook for 20 minutes and serve on the side. If you have any leftover leaves use them to cover the rolled ones.

Pour some water in the empty stuffing bowl, swirl it around to extract the last bits of flavoring and pour over the stuffed leaves until you barely cover them. Add salt to taste, bearing in mind that the stuffing is already seasoned, and put an overturned heat-proof plate over the leaves to stop them from unrolling during cooking. Cover the pan and place over a high heat. Bring to the boil, then reduce the heat to medium and boil gently for 30 minutes.

Meanwhile blend the crushed garlic, fresh or dried mint and lemon juice in a small mixing bowl, add salt to taste, and mix together. Cover and set aside.

When the 30 minutes are up, uncover the pan and remove the plate covering the leaves. Stir the garlic and mint mixture into the broth, tilting the pan to bring enough juice to the surface. Taste and add salt if needed and cook, covered, for another 20 minutes. Take off the heat and leave to sit for a few minutes, then gently lift the stuffed leaves – you might have to use two spoons for the long rolled leaves so as not to break them – and arrange on a serving platter. Ladle some sauce into a sauce boat and serve hot with a bowl of yogurt at the side.

● I have devised a time-saving variation which is nearly as good, though not as attractive, as the traditional recipe where the stuffing is sandwiched between two layers of shredded cabbage instead of being rolled inside individual leaves.

Shred the cabbage leaves either by hand using a sharp knife or by using the fine slicer attachment on your food-processor. Blanch the shredded leaves for 2 minutes, then prepare the stuffing. Line the bottom of a large casserole with the bones and tomatoes and divide the shredded cabbage in two equal heaps. Lay one lot of shredded cabbage over the bones and tomatoes, spread the stuffing over it and cover well with the rest of the shredded cabbage. Put an overturned heat-proof plate over the shredded cabbage and add water until you barely cover it. Place over a medium heat and cook as above. Add the crushed garlic and mint, finish cooking and serve as in main recipe.

VEGETARIAN STUFFED ZUCCHINI

Mehshi Koossa bil-Zeyt

SERVES 4

about 3½ lb small white or young green zucchini, approximately 24	vegetarian stuffing, p. 142
	2 large ripe tomatoes, peeled and sliced
salt	

Core the zucchini following the instructions on p. 137.

Prepare the vegetarian stuffing, p. 142, and line the bottom of a casserole, large enough to fit the zucchini half-standing comfortably, with the sliced tomatoes. Drain and rinse the zucchini under cold water, then fill, arrange and cook following the same instructions as in stuffed eggplants, p. 146.

Take off the heat, keep covered and leave to cool before lifting them out of the pan gently. The best way to lift the soft, cooked zucchini intact is to use both your hand and a spoon. Pull away one zucchini at a time with your fingers, gently slide a spoon underneath it and lift holding it against the spoon with your fingers. Arrange on a serving platter and either discard the cooked tomatoes and sauce or serve on the side. Serve at room temperature.

● You can also stuff small eggplants in the same way (*mehshi batinjen bil-zeyt*). Use about 2½ pounds of small eggplants (approximately 24; they weigh less than zucchini, and follow the recipe as above. (See p. 135 for instructions about coring the zucchini.)

MARROW STUFFED *with* MEAT, RICE *and* TOMATOES
Mehshi ʾAraᶜ

SERVES 4

8 medium marrows, or zucchini if not available (about 2 lb)	⅓ oz fresh mint leaves, crushed (or 1 tablespoon crushed dried mint)
meat, rice and tomato stuffing, p. 141	
3 or 4 lamb bones (optional)	2 tablespoons lemon juice, or to taste
3 small ripe tomatoes (about ¾ lb), peeled and sliced, or same amount Italian canned (12 oz)	salt to taste
	2 cups (1 pint) plain yogurt
7 large garlic cloves, peeled and crushed	

Core the marrows following the instructions on p. 138.

Prepare the meat, rice and tomato stuffing, p. 141, then arrange the bones (rinsed under cold water) over the bottom of a large casserole and spread the sliced or canned tomatoes over them.

Fill three-quarters of the marrows, leaving enough room for the rice to expand during cooking, and pack them snugly in the casserole, with the open ends slightly raised. If available, make full use of the bones to prop them up.

Put some water in the empty stuffing bowl, swirl it around to extract the last bits and pour over the marrows to barely cover them. Add salt to taste, bearing in mind that the stuffing is already seasoned, cover the pan and place over a high heat. Bring to the boil, then reduce the heat to medium and boil gently for 40 minutes.

In the meantime blend the crushed garlic, fresh or dried mint and lemon juice together in a small mixing bowl and add salt to taste. Cover and set aside.

When the 40 minutes are up, stir the garlic, mint and lemon mixture into the broth. You will have to tilt the pan to bring enough juice to the surface, taste, add salt if necessary and cook for another 10 minutes.

Take off the heat and leave to sit, covered, for about 10 minutes, then transfer the marrows delicately to a serving dish. Ladle some sauce into a sauce boat and serve hot with a bowl of yogurt on the side.

VEGETARIAN STUFFED PEPPERS
Mehshi Fleyfleh bil-Zeyt

SERVES 4

8 red or yellow peppers (about 5 oz each)	2 large ripe tomatoes, peeled and sliced
vegetarian stuffing, p. 142	salt to taste

Prepare the peppers following the instructions on p. 139.

Prepare the vegetarian stuffing, p. 142, and line the bottom of a casserole, large enough to fit the peppers standing quite close together, with the sliced tomatoes.

Put enough stuffing in one pepper to fill three-quarters of it, leaving enough room for the rice to expand. Fit the stem top over the opening (make sure you align the cut sides to keep the top from falling inside the peppers) and stand against the edge of the pan. Fill, close and arrange the rest of the peppers in the same way. Because of the large openings of the stuffed peppers, make sure the tops fit well and the peppers stay upright in the pan so that the rice does not spill out during cooking.

Pour some water in the empty stuffing bowl, swirl it around to extract the last bits of flavouring, and pour over the peppers up to about ¾ inch short of their tops. Cover the pan, place over a high heat and bring to the boil. Reduce the heat to medium and boil gently for about 45 minutes. Uncover one pepper and taste a little stuffing to check that it is done before taking off the heat. Keep covered until cooled, then use your hand and a spoon to remove the peppers carefully onto a serving platter. Ladle some of the sauce into a sauce boat and serve with the peppers at room temperature.

STUFFED SWISS CHARD LEAVES
*Mehshi Sille^*

The velvety texture of stuffed Swiss chard is quite unlike that of other stuffed leaves and the tartness of the stuffing makes an interesting contrast to the earthy taste of the chard. If you have an oval pan use it to cook the leaves in. This will allow you to lay the longest rolled leaves straight thus minimizing the risk of breaking them when you lift them out after cooking.

SERVES 4

about 2 lb Swiss chard	1 large ripe tomato, peeled
vegetarian stuffing, p. 142	and sliced
	salt to taste

Prepare the Swiss chard leaves following the instructions on p. 139.

Line the bottom of a large casserole with the tomato slices. Rinse the reserved stalks and stems, blanch them in boiling water and spread them over the tomatoes.

Prepare the vegetarian stuffing recipe on p. 142, then take one leaf and lay it, smooth side down, on your working surface with the cut side nearest to you and the veins running away from you. Spread 1 teaspoon of stuffing (or more depending on the size of the leaf), in a long, thin and slightly raised line, the thickness of your little finger, about ½ inch inside the edge nearest to you and the same distance short of the side edges. Fold the narrow strip of leaf over the stuffing and roll into a flat and loosely packed roll so that the rice has enough room to expand. Flatten the empty edges, lift the rolled leaf carefully onto the pan and lay over the stems with the loose end down.

Continue stuffing, rolling and arranging the stuffed leaves side by side, doing one layer at a time until you have finished both leaves and stuffing. If you have any stuffing left over, put it in a small pan, cover it with water and cook over a low heat to serve on the side. Use the leftover leaves, if any, to cover the rolled ones.

Pour enough water into the casserole to barely cover the stuffed leaves and add salt to taste, bearing in mind that the stuffing is already seasoned. Cover the leaves with an overturned plate to stop them from unrolling during cooking, put the lid on the pan and place over a high heat. Bring to the boil, then reduce the heat to medium and boil gently for 45 minutes or until the stuffing is done. Two thirds of the way through cooking, taste the broth to check the salt content and add some more if necessary.

When the 45 minutes are up, it is a good idea to taste a filled leaf to make sure the rice is done. If it is cooked through, turn off the heat and leave to cool before transferring the leaves delicately onto a serving dish (I usually pick up the rolled leaves with my fingers to keep them intact; if you don't like using your fingers you may have to use two spoons for the longest leaves). Ladle some of the sauce into a sauce boat and serve with the leaves at room temperature.

STUFFED VINE LEAVES
with LAMB CHOPS
Mehshi Wara^ ᶜEnab ma Kastalettah

This dish can be prepared with either fresh or preserved vine leaves. It is best to use fresh ones but in England these can be found only during early summer at Greek, Turkish or Lebanese shops or in gardens where there is a vine. The season is short and they quickly grow tough and stringy. In the U.S., check with your local Middle

Eastern grocer. The preserved ones (the vacuum-packed being generally superior to those preserved in brine) are widely available all year round. These are bigger, as the small fresh leaves do not keep very well. When using preserved leaves, be sparing with the salt as they remain quite salty even after rinsing.

The time you should allow to make this dish will depend largely on the speed with which you roll the vine leaves. A practiced cook will stuff and roll the amount of vine leaves given in the following recipe in an hour, whereas a novice will spend nearly twice as long preparing the same amount.

SERVES 4

8 thin lamb chops (about 1½ lb), most of the fat cut off	salt to taste
	meat and rice stuffing, p. 140
1 cinnamon stick	stock from the lamb chops
7 oz medium-sized fresh	juice of 1 lemon, or to taste
or preserved vine leaves	2 cups (1 pint) plain yogurt

Put the lamb chops in a pan, cover with water and place over a medium heat. As the water is about to boil, skim the surface clean (make sure you do that before the water boils or else the scum will break down and sink back into the water), then add a little salt and the cinnamon stick. Cover the pan and boil for 15 minutes. Lift the chops out onto a plate and reserve the stock for later.

Prepare the meat and rice stuffing, p. 140, then choose a casserole with straight sides, large enough to arrange the lamb chops in a tight and even layer on the bottom.

Put the vine leaves (fresh or preserved) in a colander and run boiling water over them. This will soften them and make them easier to roll. If you are using preserved ones rinse them beforehand in cold water, at least a couple of times, to get rid of some of the briny taste.

Take one vine leaf, cut away the stem, if any, and lay it flat on your working surface, smooth side down with the stem end nearest to you. Arrange from ½ to 1½ teaspoons of stuffing (depending on the size of the leaf) in a thin raised line across the top of the leaf. The line should be thinner than your little finger, about ½ inch away from the tip of the stem and again the same distance short of either side. Fold the sides over the rice, in a line that slightly tapers towards the bottom, then fold and tuck the top edges over the stuffing and

154

roll neatly but loosely, leaving enough space for the rice to expand during cooking. Place the rolled vine leaf, with the loose end down on the lamb chops, starting from the side of the pan. Continue filling, rolling and arranging the vine leaves, side by side, doing one layer at a time until you have finished them. If you have any leftover stuffing put it in a small pan, add an equivalent amount of water, cook for 20 minutes and serve on the side.

Pour some, or all, of the reserved stock over the rolled leaves so as to barely immerse them (if you do not have enough stock add water), add salt to taste, and swirl the water around to dilute it. Put an overturned heat-proof plate over the leaves, to stop them from unrolling during cooking, cover the pan and place over a high heat. Bring to the boil, reduce the heat to medium and boil gently for 50 minutes. Add the lemon juice and cook for another 10 minutes. It is a good idea to test one vine leaf, before you take them off the heat, to make sure that the rice inside is done.

Serving

Once the leaves are done, turn off the heat and leave to sit, covered, for about 10 minutes. The traditional way of serving this dish is to turn the vine leaves over onto a serving platter like an upside down cake, which is why you need a pan with straight sides.

Wear heat-proof gloves while performing this operation. First pour out the cooking juices into a bowl while holding the leaves back with the plate covering them. Remove the plate, turn a big round, flat serving dish over onto the top of the pan, and hold it firmly against the pan with the flat of one hand. Slide the pan slowly over the edge of your surface and put the other hand underneath it. Lift the pan off and quickly turn it upside down, then slide the platter back onto your working surface and slowly lift the pan off to uncover a cake of vine leaves topped with juicy lamb chops.

Alternatively you can spoon the rolled leaves out, a few at a time and arrange them in neat layers onto a serving dish, putting the lamb chops on top or around them. Baste with some of their cooking juice and serve immediately with a bowl of yogurt.

155

VEGETARIAN STUFFED VINE LEAVES

Mehshi Wara^ Enab bil-Zeyt

This dish is served at room temperature either as a main course or as a starter. The quantities given below will serve four vegetarian main courses. If you want to serve it as a starter, either reduce the quantities by one third or prepare for eight.

SERVES 4

1 large potato, peeled and sliced	vine leaves or preserved ones
1 large tomato, peeled and sliced	(see p. 153)
vegetarian stuffing, p. 142	salt to taste
7 oz medium-sized fresh grape	1 lemon, cut into thin wedges

Line the bottom of a large saucepan, large enough to contain the rolled vine leaves, with the potato and tomato slices.

Prepare the vegetarian stuffing, p. 142.

Prepare, stuff and arrange the vine leaves, following the instructions on pp. 154-155.

Pour some water into the empty stuffing bowl, swirl it around to extract the last bits of flavoring, and pour just enough over the leaves as to barely cover them – about half way up the top layer. Add salt to taste and put an overturned heat-proof plate over the stuffed leaves to stop them from unrolling during cooking. Cover the pan and place over a high heat. Bring to the boil, then reduce the heat to medium and boil gently for 1 hour, or until the vine leaves are done. It is prudent to taste one stuffed leaf to make sure that the rice is cooked before taking them off the heat and leaving to cool, covered.

Transfer the stuffed vine leaves to a serving dish, arranging the leaves neatly in several layers, then garnish them with thinly sliced lemon wedges. You can either discard the potatoes and tomatoes or eat them separately. Serve at room temperature.

Poultry and Game
Al-Toyoor

**Garlic Dip   Chicken Braised with Potatoes
Chicken Kebabs   Chicken with M'lookiyeh
Chicken with Moghrabbiyeh
Chicken and Whole Wheat (or Barley) Porridge
Chicken with Rice and Nuts
Chicken with Roasted Green Wheat   Grilled Chicken**

"Lady Hester, it seemed, had rather arbitrarily abridged the amusements of her secretary; and especially she had forbidden him from shooting small birds on the mountain side."

Alexander Kinglake, *Eothen*, 1906

 Although chicken is now considered an ordinary food, it was not so in the recent past when it was the main festive meal for town and mountain dwellers alike. Sheep were too big to slaughter for one meal, and many families had only one which they saved to make their winter meat reserve of ʾawarma. Those who kept their own chickens reserved the cock for one of the most important religious feast. They force-fed the cock in preparation for the celebration and kept the chickens for lesser feasts or special meals.

The Lebanese are also fond of other birds such as larks (or sparrows) ʿasafeer. These were shot during the fig season in the summer when the birds fed greedily on the fruit. Their plump little bodies were plucked and gutted, their long beaks cut off but the heads kept on. The cleaned birds were then threaded onto skewers and grilled over an open charcoal fire and served like kebabs wrapped in pita bread. Some preferred fried larks seasoned with lemon juice. Unfortunately the killer instinct of the Lebanese and their pronounced taste for these unfortunate little creatures was such

157

that the birds are now rarely available locally and have to be imported frozen from China.

Game is also scarce now but until it became so we had a strong tradition of eating partridge (*hajal*), pheasant (*d'jej el-ard*), and wild quail (*firreh*). These were prepared more or less in the same way as chicken.

⊿ ⊿ ʔ̣ ⌊ ʃ) ─Ɛ Ⱶʔ̣ ꟼ { ꟻ ꟻ Υ �7�7

GARLIC DIP
Toom

Toom is an essential accompaniment to grilled chicken or quail. It is particularly tasty except that it will turn you into a social leper for a good 24 hours after you eat it. Still garlic is reputed to be very healthy and as long as you share this dip with the people you will spend time with afterwards, you don't need to worry. The traditional garlic dip is made with only garlic, lemon juice and olive oil but it does not rise as well as when you add an egg yolk, so I have given the choice to make a proper *aïoli* with an egg yolk.

SERVES 4

8 large garlic cloves	1 tablespoon strained yogurt
¼ teaspoon sea salt	(see Lebanese larder, p. 19, to
1 egg yolk (optional)	mellow the taste of the sauce,
juice of ½ lemon, or to taste	optional)
4 tablespoons extra virgin olive oil	

Peel the garlic and chop it in small pieces before putting it in a mortar. Add the salt and pound the garlic with a pestle until you have a smooth paste.

Whisk the egg in a mixing bowl and add the garlic paste. Stir in the lemon juice, then slowly whisk in the olive oil to achieve a creamy *aïoli*; if the dip is not thick enough, add more olive oil, and, if you find the taste too strong, add a tablespoon (or more) strained yogurt.

● It would be easier to prepare this dip in the blender or food processor, but you will need a larger quantity of garlic for the size of the blender's bowl; double or triple the quantities but keep to 1 egg yolk (if you are using it).

CHICKEN BRAISED *with* POTATOES
D'jej Mohammar Ma Batatah

This must be a Maronite adaptation of a western dish, as they are the keenest of their compatriots to assimilate western influences. As with the bean stew (see p. 188) the taste is unmistakably Lebanese with the addition of the eternal cinnamon and allspice seasoning.

SERVES 4

1 medium chicken, free-range if possible, whole (3 lb)	8 large garlic cloves, peeled
salt and finely ground black pepper	about 1 lb small potatoes, peeled
4 tablespoons unsalted butter	1 teaspoon ground cinnamon
16 baby onions, peeled	1 teaspoon ground allspice
	½ cup plus 2 tablespoons water

Rinse the chicken under cold water and pat it dry with paper towels. Rub with salt and pepper to taste. Melt the butter in a large casserole over a medium heat and brown the chicken all over. Remove the chicken from the saucepan and set aside.

Sauté the baby onions and garlic cloves in the same butter until they soften, stir in the potatoes, let them brown a little then remove the vegetables onto a plate. Return the chicken to the casserole, laying it on its side, add the water, cinnamon, allspice and more pepper and salt to taste, cover the pan and simmer for 15 minutes. Turn the chicken onto its other side, simmer for another 15 minutes, then lay it onto its back. Arrange the sautéed vegetables around it and simmer, covered, for another 45 minutes, occasionally stirring the vegetables – if you find that the water is evaporating too quickly, add a little at a time, as you want a thick sauce to serve with the chicken and vegetables.

When the chicken is ready, remove it onto a chopping board and cut it into four or eight pieces. Put the vegetables in the middle of a serving dish, surround with the chicken pieces and serve hot.

● You can prepare this stew without the potatoes, in which case increase the amount of onion and garlic to your liking.

● A simpler and more refined variation is to replace the whole chicken with boned and skinned chicken fillets (about 1¾ pounds), both white and dark meat. Prepare as above, but instead of removing the vegetables, add the chicken pieces to the sautéed vegetables, season, add water as above and simmer for 45 minutes.

CHICKEN KEBABS

*Sheesh Tawoo^*

An exciting variation on the meat kebabs, p. 133.

SERVES 4

about 1¼ lb boneless chicken meat, (white and/or dark), cut into bite-sized pieces, preferably from a free-range chicken	garlic marinade, p. 63
	garlic dip, p. 158
	2 or more large pita bread

Four hours in advance

Prepare the garlic marinade, p. 63, in a large mixing bowl and add the bite-sized pieces of chicken to marinate for 4 hours at room temperature or overnight in the refrigerator. Turn the chicken over at intervals.

Preparation

Prepare a charcoal barbecue fire if you can or turn your grill on to maximum heat.

Open up one large pita bread and place it on a plate by the heat to use for soaking up the juices of the grilled kebabs during cooking (see p. 129). Thread 6 pieces of chicken onto each of the eight long metal skewers, leave a little space between each to allow them to cook evenly and grill for 5 minutes on each side or until they are done. Take a few skewers at a time to press inside the bread, do this two or three times during cooking, to soak up the juices.

Once you have finished cooking the meat, wrap the juicy bread round the skewers and pull the skewers out of the meat. Serve the kebabs hot with the garlic dip on p. 158 and extra supplies of fresh bread.

CHICKEN *with* M'LOOKHIYEH

M'lookhiyeh ala D'jej

This dish is originally Egyptian but has become so much part of the Lebanese repertoire that it has its place in this book. The mention of *m'lookhiyeh* never fails to bring back memories of summer days at the St George beach and restaurant in pre-war Beirut. It was one of the restaurant's star dishes of the day and on that given day, the beach restaurant filled up with not only habitué members but also non-members who came especially to eat this elaborate preparation. I disliked the slimy texture of *m'lookhiyeh* and always felt isolated in my rejection of this much-sought-after delicacy, being one of very few left lounging on the beach. Since then my mother gave me a few hints on how to prepare a mucus-free *m'lookhiyeh* and I now enjoy eating it, albeit in moderation. The secret lies in how you pick the leaves off the stalk. It is in the stems that the mucilaginous substance lurks and unless the leaves are picked clean off it, just under the funny whiskers at the bottom of the leaf, you will end up with a panful of green slime. It is also important to pour the lemon juice into the broth before you drop in the leaves and finally not to overboil them.

M'lookhiyeh ala d'jej is a composite dish consisting of toasted bread, rice, chicken, *m'lookhiyeh* and onion in vinegar all of which are arranged in layers in a soup plate and served hot.

SERVES 6 TO 8

1 medium frying chicken, free-range if possible (about 3 lb)	½ teaspoon ground coriander
8 cups water	juice of 2 lemons, or to taste
2 medium onions, peeled	½ teaspoon ground cinnamon
3 sticks cinnamon	1 teaspoon ground allspice
1 tablespoon coarse sea salt	½ teaspoon finely ground black pepper
3½ oz dried *m'lookhiyeh* leaves, or about 2 lb frozen leaves, or 7 oz fresh leaves (approximately 1¼ lb on the stalk; see Lebanese larder, p. 23)	salt to taste
	1 large onion, very finely chopped (try using a red onion, which will set off delightfully against the green sauce)
7 tablespoons unsalted butter	½ cup plus 2 tablespoons red wine vinegar
12 garlic cloves, peeled and crushed	2 medium pita breads, opened up, toasted and broken into bite-sized pieces
1 bunch coriander (7 oz on the stalk), washed, dried, most of the stalk cut off, finely chopped	plain rice, p. 187

Preparing the chicken

Put the chicken and water in a large saucepan, place over a high heat and bring to the boil. As the water is about to boil, skim the surface clean, then add the onions, cinnamon sticks and 1 tablespoon of sea salt. Reduce the heat to medium and boil gently for 1 hour or until the chicken is cooked.

Making the m'lookhiyeh sauce

If you are using dried *m'lookhiyeh* leaves, crumble the ready-picked leaves with your hands, remove and discard any stalks and set aside. If you are using frozen *m'lookhiyeh* leaves, take them out of the freezer some 30 minutes before you are ready to drop them into the broth. The *m'lookhiyeh* sauce made with dried leaves will taste quite differently from that prepared with frozen and both are different, and in my opinion inferior, to that prepared with fresh leaves.

If you are using fresh *m'lookhiyeh* leaves, start before you put the chicken to boil. Prepare as described in the Lebanese larder (see p. 23) and chop the leaves while the chicken is boiling.

Melt the butter in a frying pan over a medium heat, add the crushed garlic, fresh and dry coriander and sauté for one minute or until the coriander softens without letting it brown. Take off the heat and set aside. Remove the boiled onions from the chicken stock, mash into a purée and blend into the coriander and garlic mixture.

Remove and discard the cinnamon sticks from the chicken stock. Transfer 5 cups plus 6 tablespoons of chicken stock into a clean saucepan and place over a medium heat. Bring to the boil, then add the lemon juice. Drop in the chopped (or whole) *m'lookhiyeh* leaves, season with cinnamon, pepper and salt to taste and bring to the boil. Stir in the coriander mixture and boil for: 10 minutes if using dried leaves, 2-3 minutes if using frozen ones and 5 minutes if using fresh leaves. Do not boil any longer as the *m'lookhiyeh* will sink in the broth instead of staying suspended in it.

Finishing and serving
Pour the vinegar into a serving bowl, stir in the chopped onion and set aside. Transfer the chicken onto a chopping board and pick the flesh off the bones, with or without the skin. Cut or tear the meat into bite-sized pieces, arrange these in a serving dish and keep warm. Put the toasted bread in another serving dish and pour the *m'lookhiyeh* into a soup tureen.

M'lookhiyeh is a composite dish that is served hot in soup plates. First spread a few pieces of toasted bread on the plate, spoon a little rice over them, scatter a few pieces of chicken on top and cover generously with *m'lookhiyeh*. The onion and vinegar mixture is sprinkled on top and can be left out, although it gives the mixture a real lift. Eat *m'lookhiyeh* with a spoon, making sure you scoop up a little of each layer on every spoonful. Personally I like eating *m'lookhiyeh* by itself as a soup, sometimes adding chicken but leaving out the other trimmings.

● You can vary on the chicken by serving *m'lookhiyeh* with lamb (2 pounds defatted shoulder of lamb, boiled) or fish (a firm white fish, poached), both large enough for four, and follow the recipe as above.

CHICKEN *with* MOGHRABBIYEH
Moghrabbiyeh ala D'jej

Our version of North African couscous, *moghrabbiyeh* meaning North African in the feminine in Arabic. The grains are bigger, more like small beads and in the Lebanon they are sold freshly made. The taste of fresh *moghrabbiyeh* is quite different and superior to that of the dried but unfortunately it is only the dried variety that is available in the West.

SERVES 4

1 medium chicken, free-range if available (3 lb)	1½ tablespoons coarse sea salt
5¼ cups water	½ teaspoon ground cinnamon (optional)
10½ oz lamb from the shanks, cut into medium-sized pieces (optional)	about 1 lb *moghrabbiyeh*, (see Lebanese larder, p. 21)
2¾ cups water (optional)	4 tablespoons unsalted butter
	16 baby onions, peeled
4 cinnamon sticks	¼ teaspoon finely ground black pepper

Rinse the chicken under cold water and put it in a large saucepan on which you can fit a steamer. Add 5¼ cups water. Rinse the lamb meat under cold water and put it in another pan together with 2¾ cups water. Place each pan over a high heat and bring to the boil. Just as the water is about to boil, skim the surfaces of both pans clean, then add 3 cinnamon sticks and one tablespoon of coarse sea salt to the chicken and 1 cinnamon stick, half a tablespoon salt and half a teaspoon ground cinnamon to the lamb. Reduce the heat to medium under both pans and boil gently for 45 minutes each. You can do the *moghrabbiyeh* with chicken alone, in which case omit the lamb, the 2¾ cups water and both cinnamon stick and powder.

While the meat is cooking, put the dried *moghrabbiyeh* in a bowl, cover it with boiling water and leave for 15 minutes – stir as soon as you pour in the water so that it does not stick (if you are using fresh *moghrabbiyeh* do not soak it). Melt the butter in a saucepan over a low heat, then drain the *moghrabbiyeh* and sauté the grains

164

in the butter until they are well coated, after which put them in a steamer and set aside.

When the 45 minutes are up, add the baby onions to the chicken and fit the steamer with the *moghrabbiyeh* onto the pan. Cover and cook for 15 more minutes or until all the ingredients are done. Turn the heat off under the lamb and leave covered until when you need it. Then preheat the oven at a low temperature.

Put the steamer with the *moghrabbiyeh* in it on a plate while you remove the chicken onto a carving board. Place the steamer back onto the pan and cover to keep warm. Cut the chicken in four or eight pieces, keeping the skin on or not, transfer the pieces to an oven-proof bowl and pop them in the oven to keep warm. Pour the *moghrabbiyeh* into a serving dish. Drain the onions, collecting the broth in a bowl, and add them together with the drained pieces of lamb (if used), to the *moghrabbiyeh*. Pour on ½ cup plus 2 tablespoons chicken stock, season with pepper and salt to taste, and mix carefully together. Taste and adjust seasoning if necessary and arrange the chicken pieces on top. Serve hot.

ᘯ ᔭ O ᐜ ᑫᑫ ᗯ ᗴ ᘯ ᘯ 日 日 エ ᗱ Υᘯ

CHICKEN and WHOLE WHEAT (OR BARLEY) PORRIDGE

H'reesseh ala D'jej

This is traditionally an alms dish made with either chicken or lamb to give to the poor. The origins of the dish go back to the times of the caliphs.

SERVES 4

1½ cups whole wheat (or barley)	9 cups water
	½ teaspoon allspice
1 medium chicken, free-range if available (3 lb) or 1 shoulder of lamb, skinned and defatted	¼ teaspoon finely ground white pepper
	salt to taste
3 cinnamon sticks	6 tablespoons butter

Spread the wheat on a platter, pick it clean of any impurities and put it in a large saucepan. Rinse the chicken under cold water and add it to the wheat together with the cinnamon sticks and water. Place over a high heat and bring to the boil. When the water is about to boil, skim the surface clean, reduce the heat to medium, cover the pan and cook for 1 hour or until the chicken is well done.

Lift the chicken and cinnamon sticks out of the pan, reduce the heat to low and leave the wheat to simmer while you are boning the chicken. Tear or cut the meat in small pieces and discard the skin. Return the chicken meat to the pan, put the lid back on and continue simmering until the wheat is cooked, about 20 minutes, stirring occasionally so that the mixture does not stick to the bottom of the pan. If you find it is too dry add a little water, though not too much as the end result should be like a thick textured porridge.

Transfer the pan to your smallest warmer (or burner) and turn it on very low. Season the chicken and wheat with allspice, pepper and salt to taste, then start beating (or stirring) the mixture with a wooden spoon, cutting into the chicken pieces to break them into thin filaments. You should make them disintegrate into the wheat until you have a homogeneous textured porridge-like mixture. Turn off the heat and keep covered.

Put the butter in a small frying pan and place over a medium heat. Cook until browned without letting it burn. Stir into the chicken and wheat until fully incorporated. Taste, adjust seasoning if necessary and serve hot.

● An interesting and smoky variation is to substitute the whole wheat with an equivalent amount of roasted green wheat (*freekeh*). If you use *freekeh*, you do not need to make the chicken meat disintegrate as finely as you do with the wheat.

● Another variation is to use a shoulder of lamb instead of chicken. Make sure you defat it well before putting it to boil. Prepare as above.

CHICKEN *with* RICE *and* NUTS
D'jej ala Rezz

A dish most commonly served on festive occasions such as Easter or Christmas, and in the past cocks were used instead of chickens.

SERVES 4

1 medium chicken, free-range if available (about 3 lb)	⅓ cup pine nuts
	5 oz lean minced (ground) lamb
ground allspice	½ teaspoon ground cinnamon
extra virgin olive oil	½ teaspoon ground allspice
7 tablespoons water	¼ teaspoon finely ground black pepper
2 tablespoons pomegranate syrup (optional)	
	salt to taste
about 1¼ cups white short grain rice	2 cups chicken stock or water
⅓ cup blanched almond halves	2 cups (1 pint) yogurt (optional)
4 tablespoons unsalted butter	

Preheat the oven to 350°F. Rinse the chicken under cold water, pat dry with paper towels and rub with allspice. Grease a baking dish with a little olive oil, place the chicken in it and put to bake for 1½ hours – 20 minutes per pound plus an additional 20 minutes. Start basting the chicken after the first half hour with part of 7 tablespoons of water and continue to do so at 15-minute interval; this should keep the chicken moist and give you a light sauce to serve with the rice. You can, as an intriguing alternative, baste the chicken with a mixture of ⅓ pomegranate syrup and ⅔ water, which will give the dish a sweet-and-sour taste.

About 45 minutes before the chicken is ready, wash the rice in several changes of cold water and drain. Melt the butter in a saucepan over a medium heat and sauté the pine nuts, stirring regularly, until golden brown. Remove with a slotted spoon and put to drain onto a double layer of paper towels. Sauté the almond halves in the same butter until they turn the same colour, and remove to drain onto paper towels. Cook the lamb also in the same butter until it loses all traces of pink. Keep stirring and mashing it with a spoon or a fork so that it separates well and does not form lumps.

Stir in the rice and three-quarters of the pine nuts and almonds; reserve one-quarter for the garnish. Pour in the chicken stock or water and season with cinnamon, allspice, pepper and salt to taste. Cover the pan and bring to the boil. Reduce the heat to low and simmer for 10 minutes. Give the rice a good stir to blend the floating nuts and minced meat and simmer for another 5 minutes, or until the rice is done and the liquid absorbed. Turn off the heat, wrap the pan lid with a clean kitchen towel, put it back on and leave the rice to sit while you prepare the chicken, which should be ready.

Cut the chicken into four or eight pieces. Put the rice in a serving dish, arrange the chicken pieces on top, sprinkle with the reserved nuts and serve immediately with or without yogurt.

● You can boil the chicken instead of roasting it. Put it in a saucepan, add 6¾ cups water and place over a high heat. Just as the water is about to boil, skim the surface clean, add 3 cinnamon sticks, one peeled onion and salt to taste and boil for 1 hour. Prepare and serve as above.

● An impressive variation is to replace the chicken with game such as pheasant (2 birds for 4 people and 40 minutes in a hot oven), partridge or wood pigeon (1 bird each and 25 minutes in a hot oven) and prepare as above.

CHICKEN *with* ROASTED GREEN WHEAT
D'jej ala Freekeh

Freekeh is a rarely used but wonderful ingredient. The farmers harvest the wheat while it is still green and roast it immediately in the fields. It has a delicate smoky flavor which is quite addictive and cooks quite differently from bulgur, keeping a fine crunch. The fact that it is not commonly used does not mean it is difficult to obtain. It is available from Middle Eastern shops, either loose or pre-packed. There are two different types. The smokier one is coarsely cracked and brownish green in color, whereas the less roasted one is more bland with the grains whole and brown in color. (See Lebanese larder, p. 29, for full details.)

SERVES 4

1 medium chicken, free-range if available (about 3 lb)	2¾ cups chicken stock
6¾ cups water	½ teaspoon ground cinnamon
1 medium onion, peeled	½ teaspoon ground allspice
3 cinnamon sticks	⅛ teaspoon finely ground black pepper
1 tablespoon coarse sea salt	2 cups (1 pint) plain yogurt
2 tablespoons unsalted butter	(optional)
1 cup *freekeh* (see Lebanese larder, p. 29)	

Rinse the chicken under cold water and put it in a saucepan. Add the water, place over a high heat and bring to the boil. Just as the water is about to boil, skim the surface clean, then add the onion, cinnamon sticks and salt. Reduce the heat to medium, cover the pan and boil gently for 1 hour.

About half an hour before the chicken is ready, remove 2¾ cups of the chicken stock for cooking the *freekeh* (the chicken will go on cooking with the stock left in the pan).

Melt the butter in a saucepan over a medium heat, add the *freekeh* and stir until it is well coated with the butter. Pour in the chicken stock, season with cinnamon, allspice, and pepper and bring to the boil. Reduce the heat and simmer for 25 minutes or more until the *freekeh* is cooked to your liking (some people like it cooked longer) and the stock is absorbed. (This cooking time is for when the *freekeh* is cracked and well roasted; if the grains are whole and not very green, increase the stock by 7 tablespoons and cook for 45 minutes.) Take the *freekeh* off the heat, wrap the lid with a clean kitchen towel, put it back over the pan and leave to sit while you prepare the chicken.

Transfer the chicken onto a chopping board and cut into slices or pieces, keeping the skin on or not. Spoon the *freekeh* into a shallow serving bowl, arrange the chicken pieces on top and serve immediately, preferably with a bowl of yogurt.

● You can vary the above by using coarse cracked wheat (*bulgur kheshin*) instead of *freekeh*, but if you do you will lose out on the smoky taste. Cook in the same way as above, allowing for a little more stock if necessary.

GRILLED CHICKEN
Farrooj Meshwi

In the Lebanon very small chickens, more like *poussins*, are used for grilling. *Poussins* hardly have any taste, so I prefer to use small free-range chickens instead.

SERVES 4

2 small free-range chickens	garlic dip, p. 158
garlic marinade, p. 63	

Cut the chickens in half, rinse under cold water and pat dry with paper towels. Mix the marinade well and rub the chicken halves all over with it, keeping any excess to baste the chicken with.

By far the best grilling method is over an open charcoal fire, weather and availability permitting. Otherwise use a hot grill, keeping the rack further away than you would with flatter pieces of meat. This will allow you to cook the chicken thoroughly without burning the skin. Cook for 30 minutes on one side, then turn over the chicken and cook for another 30 minutes or until done.

You can also roast the chicken in a preheated 400°F, hot oven putting the halves on a rack. Cook for 1 hour, basting with the marinade and a little water during cooking. Serve hot with the garlic dip on p. 158.

● You can prepare and grill quails the same way. Instead of cutting them in half, flatten them out by cutting them open at the spine, force the birds open so that the breasts are flat. Grill for about 15-20 minutes on each side.

Yogurt Dishes
Al-Aklat bil-Laban

DISHES STEWED IN YOGURT
Al-Aklat bil-Laban
Cooked Yogurt Sauce
Stuffed Zucchini in Yogurt Sauce
Lamb Stewed in Yogurt
Meat Dumplings in Cooked Yogurt

DISHES WITH FRESH YOGURT TOPPING
Al-Fattat
Lamb and Chick Peas with Yogurt Topping
Eggplants and Lamb with Yogurt Topping
Chick Peas with Yogurt Topping
Chicken and Chick Peas with Yogurt Topping

 Yogurt is thought to have been discovered accidentally by nomadic tribes in Central Asia. The nomads carried their milk in camel bags during their peregrinations. These got so hot and shaken *en route* that the milk turned into yogurt. It was then said to have been introduced into the eastern Mediterranean area by the invading Persian armies and since then has become a much used ingredient in our cuisine.

The following dishes fall into two categories: those which are cooked in yogurt (*bil-laban*) and those built in layers of different ingredients topped with fresh yogurt which is seasoned with garlic (*fatteh*).

You can make yogurt at home with the help of a special yogurt maker or if you do not own one you can make it as described in the Lebanese larder on p. 19.

171

COOKED YOGURT SAUCE
Laban Matbookh

This is the basic sauce for all the dishes cooked in yogurt. Although the sautéed coriander and garlic mixture is eventually mixed into the cooked yogurt, you should keep it separate until you use the sauce with the various garnishes. Some of the recipes will call for the coriander and garlic mixture to be added after the main garnish is dropped into the yogurt. Ordinary yogurt curdles if cooked without a stabilizer. It needs to be stirred constantly during cooking. You can use goat's yogurt, which does not need the egg to stabilize it, but the taste of the sauce will be stronger and you will still need to stir the sauce during cooking.

SERVES 4

2 tablespoons unsalted butter	7 large garlic cloves, peeled and crushed
½ bunch fresh coriander (3½ oz on the stalk), washed, dried, most of the stalks cut off, finely chopped	about 4 cups (1 quart) yogurt
	1 egg, free-range if available, whisked

Melt the butter in a frying pan over a medium heat, add the chopped coriander and crushed garlic and sauté for one minute or until the coriander softens without letting it brown. Take off the heat and set aside.

Put the yogurt in a large heavy saucepan, add the whisked egg, mix well together with a clean wooden spoon and place over a medium heat. Bring to the boil, stirring constantly in the same direction, so the yogurt will not curdle. When the yogurt has come to the boil, reduce the heat to low and simmer for 3 minutes, still stirring. Use with any of the following *bil-laban* recipes.

● You can vary the taste by replacing the coriander with fresh mint leaves (about 2 oz), finely chopped, or 3 tablespoons dried mint. The mint seasoning is more suited to certain garnishes than the coriander one.

STUFFED ZUCCHINI
in YOGURT SAUCE

Mehshi Koossa bil-Laban

This dish is usually prepared with a meat and rice stuffing, but I have devised a vegetarian version by replacing the meat in the stuffing with sautéed pine nuts.

SERVES 4

about 1½ lb small white or green zucchini, approximately 20	yogurt sauce, p. 172
	¾ cup plus 2 tablespoons zucchini cooking stock
meat and rice stuffing, p. 140	salt to taste
2¾ cups water	

Prepare and core the zucchini as explained on p. 137 and stuff then three-quarters full.

Arrange the zucchini with the open end slightly raised in a saucepan where they fit comfortably half-standing. Add the water, cover the pan and place over a high heat. Bring to the boil, then reduce the heat to medium and boil gently for 25 minutes.

Prepare the yogurt sauce, p. 172. Stir in the coriander and garlic mixture before carefully removing the nearly cooked zucchini from the pan and folding them into the yogurt. Measure ¾ cup plus 2 tablespoons of zucchini stock and gently stir into the simmering yogurt, but be careful not to break the zucchini. Simmer uncovered for 10 minutes. Leave to sit for a few minutes, taste, adjust seasoning if necessary, and serve hot.

● You can vary the stuffing by using double the amount of meat and pine nut stuffing on p. 141 or the vegetarian version on p. 142. The Arabic name of this variation is *ablamah bil-laban*. Follow the instructions as above but use mint instead of coriander in the yogurt sauce.

LAMB STEWED *in* YOGURT

Laban Emmo

Laban emmo means 'yogurt of his mother' in Arabic. Sadly I do not know why this dish has such an evocative name.

SERVES 4

about 2 lb lean lamb from the shank end of the leg, boned and cut into 1-inch cubes	about 5¼ cups water
	1 tablespoon coarse sea salt
	16 baby onions, peeled
the leftover lamb bones	yogurt sauce, p. 172

Put the meat, bones and water in a large saucepan, place over a medium heat and bring to the boil. As the water is about to boil, skim the surface clean, then add the salt, cover the pan and boil gently for 45 minutes. Add the peeled onions and simmer for 15 minutes more, or until both onions and meat are cooked.

Prepare the yogurt sauce, p. 172. Add the meat and onions to the simmering yogurt and stir in the coriander (or mint) and garlic mixture. Measure a scant 2 cups meat stock, add to the yogurt and simmer for 3 minutes more. Serve hot with vermicelli rice, p. 187.

● If you serve this dish without rice, reduce the amount of stock to 5 tablespoons to have a thicker sauce.

● For a vegetarian and not particularly Lebanese version, omit the meat, increase the amount of baby onions by half, and add about 1 pound of another vegetable of your choice – cooked chick peas, mini cauliflower or zucchini or any other which will suit the yogurt sauce. There is a Lebanese vegetarian version using eggs but I find the combination so unappealing that I decided not to include it here.

MEAT DUMPLINGS
in COOKED YOGURT

Sheesh Barak

Many Lebanese dishes freeze very well and *sheesh barak* is no exception. You can freeze it either finished or in its three separate stages (sautéed coriander and garlic mixture, cooked yogurt and raw meat dumplings, each packaged and frozen separately) without affecting the taste. You can also make and freeze the dumplings and prepare the yogurt sauce just before serving. Either way will enable you to plan and serve an elaborate meal without much preparation time on the day.

A similar recipe for this dish is given in a 15th-century Syrian cookery book, *Kitab al-Tibakhah* (the *Book of Cookery*) written by a legal scholar from Damascus, *Ibn al-Mabrad* or *Ibn al-Mubarrad*. "*Shushbarak:* You take minced meat and stuff it in dough rolled out like cut tutmaj (unfilled dough cooked in yogurt). It is cooked in water until done. Then take off the fire and put yogurt, garlic and mint in it." [1]

SERVES 4 TO 6

dough	pinch of ground cinnamon
1¾ cups (6 oz) all-purpose flour	¼ teaspoon ground allspice
7 tablespoons water	⅛ teaspoon finely ground black
pinch of salt	pepper
stuffing	salt to taste
1 small onion, finely chopped	5 oz lean minced (ground) lamb
	yogurt sauce, p. 172

Sift the flour onto a large pastry board. Make a well in the centre, add the water and a pinch of salt and knead with your hands until you have a smooth, malleable and firm dough. Cover with a damp cloth and leave to rest for about 15 minutes.

Put the chopped onion in a medium mixing bowl, sprinkle with

[1] From "*Kitab al-Tibakhah*; a fifteenth century cookbook." PPC 21 November 1985.

cinnamon, allspice, pepper and salt to taste and firmly rub the seasonings in with your fingers until the onion softens. Add the minced meat and mix with your hands until the meat and onion are well blended. Taste, adjust seasoning if necessary and set aside.

Sprinkle a large freezer-proof platter with a little flour and have it on hand to put the meat dumplings on. Divide the dough in two balls. Flatten one slightly, dip both surfaces in flour, shake the excess flour off and roll out into a large circle, about ⅒ inch thick. Use a round pastry cutter, 2 inches in diameter, and cut the flattened dough into as many circles as you can, starting from the very edge and working your way round the outside then the inside. If you do not have pastry cutters, use a thin edged glass or cup. Pick up the excess dough, knead it into a small ball and let it rest.

Turn the circles over, then lift one and lay it on the fingers of one hand. Place ¼ teaspoon of stuffing in the middle, fold the dough over the filling, aligning the edges together to form a half circle. With your free thumb and index finger pinch the edges tightly together into a thin flat wedge, starting at one end of the half circle. Fold the half-moon-shaped dumpling until the tip ends of the half circle meet, pinch them well together and stand the curled dumpling onto the floured platter, with the thin flat wedge up – it should look like a tortellini with a narrower uncurled rim. Continue making the dumplings and arranging them neatly onto the platter until you finish both dough and filling.

Put the dumplings in the freezer and leave until you need them. This should stiffen them a little and stop their shape being spoilt by handling when you drop them into the yogurt sauce. If you are freezing them for much later use, wait until they have frozen before covering them with plastic wrap to avoid squashing them.

Prepare the yogurt sauce on p. 172. Take the dumplings out of the freezer and carefully drop them into the simmering yogurt. Bring back to a simmer and stir in the coriander and garlic mixture. Simmer for 5 more minutes or until the dumplings are cooked. Serve hot with or without vermicelli rice.

● Some people like to add kibbé balls (see p. 119) to the dumplings, in which case plan the dish for more people and double the amount of yogurt sauce. Personally I do not like mixing the two as I do not think that the tastes complement each other.

Fatta means 'break in pieces' in Arabic and the various dishes given below consist of several layers of crumbled, broken or cut ingredients, hence the name *fatteh*. All of the following dishes are topped with yogurt mixed with crushed garlic and sometimes crushed fresh mint or coriander.

There are variations on how each layer is prepared, some preferring to sauté the toasted bread in butter, crushed garlic and herb of their choice before laying it under the other ingredients and leaving the yogurt topping plain. I find this variation rather heavy and not in keeping with our present health concerns and therefore I did not include it in the recipes below. Instead I am giving a selection of traditional recipes, with an added lighter touch which is mine.

目 日 乙 乚 干 ○ Φ Φ ᴡ × ﾗ ﾗ 干 ⊲ ﾀ ﾘ

LAMB *and* CHICK PEAS
with YOGURT TOPPING
Fattet Ghanam

SERVES 4

1 cup dried chick peas	1 large pita bread, opened and
1 teaspoon baking soda	toasted
about 2 lb boned lamb meat,	3 tablespoons unsalted butter
from leg or shoulder, left in 1 piece	⅓ cup pine nuts
4 or 5 lamb bones (optional)	2 large garlic cloves, peeled
about 5¼ cups water	and crushed
3 cinnamon sticks	⅓ oz fresh mint leaves,
1 tablespoon coarse sea salt	crushed with the garlic (optional)
	4 cups (1 quart) yogurt

The night before
Put the chick peas to soak in three times their volume of water, as they will double in size. Stir in one teaspoon of baking soda, which should soften them and therefore help reduce their cooking time.

177

Preparation
Rinse the chick peas under cold water, put them in a saucepan, cover with fresh water and place over a medium heat. Bring to the boil, cover the pan and cook for 1 hour or until they are done.

Put the meat in a saucepan, add the water and place over a medium heat. As the water is about to boil, skim the surface clean, add the cinnamon sticks and salt, cover the pan and boil gently for 45 minutes or until the meat is very tender.

While the chick peas and meat are cooking, toast the bread in a hot oven or under the grill until golden and leave to cool.

Melt the butter in a frying pan and sauté the pine nuts, stirring regularly, until golden brown. Remove with a slotted spoon onto a double layer of paper towels and leave to drain. Or do them like most Lebanese who prepare the pine nuts at the last minute and pour both nuts and butter over the yogurt. Personally I hate seeing the white velvety yogurt smeared with the browned butter instead of being crisply decorated with the drained golden pine nuts.

Mix the crushed garlic (and mint if you chose to use it) into the yoghurt, add salt to taste and set aside.

Finishing and serving
Break the toasted bread into bite-sized pieces and spread over the bottom of a deep serving dish. Lift the meat out of the stock, cut into bite-sized pieces and put over the bread. Drain the chick peas and spread them over the meat. Sprinkle the chick peas, meat and bread with 6 tablespoons lamb stock and cover with the seasoned yogurt. Garnish with the sautéed pine nuts and serve immediately.

EGGPLANTS *and* LAMB
with YOGURT TOPPING
Fattet Batinjen

Replace the chick peas in the main recipe with 2 large eggplants (about 1¼ pounds). Peel the eggplants, dice into ¾-inch cubes, sprinkle with salt and leave to sweat for half an hour. Rinse them under cold water, pat dry with paper towels and deep fry in vegetable oil until golden on all sides. Remove with a slotted spoon, put to drain on a double layer of paper towels and keep warm. Finish as in main recipe, p. 178.

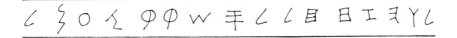

CHICK PEAS
with YOGURT TOPPING
Fattet Hommus

Omit the lamb meat and increase the quantity of chick peas to 3 cups. Prepare the chick peas and finish as in the main recipe on p. 178.

CHICKEN *and* CHICK PEAS
with YOGURT TOPPING
Fattet D'jej

Replace the lamb meat with a medium chicken (about 3 pounds). Boil the chicken for 1 hour and prepare as in the main recipe on p. 178.

Rice and Bulgur Dishes

Al-Aklat bil-Rezz wa bil-Bulgur

NON-VEGETARIAN
Ma Lahmeh
Eggplant, Rice and Nut Cake
Rice with Broad Beans   Chick Peas and Bulgur

VEGETARIAN
Bedoon Lahmeh
Rice in Tomato Sauce   Rice and Lentils
Vermicelli Rice

 Our repertoire of rice and bulgur dishes is rather limited. Rice is usually cooked plain (*rezz m'falfal*) or with vermicelli (*rezz bil-sh'ayriyeh*) and served as a side dish with stews or dishes cooked in a sauce; or in small quantities in stuffings, soups or puddings. Bulgur is also used more as an accessory ingredient than a basic one. The few rice and bulgur dishes which are served on their own are non-vegetarian main courses, with one or two Lenten exceptions.

EGGPLANT, RICE
and NUT CAKE
Ma'loobeh

This dish should be cooked in a round two-handled pan, about 9 inches wide, with straight sides that are not too high. This will allow you to turn it over (*ma'loobeh* means upside down in Arabic) into a shallow cake. It is a good idea to try and chose the eggplants all the same size in order to achieve an attractive presentation.

SERVES 4

4 large eggplants (about 2 lb)	⅓ cup blanched almond halves
salt	about 1 lb lean minced (ground) lamb
about 1 cup (7 oz) white short grain rice	1 teaspoon ground cinnamon
3 cups boiling water	1 teaspoon ground allspice
4 tablespoons butter	¼ teaspoon finely ground black pepper
⅓ cup pine nuts	vegetable oil for frying

Cut off and discard the stem ends of the eggplants. Peel off most of the skin, lengthways, leaving thin strips, about ½ inch wide, of skin unpeeled. Cut the peeled eggplant in long slices about ½ inch thick and arrange these in salted layers in a colander. Leave to sweat for about 30 minutes.

Put the rice in a bowl and pour 1⅜ cups boiling water over it. Stir in half a teaspoon of salt and leave to soak. This will make the rice swell and therefore need less cooking water to help the final cake stay firm.

Melt the butter in a frying pan over a medium heat and sauté the pine nuts, stirring regularly, until they turn golden brown. Remove with a slotted spoon and put to drain on a double layer of paper towels. Do the same with the almond halves, then cook the minced meat in the same butter until it loses all traces of pink. Keep stirring and mashing the meat with a spoon or fork so that it separates well and does not form lumps. Turn off the heat, season with cinnamon, allspice, pepper and salt to taste and mix in most of the nuts – hold back a tablespoon or two for the garnish. Taste, adjust seasoning if necessary, and set aside.

Rinse the eggplant slices in cold water and pat them dry with paper towels. Put enough vegetable oil in a large frying pan to deep fry the eggplant and place over a medium heat. When the oil is hot (to test the heat, dip the end of an eggplant slice; if the oil bubbles around it, it is ready), fry the eggplant until golden on both sides. Remove with a slotted spoon and put to drain on several layers of paper towels.

Take a round two-handled pan (see introductory paragraph) and spread half of the minced meat in an even layer on the bottom. Arrange two thirds of the eggplant in a layer over the meat and against the sides of the pan. Use the best slices for the sides, as these will be the ones to show. Drain the rice, spread it over the eggplant, cover with the remaining meat and finish off with a layer of eggplant. Season 1⅝ cups of boiling water with a little cinnamon, pepper and salt to taste. Bear in mind that this seasoning is just for the rice. Gently pour in the seasoned water, cover the pan, place over a medium heat and bring to the boil. Reduce the heat to low and simmer for 15-20 minutes or until the rice is cooked and the water is absorbed.

Take off the heat, wrap the lid of the pan with a clean kitchen towel, put it back on and leave to sit for about 10 minutes.

The traditional way of serving this dish is to turn it over onto a round serving platter as if it were a cake. Wear oven mitts while performing this operation. Take a round flat serving dish and turn it over onto the top of the pan. Hold the plate down firmly with one hand and with the other, slide the pan slowly over the edge of your surface. Put your hand underneath the pan, pick it up and quickly turn it upside down. Slide the platter back onto your working surface and slowly lift the pan off to uncover the rice and eggplant cake. Sprinkle the reserved nuts on top and serve immediately with yogurt.

● In case you find the turning-over trick too tiresome, bake the *ma'loobeh* in a transparent bake-and-serve dish in a preheated 350°F oven for 45 minutes, or until the rice is done and the water is absorbed. Serve hot straight from the dish.

RICE *with* BROAD BEANS
Rezz ala Fool Akhdar

A very versatile dish typical of mountain family food.

SERVES 4

4 tablespoons unsalted butter	½ teaspoon ground allspice
1 medium onion, very finely chopped	¼ teaspoon finely ground black pepper
5 oz lamb from the shoulder, cut into bite-sized pieces	salt to taste
	2¾ cups water
about ½ lb fresh or frozen broad beans (fava beans)	about 1 cup (7 oz) white short grain rice
½ teaspoon ground cinnamon	

Melt the butter in a large saucepan over a medium heat and sauté the chopped onion until soft and transparent. Add the meat and brown it before adding the broad beans. Season with cinnamon, allspice, pepper and salt to taste, pour in the water and bring to the boil. Reduce the heat to low, cover the pan and simmer for 15 minutes.

Wash the rice in several changes of cold water, drain and stir into the meat and vegetables. Put the lid back on and simmer for 20 minutes, checking the water halfway through cooking as you may need to add a little more. The rice should be quite moist, a bit like an Italian *risotto*. Serve hot with yogurt.

● You can vary on this dish by using any of the following and still preparing as above:

1 – Green beans (*loobyeh*), topped, tailed, stringed and cut into medium pieces. (If you have dried green beans [see the Lebanese larder, p. 23] use them, as they will give the dish an unusual and slightly smoky taste.)

2 – Zucchini (*koossah*) or carrots (*jazar*), sliced into ½-inch circles.

3 – Desert truffles (*kamah*), scrubbed clean, rinsed under cold water, then peeled and cut into bite-sized pieces.

● You can also do a vegetarian version by replacing the butter with 3 tablespoons of extra virgin olive oil. Omit the lamb and increase the quantity of raw rice to about 1½ cups. Fry the chopped onion in the olive oil until golden, stir in the broad beans and washed and drained rice, increase the quantity of water to about 13 cups and cook as above.

183

CHICK PEAS *and* BULGUR

Bulgur bi-Dfeeneh

SERVES 4

¾ cup dried chick peas	2 cinnamon sticks
½ teaspoon baking soda	1½ cups coarse bulgur,
4 tablespoons butter	(see Lebanese larder, p. 16)
2 or 3 pork or lamb bones (optional)	½ teaspoon ground cinnamon
	1 teaspoon ground allspice
about 1 lb pork or lamb meat from the shanks, cut into medium-sized pieces	¼ teaspoon finely ground black pepper
	salt to taste
1 medium onion, finely chopped	2 cups (1 pint) yogurt
6¾ cups water	

The night before

Put the chick peas to soak in three times their volume of water. Stir in half a teaspoon baking soda. This should soften them and therefore help reduce their cooking time.

Preparation

Melt the butter in a casserole over a medium heat and brown the bones. Remove onto a plate, then brown the meat, after which add the chopped onion and sauté until the onion is soft and transparent. Drain the chick peas, rinse under cold water and add to the meat and onion. Sauté for a few minutes until they are well coated in butter. Return the bones to the pan and add the water and cinnamon sticks. Cover the pan and boil gently for one hour or until the chick peas and meat are tender.

Remove and discard the bones and cinnamon sticks, add the bulgur and season with cinnamon, allspice, pepper and salt to taste. Reduce the heat to low and simmer for about 25 minutes or until the bulgur is done and the liquid is absorbed. Wrap the lid in a clean kitchen towel, put it back over the pan and leave to sit for a few minutes. Serve hot with yogurt.

● You can use rice or *freekeh* instead of bulgur. Follow instructions as above but use only lamb meat as pork does not really go with either.

184

RICE *in* TOMATO SAUCE
Rezz bil-Banadoorah

This dish can be served cold provided you replace the butter with extra virgin olive oil.

SERVES 4

6 tablespoons butter or scant ½ cup extra virgin olive oil	1⅜ cups water
2 medium onions, very finely chopped	1 teaspoon finely ground black pepper
	salt to taste
2½ lb ripe tomatoes, peeled and chopped, or same amount Italian canned	about 2¼ cups (14 oz) white short grain rice
	a few basil leaves for garnish

Melt the butter (or heat the oil) in a large saucepan over a medium heat. Add the chopped onion and sauté until golden. Add the chopped tomatoes and bring to the boil. Then cover the pan and boil gently for 5 minutes.

Pour in the water, add the pepper and salt to taste and bring back to the boil. Stir in the rice and boil for 2 minutes before putting the lid back on. Reduce the heat to low and simmer for 15 minutes or until the rice is cooked but without having dried up completely. The rice should be quite moist, like that of Italian *risotto*. Garnish with a few basil leaves and serve hot (or at room temperature if it is cooked in olive oil).

● You can replace the rice with coarse bulgur, a delicious variation typical of Lenten mountain food.

RICE *and* LENTILS
M'dardarah

The amounts given below are for four generous starters. If you want to serve it as a vegetarian main course, increase the quantities by half (or double them for healthy appetites).

SERVES 4

¾ cup brown lentils	½ teaspoon ground cinnamon
4½ cups water	½ teaspoon ground allspice
⅝ cup extra virgin olive oil	½ teaspoon finely ground black
3 medium onions, thinly sliced	pepper
about ¾ cup (5 oz) white short grain rice	salt to taste

Spread the lentils on a platter and pick them clean of any impurities. Put the lentils in a saucepan, add the water and place over a high heat. Bring to the boil then reduce the heat to medium, give the lentils a good stir in case some have stuck to the bottom, cover the pan and simmer for 45 minutes or until the lentils are nearly cooked.

While the lentils are cooking, heat the olive oil in a large frying pan over medium heat. When it is hot (to test the heat, dip in an onion slice, and if the oil bubbles around it, it is ready) insert the onion slices and fry until they turn a rich dark brown without letting them burn and blacken. Remove three quarters of the onion slices with a slotted spoon and spread them thinly on a double layer of paper towels so that they drain well and become crispy.

Wash the rice in several changes of cold water, drain and add to the lentils. Season with cinnamon, allspice, pepper and salt to taste and bring back to the boil. Reduce the heat, stir in the onions left in the pan and their oil, put the lid back on and simmer for 15 minutes. Turn off the heat, wrap the lid with a clean kitchen towel, put it back over the pan and leave to sit for 5 minutes. Stir the lentils and rice before transferring to a serving dish. Scatter the crisp onion slices over the top before serving hot with a white cabbage salad, p. 75. You can serve this dish tepid or at room temperature, in which case garnish with the crisp onion slices at the last minute; if not they will go soft with the steam rising from the lentils and rice.

● A variation from the south is to replace the rice with coarse bulgur. Prepare as above but you may need to add more water (up to ⅝ cup depending on how coarse the bulgur is; the coarser the bulgur, the more water needed.

186

VERMICELLI RICE
Rezz bil-Sh'ayriyeh

This rice, also called rice pilaf, is normally served with dishes stewed in yogurt or in tahini sauce.

SERVES 4

2 tablespoons unsalted butter	1¾ cups water
1 oz vermicelli	salt to taste
about 1 cup (7 oz) white short grain rice	

Wash the rice in several changes of cold water and drain well. Melt the butter in a saucepan over a medium heat. Break the vermicelli into small pieces, about ¾ inch long, before adding to the butter. Sauté the vermicelli pieces, stirring regularly, until they turn golden brown. Stir in the rice and sauté until it is well coated with the butter. Pour in the water and add salt to taste. Cover the pan and bring to the boil. Then reduce the heat to low and simmer for 15 minutes or until the rice is done and the water absorbed.

Take off the heat, wrap the lid with a clean paper towel, put it back over the pan and leave to sit for 5 minutes. Serve hot with any of the dishes that call for vermicelli rice.

● You can make a plain version, *rezz m'falfal*, which is more commonly served by omitting the vermicelli and preparing as above.

Stews
Al-Yakhnat

Cannellini Beans and Meat Stew
Zucchini and Meat Stew
Green Beans and Meat Stew   Meatball Stew
Okra and Meat Stew   Peas, Carrots and Meat Stew
Spinach, Fresh Coriander and Meat Stew

 Stews are some of the dishes we eat most regularly. They are usually a mixture of meat and vegetables cooked in three different sauces. One made with fresh (or canned) tomatoes, another with tomato concentrate diluted in the cooking water and a third with a little water thickened with flour and flavored with lemon juice.

Our stews are both economical and well balanced, nourishing meals. They are traditionally served with rice but you can also serve them on their own with Arabic bread.

CANNELLINI BEANS
and MEAT STEW
Fassolyah bil-Lahmeh

Although this dish is very much part of our home cooking repertoire, it is quite similar to western bean dishes such as *cassoulet* or baked beans except for the strong flavor of cinnamon and allspice as well as the copious use of tomato paste.

SERVES 4

1½ cup dried cannellini, kidney, lima, or navy beans	4½ cups water
1 teaspoon baking soda	5 oz tomato paste
about 1 lb pork meat from leg or shoulder or lamb meat from the shoulder	1 teaspoon ground cinnamon
	1 teaspoon ground allspice
	½ teaspoon finely ground black pepper
2 or 3 bones (optional)	¼ teaspoon ground nutmeg
4 tablespoons unsalted butter	salt to taste
1 large onion, sliced medium-thin	

The night before

Put the beans to soak in three times their volume of water as they will double in size. Stir in one teaspoon baking soda. This should soften them and help reduce their cooking time.

Finishing and serving

If you are using pork, rinse the meat under cold water and cut it in chunky pieces, separating the skin from the meat (if the skin is very fatty cut off and discard any excess fat). If you are using lamb, strip the skin off, discard it, and get rid of as much fat as you can and cut as with the pork.

Melt the butter in a saucepan over a medium heat and sauté the pork skins (if you are using them) until crisp and golden. Remove them onto a plate and brown the meat. Remove the meat onto the same plate as the skins. Add the sliced onion and cook, stirring occasionally, until soft and transparent. If you are using the bones, rinse them under cold water before adding to the onion. Sauté the bones until they lose all traces of pink. Return the skins and meat to the pan, add the water, cover and bring to the boil. When the water is about to boil, skim the surface clean and boil gently for 15 minutes.

Drain the soaked beans and rinse them under cold water. Add to the meat and onion and boil gently, covered, for 45 minutes or until the beans are tender.

Dilute the tomato paste in a little water and stir into the broth. Season with cinnamon, allspice, pepper, nutmeg and salt to taste, put the lid back on and simmer for 10 more minutes or until the sauce has thickened and the beans are cooked. Taste, adjust seasoning if necessary, and serve hot with plain rice.

ZUCCHINI *and* MEAT STEW
Yakhnet Koossa bil-Lahmeh

Ideally you should use small, tender white zucchini. I rather like using whole mini ones, as they do not break as easily as those cut in halves. If you cannot find white zucchini, select small green zucchini, all about the same size, and slice them in ½-inch circles.

SERVES 4

1½ to 1¾ lb small white or green zucchini	½ teaspoon ground cinnamon
4 tablespoons unsalted butter	½ teaspoon ground allspice
1 medium onion, very finely chopped	¼ teaspoon finely ground black pepper
about ¾ lb lean minced (ground) lamb	salt to taste
1¾ lb ripe tomatoes, peeled and chopped, or same amount Italian canned	

Cut off and discard the stem ends of the zucchini and shave off the round brown skin on the bottom. Rinse under cold water and cut them in half, lengthways (not if you are using mini zucchini, which you should leave whole). Set aside.

Melt the butter in a saucepan over a medium heat and sauté the chopped onion until soft and transparent. Stir in the minced meat and cook until it loses all traces of pink. Keep stirring and mashing the meat with a wooden spoon or fork so that it separates well and does not form lumps. Add the zucchini, sprinkle with a little salt and carefully mix them with the meat and onion. Reduce the heat to low, cover the pan and cook for 5 minutes.

Add the chopped tomatoes, season with cinnamon, pepper and salt to taste, increase the heat back to medium and cook for 15-20 minutes, or until the zucchini are done to your liking and the sauce thickened. Taste, adjust seasoning if necessary, and serve hot with plain rice.

● You can make a variation by using potatoes instead of the zucchini, cutting them into medium-sized chunks; or you can substitute eggplant diced into ¾-inch cubes which you will need to salt first before leaving them to sweat for about 30 minutes, after which rinse and dry them, then prepare as above. Both the potatoes and the eggplant will take a little longer to cook, so allow 10 minutes extra cooking time.

GREEN BEANS *and* MEAT STEW
Loobyeh bil-Lahmeh

SERVES 4

about 1 lb fresh green beans	3 to 4 small (14 oz) ripe
4 tablespoons butter	tomatoes, peeled and chopped,
2 medium onions, thinly sliced	or same amount Italian canned
about ¾ lb lamb, cut in	1 teaspoon ground cinnamon
bite-sized pieces	1 teaspoon ground allspice
salt	¼ teaspoon finely ground black pepper

Top, tail and string the beans. Put in a colander, rinse under cold water and set aside.

Melt the butter in a large saucepan over a medium heat and sauté the onions until soft and transparent. Add the meat and brown stirring regularly for about 5 minutes. Stir in the beans, sprinkle with a little salt, mix well together, cover the pan and cook for another 5 minutes, lifting the lid to stir the beans from time to time.

Pour in the chopped tomatoes. Season with cinnamon, allspice, pepper and more salt to taste. Bring to the boil, then cover the pan and boil gently for 15-20 minutes or until both beans and meat are done. If the tomato sauce has not thickened enough, uncover the pan and boil away the excess liquid. Taste, adjust seasoning if necessary, and serve hot with plain rice.

MEATBALL STEW
Dawood Basha

Dawood Basha was appointed first *mutasariff* (governor) of the Lebanon in 1861 to help reunite the Ottoman province, as Lebanon stood at that time, after its second bout of serious sectarian fighting. He proved to be a wise and honest governor. I presume this dish was either created for him or else named after him, as his favorite dish, to honour him as a much loved and just ruler.

SERVES 4

1 medium onion, peeled and quartered, grated	½ tablespoon all-purpose flour
	scant ¼ cup water
1¾ lb lean coarse minced (ground) beef	¼ teaspoon ground cinnamon
	½ teaspoon ground allspice
cinnamon, allspice, finely ground black pepper and salt to taste	¼ teaspoon finely ground black pepper
2 tablespoons club soda or seltzer	salt to taste
	juice of ½ lemon, or to taste
4 tablespoons unsalted butter	(or ½ tablespoon pomegranate syrup; see Lebanese larder, p. 28)
⅓ cup pine nuts	
1 lb baby onions, peeled	

Grate the quartered onion and put it in a mixing bowl. Add the minced meat, season with a little cinnamon, allspice, pepper and salt to give the meatballs some taste; bear in mind that the main seasoning will be in the sauce, and blend until the texture of the meat is smooth. Next pour in the club soda or seltzer and mix well together with your hand. The soda water gives the meatballs a lighter texture. Shape the meat into walnut-sized balls, put on a plate and set aside.

Melt the butter in a large sauté pan over a medium heat and sauté the pine nuts, stirring regularly, until golden brown. Remove onto a plate and put the baby onions in the pan. Cook until they soften and start changing color. Remove the onions onto a separate plate, then brown the meatballs, still in the same butter and put on the same plate as the pine nuts.

Brown the flour in the butter, stir in the water, season with cinnamon, allspice, pepper and salt to taste and add the onions. Bring to the boil, reduce the heat to low, cover the pan and simmer for 15 minutes or until the onions are cooked.

Add the meat, pine nuts and lemon juice and simmer for 2 more minutes. Taste, adjust seasoning if necessary and serve hot with vermicelli rice.

● You can vary on this dish by cooking the meat in tomatoes, in which case leave out the flour, water and lemon juice. After you have sautéed the pine nuts, onions and meat and set them aside, put 1¾ pounds ripe tomatoes, peeled and coarsely chopped, or same amount Italian canned, in the pan and boil uncovered for 20 minutes or until the tomatoes have lost most of their liquid. Drop in the onions, cover the pan and simmer for 15 minutes, then add the meatballs and pine nuts and simmer uncovered for another 2 minutes. Serve with plain rice.

⟃⟄⟩⟩ ⟨⟨⟩ ⟩－Ε⟩⟨⟩ ⟩ ⟨ ⟩ ⟩Υ⟩⟩

OKRA *and* MEAT STEW
Bamya bil-Lahmeh

SERVES 4

about 1½ lb okra	¼ teaspoon ground coriander
vegetable oil for frying	salt
2 tablespoons unsalted butter	6 to 8 small (1¾ lb) ripe
1 medium onion, thinly sliced	tomatoes, peeled and chopped,
¾ to 1 lb lamb from the	or same amount Italian canned
shoulder, cut into bite-sized	¼ teaspoon cinnamon
pieces	½ teaspoon allspice
7 garlic cloves, peeled and	¼ teaspoon finely ground black
crushed	pepper
½ bunch fresh coriander	
(3½ oz on the stalk),	
washed, dried, most of the stalk	
cut off, finely chopped	

Prepare and sauté the okra as in the recipe on p. 58.

Melt the butter in a large saucepan over a medium heat and fry the onion slices until soft and transparent. Stir in the meat and brown for 5 minutes. Add the crushed garlic, chopped and ground coriander, a pinch of salt and sauté for one minute, or until the coriander softens without letting it brown.

Pour in the chopped tomatoes, season with cinnamon, allspice, pepper and salt to taste and bring to the boil. Cover the pan and boil gently for 15 minutes. Add the sautéed okra, bring back to the boil then reduce the heat and simmer, covered, for 15 minutes or until the okra is done and the tomato sauce has thickened. Taste, adjust seasoning if necessary, and serve hot with plain rice.

PEAS, CARROTS *and* MEAT STEW
Yakhnet Bazella wa Jazar

A delicious stew with an unusual taste of orange peel that is well suited to the carrots and peas.

SERVES 4

4 tablespoons unsalted butter	peel of 1 small orange, cut in one piece
1 medium onion, finely chopped	small piece of lemon peel
¾ to 1 lb lamb meat from the shoulder, cut into bite-sized pieces	½ teaspoon ground cinnamon
	½ teaspoon ground allspice
3 medium carrots, peeled and sliced into ¼-inch circles	¼ teaspoon finely ground black pepper
6 to 8 small (about 1¾ lb) ripe tomatoes, peeled and chopped, or same amount Italian canned	salt to taste
	about 1 lb fresh peas (or frozen, in which case defrost before using)

Put the chopped tomatoes in a saucepan and boil for 10 to 15 minutes to get rid of some of their excess liquid.

Melt the butter in a large saucepan over a medium heat, add the onions and sauté until golden. Add the meat to the onion and cook until browned. Stir in the carrots, reduce the heat to low, cover the pan and cook for 5 minutes, stirring occasionally.

Add the chopped tomatoes, orange and lemon peel. Season with the cinnamon, allspice, pepper and salt to taste and increase the heat to medium. Cover the pan and bring to the boil. Boil gently for 10 minutes before removing and discarding both peels. Then add the peas and cook for another 10 minutes or until the vegetables and meat are cooked and the tomato sauce has thickened. Serve hot with plain rice.

SPINACH, FRESH CORIANDER and MEAT STEW

S'banegh bil-Lahmeh

This dish is equally delicious without meat and makes an unusual vegetarian main course. Just leave out the minced meat and prepare all the other ingredients as below.

SERVES 4

about 2 lb fresh spinach	½ bunch fresh coriander
4 tablespoons butter	(3½ oz on the stalk),
1 medium onion, finely chopped	washed, dried, most of the stalks
½ teaspoon ground coriander	cut off, finely chopped
½ lb or a bit more minced (ground) lean lamb	juice of 1 lemon
5 garlic cloves, peeled and crushed	¼ teaspoon finely ground black pepper
	salt to taste

Wash and drain the spinach well, then cut into strips, about ½ inch wide. Melt the butter in a large saucepan over a moderate heat, put in the chopped onions and ground coriander and fry until

195

golden. Add the minced meat and cook until all traces of pink have disappeared. Keep stirring and mashing the meat with a wooden spoon or fork so that it separates well and does not form lumps.

Stir in the crushed garlic and chopped coriander, add the spinach, sprinkle with a generous pinch of salt and cover the pan. Wait for a couple of minutes for the spinach to wilt before uncovering the pan and mixing the ingredients well together. Put the lid back on and cook over a medium heat for 10 minutes. If the spinach has released too much water, increase the heat and boil quickly, uncovered, until most of the excess liquid has evaporated. Stir in the lemon juice and cook for another 2 minutes. Taste, adjust seasoning if necessary, and serve hot with plain rice.

● You can replace the minced meat with ½-inch meat cubes or chicken pieces. If you are using the latter, make sure you cook them thoroughly before adding the spinach.

Pickles

Al-Mukhallalat

PICKLES IN VINEGAR
Al-Kabees bil Khal
Eggplant   Cabbage   Cauliflower   Cucumber
Green Tomato   Baby Onion
Sweet Green Chili Pepper   Fresh Thyme   Turnip

PICKLES IN OLIVE OIL
Al-Kabees bil-Zeyt
Eggplant with Walnuts and Garlic
Strained Yogurt Balls

Pickling was an essential part of Lebanese cuisine when refrigeration and easy transport were not readily available. It was a way of preserving fresh produce that could not be dried. But even now almost every family in the Lebanon makes its own pickles (commonly known as *kabees*). Farmers pickle their excess fresh produce for their own use and to send to relatives and friends as 'blessings of the season' (*barakat al-mowssem*). Town dwellers wait until the height of the season before buying their choice of pickling vegetables when prices are at their lowest.

Pickles are one of several ingredients always present at our table together with olives, bread and a plate of fresh salad ingredients. This initial spread is what we call 'the decoration of the table' (*zeynet al-towleh*). A home-served meal will usually feature one type of pickle, the choice of which depends on what is eaten on the day. In restaurants, or at dinner parties, you will be served a classic selection of steel gray eggplants and pale green cucumber wedges, long sweet chili peppers and bright pink turnip roundels (a color imparted by

197

adding beetroot to the pickling solution). We also eat them as a snack to stave off hunger between meals and serve them with other nibbles when offering *arak* or other drinks.

The common pickling solution is a salted mixture of vinegar and water in the proportions of ½:1, or ⅓:1 if you prefer a less sharp taste. Some people add peeled garlic cloves and/or hot chilies to their pickles. Both of these are optional and I personally do not use either. If you decide to use chilies, cut into the bottom tip, to open the flesh and release the hot juices into the liquid. Make sure you remove them as soon as the pickles have reached the right degree of piquancy, otherwise they will become too hot. We also use olive oil to preserve eggplant, filled with a walnut and garlic paste and *labneh* balls. Olive oil preserves take longer to mature than vinegar/water ones.

There are several basic requirements in producing successful pickles. The first is to choose both vegetables and vinegar carefully. The vegetables need to be very fresh, without blemishes or rot spots, and the smaller they are the better. Special attention should be paid to the selection of vinegar if it is not home-made. Try and buy the very best red wine vinegar you can afford as it will make a difference to how good your pickles are.

Cleanliness is all important; hands and utensils must be thoroughly cleaned and jars (*maratbeen*) sterilized. You can sterilize the jars in the oven. Wash them well in soap first, rinse and dry them, then stand them on a baking tray and put them in the oven. Turn the oven on to 275°F. Leave for half an hour or until they reach that temperature, then turn the oven off and let the jars cool before using them.

The finished pickles should be stored in airtight containers that are then placed in a cool dark place. If you are in a hot area, refrigerate pickles as soon as they are ready to eat. A layer of mold can develop sometimes on the surface, in which case skim it off and rinse the pickles before serving.

PICKLING SOLUTION
Al-Mukhallal

The following quantities will make enough pickling solution for a 36-fluid-ounce jar packed full of vegetables. The weight of the vegetables will vary from about 1 to 1¾ pounds, as some will weigh more (or less) for the same volume.

MAKES ABOUT 16 FL OZ (1 PINT)

1⅜ cups water	2 tablespoons of sea salt
⅝ cup red wine vinegar	1 teaspoon sugar

Put the vinegar, water, salt and sugar in a clean jug and mix well together until the salt and sugar are completely diluted. Use with any of the vegetables listed below.

⊲⊲ ⊐ ⅄ Υ ⊟ ⅄ ⌐ ↓ ○ ○ ⌶)⁊⁊ ↓○

EGGPLANT
Batinjen

MAKES A 36-FL-OZ JAR

about 1¾ lb small eggplants	¼ teaspoon cayenne pepper or
½ tablespoon coarse sea salt	1 fresh green chili pepper,
2 heads of garlic (about 3 oz),	topped and seeded
cloves peeled	half the amount of
1 teaspoon fine sea salt	pickling solution
	(about 8 fl oz/½ pint), above

Peel and discard the husks and stalks of the eggplants, leaving a rounded, uncut top. Put the eggplants in a saucepan, cover with water, add the salt and place over a high heat. Bring to the boil, then reduce the heat to medium, cover the pan and boil gently for 5 minutes or until the eggplants are half cooked. Drain the

199

eggplants and leave until they are cool enough to handle.

In the meantime put the peeled garlic cloves in a blender or food processor with the fine sea salt and the cayenne pepper (or fresh chili pepper) and process until nearly smooth. The garlic paste should have a fine crunch.

Take one eggplant and make a slit down the middle, lengthways, cutting half way into the flesh – make sure you do not cut through the other side. Prise the flesh open to create a pocket for the filling and press half a teaspoon of garlic paste into the eggplant. Smooth the filling with your finger or spoon to level it with the eggplant skin, put on a plate and finish doing the rest of the eggplants in the same way.

Take a 36-fluid-ounce sterilized glass jar and arrange the eggplants in layers with the filled side facing upwards, packing them quite snugly together without crushing them.

Prepare half the amount of the pickling solution in the recipe on p. 199 and pour it over the eggplants to cover them. Close the jar and store in a cool, dark place. Eat after two weeks or more.

CABBAGE
Malfoof

MAKES A 36-FL-OZ JAR

about 1 lb white or young green cabbage leaves	1 fresh red chili pepper (optional)
4 garlic cloves, peeled (optional)	full amount of pickling solution (about 16 fl oz/1 pint), p. 199

Wash and drain the cabbage leaves, then roll them, or cut them in medium-sized pieces – you will be able to fit more cabbage in the jar if you cut the leaves. Pack the leaves in a 36-fluid-ounce sterilized glass jar. You can add peeled garlic cloves and one chili pepper to pep up the taste.

Prepare the pickling solution in the recipe on p. 199 and pour it over the cabbage leaves to cover them. Close the jar and store in a cool, dark place. Eat after two to three weeks.

CAULIFLOWER
^Arnabeet

MAKES A 36-FL-OZ JAR

about 1 lb cauliflower	1 fresh hot chili pepper (optional)
4 garlic cloves, peeled (optional)	full amount of pickling solution (about 16 fl oz/1 pint), p. 199

Cut the cauliflower in medium florets. Wash and drain these and pack them in a 36-fluid-ounce sterilized jar, interspersing the garlic and chili between the layers, if you are using them.

Prepare the pickling solution in the recipe on p. 199 and pour it over the cauliflower. Close the jar and store in a cool, dark place. Eat after two to three weeks.

CUCUMBER
Khyar

MAKES A 36-FL-OZ JAR

about 1 lb small cucumbers	4 garlic cloves, peeled (optional)
1 fresh red chili pepper (optional)	full amount of pickling solution (about 16 fl oz/1 pint), p. 199

Wash and drain the cucumbers, then prick each with a toothpick or a small fork in several places. Stand them upright quite tightly together in a 36-fluid-ounce sterilized glass jar, interspersing the garlic and chili between the layers, if you are using them.

Prepare the pickling solution in the recipe on p. 199 and pour it over the cucumbers to cover them. Close the jar and store in a cool, dark place. Eat after two weeks.

● You can also prepare wild cucumber (see p. 73) (*kabees me'teh*) in the same way. Make sure you choose small ones though, or else cut big ones in pieces the length of the jar so that you can stand them in it.

GREEN TOMATO
Banadoorah

MAKES A 36-FL-OZ JAR

about 1 lb medium green tomatoes	**full amount of pickling solution (about 16 fl oz/1 pint), p. 199**
4 garlic cloves, peeled (optional)	
1 fresh red chili pepper (optional)	

Wash and drain the tomatoes, then cut a deep cross into each tomato at the smooth end without going through the other side. The idea is that you will be able to break off one quarter by hand when the tomatoes are pickled. Arrange the tomatoes with the stalk end up, in a 36-fluid-ounce sterilized glass jar, together with the garlic and chilli if you are using them.

Prepare the pickling solution in the recipe on p. 199 and pour it over the tomatoes to cover them. Close the jar well and store in a cool, dark place. Eat after two to three weeks.

BABY ONION
Bassal

MAKES 36-FL-OZ JAR

about 1 lb baby onions, peeled 1 fresh red chili pepper (optional)	full amount of pickling solution (about 16 fl oz/1 pint), p. 199

Pack the peeled onions in a 36-fluid-ounce sterilized glass jar together with the chili pepper if you are using it.

Prepare the pickling solution, p. 199, and pour it over the onions to cover them. Close the jar and store in a cool, dark place. Eat after two to three weeks.

⌐◻ ◸ △ 𝘺 Y ⊟ ⊕ ⌄ ⅄ 𝙨 ⅄ ◇ Ɇ𝘞𝘚

SWEET GREEN CHILI PEPPER
Felfel

MAKES A 36-FL-OZ JAR

about 1¼ lb sweet green chili peppers 4 garlic cloves, peeled (optional) 1 fresh red chili pepper (optional)	full amount of pickling solution (about 16 fl oz/1 pint), p. 199

Wash and drain the peppers. Pack them in a 36-fluid-ounce sterilized glass jar together with the garlic and chili pepper if you are using them.

Prepare the pickling solution in the recipe on p. 199 and pour it over the peppers to cover them. Close the jar and store in a cool, dark place. Eat after two to three weeks.

◿◺ ⁊⁊ ⊂ 𝘚) ⊣Ɇ⊢⁊ ⅁ ⁂ ⅂ ⅂ Y ⁊⁊

FRESH THYME

Za'tar

These pickles are served separately and are quite pungent. People usually nibble on them while drinking arak (see Lebanese larder, p. 35) or eat them as part of a *mezze*.

MAKES A 36-FL-OZ JAR

3 bunches of fresh thyme, (about 10½ oz)	1 fresh red chili pepper (optional)
4 garlic cloves, peeled (optional)	full amount of pickling solution (about 16 fl oz/1 pint), p. 199

Trim the stalk ends of the thyme. Wash and drain the thyme, then pack it, together with the garlic and chili if you are using them, in a 36-fluid-ounce sterilized glass jar.

Prepare the pickling solution in the recipe on p. 199 and pour it over the thyme. Close the jar and place in a cool, dark place. Eat after two to three weeks.

999 w + ⊕ 日 日 ≳ ∨ ⟨ ⟩⟩ο 𝒴 Υ Ɪ+

TURNIP

Lefet

MAKES A 36-FL-OZ JAR

about 1 lb small turnips	1 fresh hot chili pepper (optional)
1 small beetroot, washed, unpeeled and cut in quarters	full amount of pickling solution (about 16 fl oz/1 pint), p. 199

Wash and dry the turnips, then trim the stalk and root ends and pull out any thin roots on the skin.

If the turnips are very small, divide them in two by making one deep incision in the middle from the root end stopping about ¼ inch short of the stalk end; if they are small to medium, divide them in thin slices by making several deep incisions every ½ inch, making sure you do not cut through the other side. Pack them in a sterilized jar, interspersing the beetroot pieces (this will give the white turnip a lovely pink color), and chili pepper.

Prepare the pickling solution in the recipe on p. 199 and pour it over the turnips to cover them. Close the jar and store in a cool, dark place. Eat after two to three weeks.

EGGPLANTS
with WALNUTS *and* GARLIC
Makdoos

This is a variation on *batinjen* (see p. 199), where the eggplants are filled with a walnut and garlic paste and preserved in olive oil instead of vinegar and water. *Makdoos* is never served as part of a selection but on a separate plate, as we consider it more of a dish than a condiment, with its rich nut filling, and usually eat it on its own with or without bread.

MAKES A 36-FL-OZ JAR

about 1¾ lb small eggplants	¼ teaspoon cayenne pepper or
1 tablespoon coarse sea salt	1 fresh green chili pepper,
3 oz walnut pieces or halves	topped and seeded
2 heads of garlic (3 oz), cloves peeled	1 teaspoon fine sea salt
	extra virgin olive oil

Prepare, cook and drain the eggplants as in *batinjen*, p. 199. Make sure you use twice the amount of salt in the cooking water, as there will be no salt added to the oil.

Put the peeled garlic cloves in a blender or food processor with 1 teaspoon salt and process until nearly smooth. Add the walnuts and cayenne pepper (or fresh chili pepper) and blend until the walnuts are ground medium-fine. The filling should have a fine crunch.

Take one eggplant and make a slit down the middle, lengthways, cutting half way into the flesh – make sure you do not cut through the other side. Prise the flesh open to create a pocket for the filling and press a teaspoon of walnut and garlic mixture into the egg-plant. Smooth the filling with your finger or spoon to level it with the eggplant skin, put on a plate and finish doing the rest of the eggplants in the same way.

Pack the eggplants in layers with the filled side up, in a sterilized glass jar, fitting them quite snugly together but without crushing them. Cover the eggplants with extra virgin olive oil, close the jar and store in a cool, dark place. Eat after one month or more.

STRAINED YOGURT BALLS
Labneh bil-Zeyt

A delicious way to preserve strained yogurt (see Lebanese larder, p. 19). The tastiest *kabees labneh* is that made with strained goat's yogurt, which is not always available in the West. You can make your own, though, at a price.

You can enliven the taste of the *labneh* balls by putting a chili pepper and/or sprigs of dried thyme or another dried herb in the oil. It is important you mix enough salt with the strained yogurt before shaping it into balls so that it does not spoil.

MAKES A 36-FL-OZ JAR

about 2 cups (1 pint) sheep's, goat's or cow's strained yogurt	1 teaspoon salt

1 fresh red chili pepper (optional)	two sprigs of dried thyme (optional)
	extra virgin olive oil

You can make your own strained yogurt from about 4 cups (1 quart) cow's, ewe's or goat's yogurt to produce the above amount of strained yogurt. Lay a double layer of cheesecloth over a colander and pour the yogurt into it. Gather the edges to make a pouch and tie the ends twice leaving a space between the two knots so that you can hang the pouch. Hang the filled pouch on the tap over the sink or anywhere else over a receptacle to receive the draining liquid, and leave to drain overnight to use as below.

Before starting to make the balls lay a clean cloth over a tray then salt the strained yogurt; be generous with the salt as you need it for the balls to last. Pinch off a little strained yogurt and shape it into a ball the size of a small walnut. Place on the cloth and shape the rest of the strained yogurt in the same way, spreading the balls on the cloth. Leave them to dry for a day or two.

Carefully pack them in a 36-fluid-ounce sterilized glass jar and cover them with extra virgin olive oil. Add the chili pepper and sprigs of dried thyme if you are using them and close the jar. Store in a cool, dark place and eat after one to two months.

Desserts
Al-Halaweyat

PASTRIES WITH SYRUP
Helo ma Ater
Sugar Syrup Bois de Panama Mousse
Lebanese Clotted Cream Aniseed Fritters
Baklawa The Bread of the Seraglio
Cheese and Semolina Pudding
Clotted Cream Fritters
Pancakes with Clotted Cream
Fried Pancakes with Walnut Stuffing
Pastries Stuffed with Semolina
Pellet Fritters Semolina Cake
Shredded Pastry and Cheese Pie Walnut Triangles

DRY PASTRIES
Helo Nashef
Date Pastries Easter Galettes Finger Fritters
Walnut Pastries White Shortbread Biscuits
Yellow Cakes

PUDDINGS

Cinnamon and Ground Rice Custard Milk Pudding
Rice Pudding Wheat Porridge with Mixed Nuts

ICE CREAMS
Booza
Fig Ice-cream Milk Ice-cream
Candied Apricot Ice-cream Pistachio Nut Ice-cream

"In the Lebanon, the infinite charm of nature leads always to the thought of death, imagined not as cruel but as a dangerous attraction to which you happily surrender and let yourself go into a deep sleep. Thus religious emotions linger between pleasure, sleep and tears. Still today, the Syriac hymns I have heard sung in praise of the Virgin ring like a kind of tearful sigh, a strange sob. This latter worship is very profound amongst the races of the Lebanon, and constitutes the great obstacle to the efforts of Protestant missionaries with these people. They give in on all points; but when it comes to the cult of the Virgin, a tie stronger than them restrains them."

Henri Renan, *Mission en Phenicie*, 1867

 The Lebanese very rarely finish a meal with a dessert; instead they serve fresh fruit and coffee and sweets are served separately in between meals. Many of these are bought commercially. They are made by professional sweet makers, mostly Sunni Muslims, who guard their secrets jealously. The recipes I give here are for those that are most commonly home-made and for those commercial preparations that are easy to reproduce at home.

Most of our sweet preparations are associated with religious feasts which are celebrated with great fervor in the Lebanon. Each religious commemoration boasts its own specialities. For instance, *kellage* (see p. 220) is a typical Muslim sweet, made daily throughout the Muslim month of fast, Ramadan, whereas walnut pastries (*ma'mool*), date pastries (^*rass bil-tamer*) and Easter galettes (*ka'k el-eed*) (see pp. 236, 231 and 233) are Easter specialities. They are amongst the few sweets that are not considered better when made commercially. The hive of activity in our house in the days leading up to Easter was quite tremendous, with my mother spending hours in the kitchen preparing industrial quantities of Easter pastries. Much more effort went into the preparations of Easter lunch and pastries than at any other time of the year, Easter being more important to Lebanese Christians than Christmas. We also prepared the traditional hard-boiled eggs, which we colored organically by boiling them with red onion skins for a deep orange colour or with beetroot for a bright purple.

The first thing we did on Easter morning when we came back from church was to break the eggs. We went round knocking our eggs against each others', counting the broken ones to announce the loser. Little did I know that the broken egg was the symbol for breaking

Christ's tomb open and the sign of renewed life. My mother used to get very annoyed with us because we did not leave any unbroken eggs for visiting relatives. We then repositioned the eggs to hide the broken ends and loved watching our relatives lift an egg, preparing to knock it against someone else's, only to find that we had beaten them to it.

I have divided the following chapter into four different sections. The first includes a wide range of creamy or nutty sweets which are made or served with sugar syrup; the second is devoted to dry pastries, cakes and biscuits with or without filling; the third features a limited selection of delicious aromatic puddings, and the fourth a luscious choice of ice-creams with a boiled milk and cream basis.

SUGAR SYRUP

Ater

The sugar we normally use for this syrup is the white granulated one which produces a transparent liquid. I prefer to use raw cane, golden superfine sugar, which is tastier and relatively healthier (if you can qualify sugar as healthy). The syrup made with the latter has a golden color, which might not meet with the approval of purists, especially if used with white puddings. On the other hand, it makes a lovely contrast and looks like honey. The quantities given below will make enough syrup in which to immerse the fritters. There will always be some syrup left over, which you can either discard or strain to get rid of any loose bits of fritters and save for another time, to use only with fritters.

MAKES ABOUT 1½ CUPS

12 oz (about 1½ cups) white granulated or golden superfine sugar	1 teaspoon lemon juice
	1 tablespoon rose water
½ cup plus 2 tablespoons water	1 tablespoon orange blossom water

Put the sugar, water and lemon juice in a saucepan and place over a medium heat. Bring to the boil, occasionally stirring the mixture. Leave to boil for 3 minutes then stir in the rose and orange blossom water and boil for a few seconds.

Take off the heat and leave to cool before using with any of the recipes that call for sugar syrup. You can store this syrup in a glass jar and keep it in the refrigerator for about two weeks or more.

BOIS DE PANAMA MOUSSE
Natef

Here is a recipe you are unlikely to make. First, it is very difficult to find bois de panama (the dried bark or root of the *Quillaja saponaria* Molina tree, see Lebanese larder, p. 14) in the West. Even if you do find it, the time and effort involved in preparing the mousse will dissuade you of ever wanting to make it. It is a delicious mousse, though, and of interest as bois de panama is a little known ingredient in the West.[1]

SERVES 4

2 oz bois de panama (see Lebanese larder, p. 14)	full recipe of sugar syrup (about 1½ cups), p. 210
2¾ cups water	

Peel the bois de panama (*shirsh el-halaweh*) and pound it in a mortar with a pestle until you have a coarse powder. Soak the powder in 2¾ cups water for 24 hours, then put the soaked powder and its water in a large saucepan. Place over a medium heat and bring to the boil. Watch it as it is about to boil as it will make quite a froth. If you leave it boiling too hard the froth might spill over, in which case reduce the heat, to bring the froth down, and leave the liquid to boil until it has reduced to ¾ cup, about a quarter of the initial amount; this will take 20-30 minutes.

[1] For added information and the definitive recipe see *PPC* 47 (1994).

While the bois de panama solution is boiling, prepare the sugar syrup recipe on p. 210 and keep warm.

Strain the reduced liquid into a medium-large saucepan and place over a low heat. Whisk the liquid until it becomes very foamy. If you are doing this by hand it will take rather a long time, or else use an electric beater, which will relieve your arm and considerably shorten the whisking time. Gradually add the warm sugar syrup, still whisking, until you have a foamy, white elastic mousse. Take off the heat and leave to cool before refrigerating. Serve as a dip with pistachio nut fingers (*karabeege*), p. 238.

LEBANESE CLOTTED CREAM
ˆAshtah

Lebanese clotted cream (ˆashtah from the verb ˆasht: to strip off) is the thick skin which forms on the milk when it has been simmered for a long time. The skin is skimmed off, chilled and used as our only type of cream. English clotted cream is basically prepared in the same way except that ours does not melt during cooking. The only time you can substitute English clotted cream to ours is when the sweet preparation does not require cooking. Even then the color, texture and taste will be quite different and the end result not very authentic.

Hardly anyone in the Lebanon makes *ashtah* at home. People usually buy it from sweet makers. It is not easily available in the West except during the month of Ramadan from some Lebanese shops where they sell sweets. I am giving two recipes for a home-made version; one which uses the natural skimming method and another where half-and-half is boiled with the white of the bread to produce an artificially thickened cream. The natural process is quite long and only yields a very small amount of cream. Although the result is excellent, it seems much easier to buy it ready-made or to prepare it by following the instructions given for the artificial method.

Natural method

MAKES ABOUT SCANT ¾ CUP

4½ cups milk	scant 1½ cups heavy (whipping) cream

Put the milk and cream in a wide, shallow round pan and place over a low heat. Use the widest pan possible for your burner so as to maximize the amount of skin formed, which will be the cream. Bring to the boil then reduce the heat to very low and leave simmering for 1½ to 2 hours.

Once ready, cover the pan and leave undisturbed for 6 to 8 hours after which put the pan in the refrigerator and leave overnight. Skim the thick skin and put it in an airtight container to use when necessary. As for the leftover liquid you can either use it for milk puddings (see pp. 242-3) to make them extra thick or discard it.

Artificial method

MAKES ABOUT 16 OZ (1 PINT)

2 slices of white bread without the crust	2¾ cups half-and-half

Cut or tear the white bread in small pieces and put in a saucepan. Pour the half-and-half over the bread and place over a medium heat. Bring to the boil, then reduce the heat to low and simmer for 10 minutes, stirring regularly.

Take off the heat and leave to cool before refrigerating in an airtight container. This cream should keep for four to five days.

ANISEED FRITTERS

Ma'caron

Ma'caron is made for Epiphany (*Ghtass*) together with other fritters such as *'owwamat* and *zellabiya* (see pp. 225 and 235). It is also one of the specialities prepared for the Assumption of the Virgin (*Eed el-Saydeh*). It can be made with flour for a softer, more syrupy texture, or with fine semolina for a crunchier *ma'caron*.

MAKES 16

full recipe of sugar syrup (about 1½ cups), p. 210	¼ teaspoon Quick Rise or active dry blend yeast
(9 oz) (about 2½ cups) all-purpose plain flour (or fine semolina)	3 tablespoons extra virgin olive oil
1¼ teaspoons ground aniseed	½ cup plus 1 tablespoon water
¼ teaspoon ground cinnamon	vegetable oil for frying

Put the flour (or fine semolina), ground aniseed, cinnamon and yeast in a mixing bowl and mix well together. Add the olive oil and work it in with your fingertips until it is fully incorporated. Add the water and knead with your hand until you have a firm, elastic dough. Cover with a damp cloth and leave for 45 minutes.

In the meantime prepare the sugar syrup as in the recipe on p. 210, keep it in the pan and have on hand to drop the fritters in when they are ready.

Divide the dough in 25 equal pieces, then shape one into a fat sausage, about 2 to 2¾ inches long. Place the rolled pastry against a flat perforated surface, like the bottom of an inverted colander, and with your fingers press the dough down and roll it towards you to make a knobbly roll. Place, joint side down, on a platter and continue treating the rest of the dough in the same way until you have finished all 25 pieces.

Pour enough vegetable oil in a large frying pan to deep fry the *ma'caron* and place over a medium heat. When the oil is very hot (to test the heat, dip in the tip of one roll, and if the oil bubbles around it, it is ready), drop in as many rolls as you can fit comfortably and fry until golden brown all over. Remove with a slotted spoon and drop into the sugar syrup. Leave until the second batch is ready so that they absorb as much syrup as possible, then lift fritters onto a serving platter before putting in the second fried batch. Finish doing the rest of the *ma'caron* in the same way and serve at room temperature.

BAKLAWA
Ba'lawa

The term baklawa designates a whole selection of elaborate sweets ranging from *kol wa shkor* (eat and be thankful) to *borma* (twist) to *ballooriyeh*, a white square version of *borma*. These are all the reserve of commercial sweet makers and are not commonly made by home cooks. Some are easier to make at home than others and here is a home-made version of *kol wa shkor* using layers of phyllo pastry instead of the traditional pastry that is far too difficult and time consuming to attempt. It will not be as melting as that made with the genuine pastry but will be equally tasty and it has the advantage of being very simple to make.

SERVES 4

½ recipe sugar syrup (about ¾ cup), p. 210	1 tablespoon orange blossom water
stuffing	1 tablespoon rose water
1 cup walnuts, (or almonds, pine nuts, pistachio nuts, or cashew nuts)	a chunk of butter to grease the baking dish
scant ½ cup (3½ oz) golden superfine sugar	*pastry*
	12 sheets phyllo pastry measuring 7 x 12½ inches
¾ teaspoon ground cinnamon	5 tablespoons butter, melted

Prepare half the amount of sugar syrup as in the recipe on p. 210 and leave to cool. Preheat the oven to 400°F

Put the walnuts (or almonds, pine nuts, pistachio nuts or cashew nuts) in the blender or food processor and process until medium fine. Transfer to a mixing bowl, add the sugar, cinnamon, orange blossom and rose water and mix well together.

Grease a medium baking dish measuring about 7 x 12½ x 1¼ inches with a chunk of butter, then spread one sheet of phyllo pastry on the bottom of the baking dish – keep the other sheets covered with a damp cloth or plastic wrap as they dry up very quickly – brush it with melted butter, lay another sheet over it, brush with more melted butter and lay another four sheets, brushing each with butter until you have six layers of phyllo pastry.

Spread the nut filling evenly over the pastry and cover with six more layers of phyllo, making sure you brush each with melted butter. Pour any leftover butter onto the pastry and cut into diamonds with sides measuring 2 inches, or into thin rectangles about 2 inches long and ¾ inch wide.

Bake in the preheated oven for 15-20 minutes, or until crisp and golden. Take out of the oven, let sit for a minute, then pour the cooled syrup all over the pastry. Serve at room temperature. This baklawa will keep for a few days if stored in an airtight container.

● You can use fewer layers of phyllo pastry for a more melting baklawa. Sandwich the nut filling between two layers of four buttered sheets of phyllo pastry and finish as above. The presentation will not be as crisp as that in the main recipe.

● You can also make rolled fingers. Cut the phyllo pastry in sheets about 3½ inches wide and 12½ inches long and lay six sheets one over the other, brushing each with melted butter. Spread a quarter of the nut filling in a thin raised line, lengthways, down the middle of the pastry and roll into a thin sausage. Cut the filled roll into pieces about 1½ inches long and arrange them onto a greased baking sheet. Do the rest in the same way, then bake and add syrup as above.

● You can also use puff pastry (about 9 ounces) for a softer texture. The use of puff pastry is not common in the Lebanon, although it is easier as you do not have to fiddle with very thin sheets of phyllo pastry and the taste is more melting. Divide the pastry in two equal parts; roll out one to the size of the baking dish and to a thickness of about ¼ inch. Lay it on the baking dish and spread the filling over it. Roll out the other piece, lay it over the filling and finish as above.

___

THE BREAD *of the* SERAGLIO
Aysh el-Saraya

I am not sure why this bread pudding has been given such a grand name. It uses stale bread which is first soaked in caramelized sugar syrup, then covered with clotted cream and garnished with nuts. The name indicates it is an Ottoman sweet, and depending on how you read seraglio (harem or Turkish palace?) it could be a cheap pudding reserved for concubines or one that was served to kings, and if the latter why the cheap basic ingredient? In any case, it is very much part of the Lebanese repertoire and is a great favorite.

SERVES 4

1 round loaf white bread, about 8 inches in diameter, 1 day old	1 tablespoon orange blossom water
about 1¼ cups (9 oz) golden superfine sugar	1 tablespoon rose water
4 tablespoons water	1¾ cups Lebanese clotted cream, p. 212, or English clotted cream
1 teaspoon lemon juice	2 tablespoons pistachio nuts, ground medium-fine (or more to taste)
scant ½ cup boiling water	

Cut off the crust of the bread and keep for bread crumbs. Slice off the top of the white of bread to leave one flat slice about 1½ inches thick and put it in a round serving dish about 8 inches in diameter. Tear the rest of the white of the bread in thick pieces and use them to fill the gaps in the dish.

Put the sugar, water and lemon juice in a deep frying pan (preferably with a spout) and place over a medium heat. Bring to the boil and cook, stirring constantly, so that the sugar does not crystallize in places, for about 15 minutes or until it is caramelized.

Towards the end of the cooking time, measure 7 ounces of water into a teakettle and bring to a boil. When the sugar is caramelized, start adding the boiling water gradually without taking the sugar mixture off the heat. This is quite a dangerous operation as the syrup will start spluttering as soon as you add the water, so make sure you do this very slowly and stir with a long handled spoon.

Pour the boiling syrup all over the bread and transfer the soaked bread to the pan. Place over a medium heat and cook pressing the bread with the back of a spoon to mash it and make it soak up the syrup.

Clean the dirty edges of the serving dish and slide the bread back onto it, spreading it evenly across the dish. Leave to cool before covering with the cream. Chill, then sprinkle with the chopped pistachio nuts before serving.

CHEESE *and* SEMOLINA PUDDING
Halawet el-Jebn

Halawet el-Jebn is a northern speciality which is very simple to make at home and has a rather interesting and delicious taste. It is served hot, lukewarm or chilled. If you want to serve it hot I suggest you prepare it just before serving as it does not reheat to the right consistency.

SERVES 4

about 1 lb *akkawi* (see Lebanese larder, p. 18) or mozzarella cheese	scant ½ cup semolina
	scant ¾ cup Lebanese clotted cream, p. 212, or English clotted cream (optional)
full recipe sugar syrup (1½ cups), p. 210	
7 tablespoons unsalted butter	1 tablespoon chopped pistachio nuts or candied rose petals (optional)

A few hours before

Cut the cheese into thin slices about ¼ inch thick and put them to soak in cold water. Change the water at regular intervals, every 15 minutes or so, until the cheese has lost all trace of saltiness. You will probably have to change the water about eight or ten times. Taste a bit of cheese before you drain it to make sure it is completely unsalted.

Finishing and serving

Prepare the sugar syrup as in the recipe on p. 210 and measure out ½ cup plus 2 tablespoons to have ready to use with the cheese and semolina. Keep the rest to serve on the side.

Put the butter in a saucepan and place over a medium heat. When it is melted, add the semolina and stir for a few minutes until the semolina has absorbed all the fat. Pour in the measured syrup and continue stirring until the mixture is smooth and well blended.

Drain the sweetened cheese slices, add to the semolina and stir, scraping the bottom so that the cheese does not stick, until the cheese is completely melted and the mixture looks like a thick purée. You can either serve it hot, in which case, beware, the cheese will stretch forever, or lukewarm, or chilled with or without clotted cream and more syrup on the side. The purée can be made to look more attractive with a sprinkling of chopped pistachio nuts or candied rose petals.

● Another way to serve this sweet is in the form of cream-filled rolls. After you have made the sugar syrup and before you start cooking the cheese and semolina mixture, take a large baking sheet and coat it evenly with a little syrup. Then cook the mixture and pour it onto the baking sheet. Dip a spatula in the leftover syrup and use it to spread the hot cheese and semolina purée into a thin layer, about ½ inch thick. Leave to cool, then cut into 2½-inch squares. Spread a tablespoon of clotted cream down the middle of each square and make a medium-thin roll. If the cheese mixture is sticky, dip your fingers in a little syrup. Arrange the filled rolls on a serving platter and dust with coarsely ground pistachio nuts or candied rose petals. Serve chilled.

999 w + ⊕ 日 日 ⸹ ∨ ⸹ ⟩⟩ o ℒ Υ ⵣ+

CLOTTED CREAM FRITTERS
Kellage

Kellage is the Muslim Ramadan sweet 'par excellence.' During that whole month of fasting, a Lebanese sweet maker will set up a deep frying pan outside his shop that he uses only for frying large quantities of *kellage*. The sweets are sold to Muslim families who eat it every day after their meals. *Kellage* is the name of the pastry. It comes in large, round, wafer-thin sheets. The one I buy in London looks and tastes like a communion wafer but my mother tells me that the pastry available in Beirut is more like *marqooq* bread (see p. 15). In the U.S., see what is available from your local Middle Eastern grocery. In either case the method for making the fritters remains the same.

MAKES 8

full recipe sugar syrup (about 1½ cups), p. 210	**a small bowl of milk**
8 round sheets *kellage* pastry	**¾ cup plus 2 tablespoons Lebanese clotted cream, see p. 212**
	vegetable oil for frying

Prepare the sugar syrup as in the recipe on p. 210, keep it in the pan and have at hand to drop the fritters in when they are ready.

Lay one *kellage* sheet on your working surface and brush with milk. Fold the sides of the circle to make a rectangle measuring about 6 x 8 inches, brushing the folds with more milk if they are too dry. Place one heaped tablespoon of clotted cream in the middle, spreading it slightly then fold over, the long sides first, then the shorter ones, to make a filled rectangle measuring about 2½ x 4 inches. Prepare and fill the other seven sheets in the same way and set aside.

Pour enough vegetable oil in a large frying pan to deep fry the rectangles and place over a medium heat. When the oil is very hot, (to test the heat, dip in the tip of one pastry, and if the oil bubbles around it, it is ready), drop in as many pastries as you can fit comfortably and fry until lightly golden on both sides. Remove with a slotted spoon and drop into the sugar syrup. Turn over a couple of times, then lift onto a serving platter. Finish doing the rest of the *kellage* in the same way and serve at room temperature.

𝅘𝅥 𝅘𝅥 𝅘𝅥 𝅘𝅥 𝅘𝅥 ○ ♀ ♀ ᴡ ✗ ⸲ ⸲ 𝅘𝅥 ◁⸲⸲

PANCAKES *with* CLOTTED CREAM
ˆAtayef bil-ˆAshtah

Lebanese pancakes are like thin muffins. They come in two sizes. The small size is about 2¾ inches in diameter and ¼ inch thick. The large size is the same thickness but about 4 inches round. The pancakes are very rarely made at home; instead they are bought from sweet shops and filled at home with clotted cream, cheese or walnuts. They are not commonly found in Lebanese shops in the West, except during the month of Ramadan. You can make them at home by following the recipe below but the home-made pancakes will not be nearly as perfect as the commercial ones. However, they will be good; and provided you do not cook them on both sides, you will be able to fill and close them without any trouble.

SERVES 4

the pancake mix to make 12 small pancakes (about 7 oz/2 cups)	syrup, filling and garnish
¾ cup (3½ oz) all-purpose flour	½ recipe sugar syrup (about ¾ cup), p. 210
½ teaspoon Quick Rise or active dry yeast	¾ cup plus 2 tablespoons clotted cream, p. 212
pinch salt	1 tablespoon chopped pistachio nuts or candied rose petals for garnish (optional)
½ cup plus 2 tablespoons water	
vegetable oil	

221

To prepare the pancakes, syrup and clotted cream

Sift the flour into a mixing bowl and mix in the yeast. Slowly stir the water into the flour and mix with a wooden spoon until smooth. Use a whisk towards the end if the batter is not smooth enough. Cover the bowl with a clean kitchen towel and leave for 1 hour until the batter has risen and its surface is bubbly.

In the meantime prepare the sugar syrup and the clotted cream (if you are making it) as in the recipes on pp. 210 and 212 and leave to cool.

Shortly before the hour is up, grease a heavy, shallow frying pan with a little vegetable oil and place over a medium heat. When the pan is very hot, measure a heaped tablespoon of batter and pour it into the pan, to have a disc about 2¾ inches wide and ¼ inch thick. You can tilt the pan to spread the batter but because the batter is quite thick , it will not spread much so it is better to try and spread as you are pouring it into the pan. Cook on one side for 2-3 minutes or until the bottom is lightly browned and the top bubbly and dry. Remove onto a plate and finish doing the rest of the batter in the same way. To make the larger pancakes measure 1½ tablespoons of batter in a ladle before pouring it into the pan as you have to pour the batter in one go.

Finishing and serving

Leave the pancakes to cool, then take one and lay it on your hand, smooth side down. Place one tablespoon of clotted cream in the middle, fold the pancake over the cream and pinch the edges tightly together halfway round, leaving the other half open to show the cream. They will look a bit like a cream-filled cone. Place on a round serving platter with the pointed end on the inside to form a rosette and continue filling and arranging the pancakes until you have finished both pancakes and cream.

Sprinkle a little chopped pistachio nuts or place a few candied rose petals on the cream. Serve chilled, with a little syrup poured over each pancake.

FRIED PANCAKES
with WALNUT STUFFING
ʾAtayef bil-Joz

These are made with large pancakes (see p. 221). Fried pancakes are at their best served soon after they are ready.

SERVES 4

1½ recipes pancake mix (10½ oz/3 cups), p. 22	1 tablespoon golden superfine sugar
full recipe sugar syrup (1½ cups), p. 210	¼ teaspoon ground cinnamon
scant ⅔ cup walnuts, ground medium-fine	¼ teaspoon orange blossom water
	vegetable oil for frying

Prepare the pancakes as in the recipe on p. 221, making the larger version, and leave to cool. Prepare the sugar syrup as in the recipe on p. 210, keep in the pan and have at hand to drop the fried pancakes into when they are ready.

Put the walnuts in a food processor and process until medium fine. Transfer to a mixing bowl, add the sugar, cinnamon and orange blossom water and mix well together.

Take one pancake and lay it on your hand, smooth side down. Spread 1 tablespoon of walnut filling in a line down the middle, leaving the edges clear, fold the pancake, aligning the edges and with your fingers pinch them tightly together so that they do not open during frying. Place the filled pancake on a platter and continue filling the rest until you have finished all the pancakes and filling.

Pour enough vegetable oil in a large frying pan to deep fry the filled pancakes and place over a medium heat. When the oil is really hot (to test the heat, dip in one corner of a pancake; if the oil bubbles around it, it is ready), slide in as many pancakes as you can fit comfortably in the pan and fry until golden on both sides.

Remove with a slotted spoon and drop into the syrup. Turn them in the syrup a few times until they are well coated and then remove onto a serving dish. Serve lukewarm or at room temperature.

● You can vary the filling by using mashed *akkawi* (see Lebanese

223

larder) or mozzarella cheese (about 5 ounces), which you will have soaked previously to remove all taste of salt (see p. 18), or Lebanese clotted cream (see p. 212, same weight as cheese). Prepare as above and serve hot.

PASTRIES STUFFED *with* SEMOLINA
Tamriyeh

In Arabic *tamriyeh* means 'made with date,' which is a very odd name for this sweet as it contains no dates at all. It is another sweet that has strong religious associations. The Greek Orthodox Christians prepare it to celebrate the day of *Mar Metr* (Saint Matthew?) and the Maronites to celebrate the Assumption of the Virgin (*Eed el-Saydeh*). *Tamriyeh* is traditionally made with a very thin phyllo-like dough, so thin that you should be able to read a newspaper through it, then fried and sprinkled with icing sugar. I found it impossible to make a successful home-made dough and have devised a baked solution, using a good commercial puff pastry, which saves time and produces a different but equally good *tamriyeh*.

SERVES 4

5 tablespoons semolina	½ recipe sugar syrup
2¼ cups milk	(about ¾ cup), p. 210
5 tablespoons golden superfine sugar	9 oz ready-made puff pastry
	vegetable oil
1 tablespoon orange blossom water	

Put the semolina, milk and sugar in a saucepan and place over a medium heat. Bring to the boil while stirring constantly. Reduce the heat to low and continue stirring for 5 more minutes. Add the orange blossom water and keep stirring for another minute.

Take off the heat and pour into a 6½-inch-square dish, spreading the mixture in an even layer, about ½ inch thick. Leave to cool

cool completely before cutting it into 1½-inch squares to end up with 16 pieces.

Preheat the oven to 400°F and prepare the sugar syrup as in the recipe on p. 210 and keep warm.

Divide the puff pastry into 16 pieces, each the size of a walnut. Place these on a lightly oiled dish then brush them with vegetable oil. Roll out one piece into a thin 4-inch square. Place a semolina piece in the middle of it, then pick up one corner and flap it over the filling, positioning the corner in the middle of the square. Pick up the opposite corner and flap it over the first and do the same with the other two corners. Press the folded pastry lightly into the filling and place onto an oiled baking sheet. Continue rolling and filling the pieces of pastry until you have finished making all 16 squares.

Bake in the preheated oven for 15-20 minutes, or until lightly golden. Remove and let cool slightly before pouring a little warm syrup over each square. Serve lukewarm or at room temperature. If you do not intend to serve the squares on the day you made them, do not add the syrup. Warm it up just before serving the pastries and pour it over them at the last minute. Serve at room temperature.

◁ ◁ ∃ ⅄ Υ ⊟ ⋌ ⌐ ∨ ○ ○ ⊥) ⑦⑦ ∨ ○

PELLET FRITTERS

ʿOwwamat

These pellets are quite simple to make, though you will have to master the art of dropping the batter into the frying oil in a ball-shape. They should be served very fresh, soon after they have been made as they go soggy quite quickly.

SERVES 4

full recipe sugar syrup (1¾ cups), p. 210	**about 1¼ cups yogurt**
about 1 cup (5 oz) all-purpose flour	**¼ teaspoon baking soda**
	vegetable oil for frying

Prepare the sugar syrup as in the recipe on p. 210, keep in the pan and have it on hand to drop the fritters in when they are ready.

Sift the flour into a mixing bowl, then add the yogurt and the baking soda. Whisk until the ingredients are well blended and the batter smooth, then cover and leave to rest for 45 minutes.

Pour enough vegetable oil in a medium-sized frying pan to deep fry the pellet fritters and place over a medium heat. When the oil is hot (to test the heat, drop in a little batter, and if the oil bubbles around it, it is ready), dip a rounded dessert spoon in a little oil, fill it with batter and drop the batter into the oil. Ideally you should drop in the batter in such a way as to have ball-shaped fritters, but this is quite difficult and you will need a little practice before achieving this. Drop in as many pellets as can fit comfortably in the pan and fry them, while stirring to brown them evenly, until they become golden all over.

Remove with a slotted spoon onto a double layer of paper towels before dropping in the syrup. Turn a few times in the syrup and remove onto a serving dish. Do the rest of the batter in the same way and serve at room temperature.

● You can also dribble the batter into the oil using a small plastic bottle with a small hole in the top – like a ketchup or mustard bottle, making thin squiggly lines, to achieve a laced disc, and these are called *m'shabbak* (entangled or 'Jackson Pollock' fritters as I call them).

SEMOLINA CAKE
Nammoorah

This is a particularly simple and delicious cake that is cut in small squares before baking and each square is decorated with an almond. It is another of the few sweets where the home-made version tastes better than the commercial one. Make sure you prepare *nammoorah* about 6 hours before you plan to serve it, as the semolina needs quite a long time to soak up the yogurt.

SERVES 4

1½ recipes sugar syrup (2¼ cups), p. 210	about 1½ cups yogurt
1½ cups semolina	¼ teaspoon baking soda
7 tablespoons unsalted butter, softened	½ teaspoon tahini to grease the baking dish
about ¼ cup (2½ oz) golden superfine sugar	⅓ cup blanched almonds

Prepare one and a half times the amount of sugar syrup as in the recipe on p. 210 and leave to cool.

Put the semolina, sugar and softened butter in a mixing bowl and work together with your hand until well blended. Add the yogurt and baking soda and mix well together until you have a firm batter.

Grease a baking dish measuring about 8¼ x 12¼ x 1½ inch deep with the tahini, then spread the batter evenly across the dish. Flatten it gently with the back of a spoon, cover with a clean kitchen towel and leave to rest for 3 hours.

Shortly before the 3 hours are up, preheat the oven to 400°F. Score the uncooked cake into 2-inch squares and press one blanched almond in the middle of each square. Bake in the preheated oven for 20-30 minutes or until golden.

Take out of the oven and pour the cooled syrup all over the squares. Leave to soak up the syrup, then serve at room temperature. You might find the traditional amount of syrup excessive, especially if you are calorie conscious; if so, reduce the quantity to your liking. But do bear in mind that the cakes need time to absorb the syrup and although they might seem to be swimming in syrup to start with, the syrup will only be fully absorbed after 30 minutes or so.

SHREDDED PASTRY
and CHEESE PIE
K'nafeh bil-Jebneh

K'nafeh is usually eaten for breakfast with sesame bread (see Lebanese larder, p. 16). It is not that commonly prepared at home though quite easy to make, provided you can get hold of the pastry. You can buy the pastry in two versions. An unprepared one, fresh or frozen, known as 'hair' (*sha'r*) as it is made in very thin, long strands that are then gathered and folded into long packs which you will have to prepare as below before making the pie. The other kind of pastry is called 'rubbed' (*mafrookeh*), which is ready to use and is usually bought fresh. In this version the strands of dough have been rubbed and rubbed until they become like fluffy bread crumbs. I have not been able to make a home-made *mafrookeh* that is nearly as fine as that made professionally.

You can order both types of fresh pastry, *sha'r* or *mafrookeh*, a day in advance from certain Middle Eastern and Lebanese stores where they sell sweets. Frozen *sha'r* is more readily available; however I suggest you plan to make the pie a day ahead of time and order *k'nafeh mafrookeh*. This will save you the preparation time needed for *k'nafeh sha'r* and it is nearer in taste to the professional one.

SERVES 4 TO 6

10½ oz *akkawi* (see Lebanese larder, p. 18) or mozzarella cheese	about 9 oz *k'nafeh* pastry
	9 tablespoons unsalted butter or *samneh*
½ recipe sugar syrup (about ¾ cup)	(see Lebanese larder, p. 20)

A few hours before

Cut the cheese into thin slices, about ¼ inch thick and put to soak in cold water. Change the water at regular intervals, every 15 minutes or so, until the cheese has lost all trace of saltiness. You will probably have to change the water about eight or ten times. Taste a bit of cheese before you drain it to make sure it is completely unsalted.

Finishing and serving

Prepare the sugar syrup as in the recipe on p. 210 and leave to cool. Preheat the oven to 400°F.

Chop the *k'nafeh sha'r* into small pieces about ½ inch long. Put the chopped pastry in a wide frying pan and make a space in the middle. Cut 7 tablespoons of the butter or *samneh* into small pieces. Put these in the middle of the pastry and place over a low heat. Rub the melting fat into the pastry with your hands until all the shreds are well coated and the fat is completely melted; this will take a few minutes.

Grease a round baking dish (which is the traditional shape) about 9 inches in diameter or a rectangular one 7 x 12½ x 2¼ inches with the rest of the butter or *samneh*. Spread the shredded pastry (or the *k'nafeh mafrookeh*) across the dish in an even layer and press it down hard with your hands. Bake in the preheated oven for 5 minutes.

Drain the cheese and when the 5 minutes are up, take out the pastry and spread the cheese slices evenly over it. Bake for 10 more minutes or until the cheese is completely melted.

This pie is served hot or lukewarm and you should ideally turn it over onto a serving dish which you will have previously brushed with sugar syrup, so that the cheese does not stick.

You can also cut the pie into pieces about 3¼ inches square and put these upside down on a platter, also brushed with syrup, to show the golden pastry. But, because the pastry is quite crumbly, this presentation will not be as nice as if you turn over the whole pie. Pour a little sugar syrup all over the pastry and serve with more syrup on the side and with or without sesame bread.

● You can also cook this pie on top of the stove, in which case it is best to use a round dish. Spread the cheese slices over the pastry before cooking and place the round baking dish over a low heat. Cook for about 20 minutes, turning the dish regularly to make sure the pastry browns evenly. When ready the pie should move in one block if you shake the dish from side to side.

● You can vary on the above by replacing the cheese with 2 cups (1 pint) Lebanese clotted cream (*ˆashtah*). Prepare and serve as above.

WALNUT TRIANGLES
Sh'aybiyatt bil-Joz

MAKES 12

½ recipe sugar syrup (¾ cup), p. 210	½ teaspoon rose water
about ½ cup walnuts, ground medium-fine	4 tablespoons unsalted butter or *samneh* (see Lebanese larder, p. 20), melted
1 scant tablespoon sugar	8 sheets phyllo pastry, measuring 11 x 17 inches
¼ scant teaspoon ground cinnamon	
½ teaspoon orange blossom water	

Prepare the sugar syrup as in the recipe on p. 210 and leave to cool. Preheat the oven to 400°F.

Put the walnuts in a food processor and process until medium-fine. Transfer to a mixing bowl and add the sugar, cinnamon, orange blossom and rose water and mix well together.

Melt the butter, brush a large baking sheet with some of it and have the rest at hand to brush the phyllo pastry with.

Lay one sheet of phyllo pastry on your working surface – keep the other sheets covered with a damp cloth or plastic wrap as they dry up quickly – and brush it with a little melted butter. Lay another piece over it, brush it with butter and lay another two layers, brushing each with butter. Cut the layered sheets into 3½-inch squares. Separate one square and spread a heaped teaspoon of walnut filling in the middle, leaving the edges clear. Fold the pastry over the filling to make a triangle and press the edges together. Brush the top and bottom with butter and place onto a large baking sheet. Continue making the rest of the triangles and arranging them on the baking sheet until you have finished the first lot of pastry and half of the filling. Do the remaining four sheets of phyllo pastry as above.

Bake in the preheated oven for 10 minutes or until crisp and golden.

● You can also make the triangles with a milk pudding filling instead of walnuts. Make this by putting 2 cups plus 2 tablespoons milk in a small saucepan. Stir in a scant ½ cup heavy (whipping) cream and 2 scant tablespoons of cornflour. Place over a medium heat and bring to the boil while stirring constantly. Boil for 1-2 minutes still stirring, then take off the heat and leave to cool. This should make about 1 cup cream filling. Prepare the triangles as above. If you are left with a little extra filling, pour some syrup over it and eat like custard.

● You can also use a clotted cream filling, about ¾ cup Lebanese clotted cream, and prepare as above.

DATE PASTRIES
ˆRass bil-Tamer

One of several sweets that are especially associated with Easter celebrations. Make sure you use unsweetened dried dates for the filling or else the pastries will be too sweet. You will save yourself the sticky chore of pitting each date individually if you buy the dates already pitted. Better still, you can buy a ready-made date paste which comes in the shape of a cake, though make sure you read the label carefully, as some manufacturers press the dates into a cake with the stones. The ready-made paste is more expensive to buy but it is easier to use and has a softer texture making for a more melting pastry.

MAKES ABOUT 40

Pastry	10 tablespoons (1½ sticks)
1¼ cups semolina	unsalted sunflower margarine
6 tablespoons (1½ oz) all-purpose flour	or butter
5 tablespoons (1½ oz) superfine sugar	1½ tablespoons orange blossom water
¼ teaspoon Quick Rise or active dry yeast	1½ tablespoons rose water
	Filling
	12 oz pitted, dried unsweetened dates or unsweetened dried date paste

½ teaspoon ground cinnamon	*Equipment*
2 tablespoons unsalted butter	special *ʿrass bil-tamer* mold
	known as *tabeʿ* (see p. 35)

One and a half hours in advance

Put the semolina, flour, sugar and yeast in a mixing bowl and mix well. Add the margarine or softened butter and work it in with the tips of your fingers until fully incorporated.

Add the orange blossom and rose water and knead with your hand until the pastry is smooth and elastic. Cover with a damp cloth and leave to rest for 1½ hours.

Preparing the filling

Put the pitted dates and ground cinnamon in a food processor and blend into a smooth paste – do not let the paste become too fine, as it should retain some texture – then remove it to a mixing bowl. If you are using a ready-made paste, it comes in a cake form and you will need to work the ground cinnamon and melted butter in with your hands until you have a malleable paste.

Melt the butter in a small frying pan over a low heat. Dribble a little melted butter over the paste and work with your hands until the butter is incorporated. Repeat until you have used up all the butter and the paste is softer.

Pinch off a small piece of date paste and shape it into a round disc about 2½ inches in diameter and ¼ inch thick and put it on a platter. Continue making the date discs until you have finished the paste. Cover with plastic wrap and keep on hand to use with the pastries.

Making the pastries

Preheat the oven to 400°F.

Pinch off a small piece of pastry and roll it into a ball the size of a walnut. Put it on your palm and with your index and middle finger flatten it evenly into a round disc about ¼ inch thick and 2¾ to 3¼ inches wide. Place one piece of date filling in the middle, flap the pastry over and pinch the sides tightly together, removing any excess pastry to end up with a smooth top. The date filling should be wrapped with an even layer of semolina pastry.

You can shape the pastry with your hands to produce a flat round cake about 2 inches in diameter and ½ inch thick or you can use the traditional mold (*tabeʿ*). If you are using the *tabeʿ*, gently press the filled cake into the mould, unpinched side down, making sure you do not press it in too hard; if not, the moulded pastry may not come out intact. Tap the pastry out onto the tip of your fingers and slide it onto the baking sheet. Continue filling and shaping the pastries until you have finished both pastry and paste. Scrape the inside of the mold every now and then to get rid of the residue pastry from inside the grooves. You should end up with about 40 pastries. If you have any leftover filling, eat it as a snack; and if you are left with any extra pastry, either shape and bake it as dry biscuits or make a small amount of nut filling, p. 236, and prepare as in the recipe on the same page.

Bake the pastries in the preheated oven for 15-18 minutes or until lightly golden. If your oven is not large enough to take the baking sheets side by side you will need to allow more time for the bottom tray. Gently remove the baked pastries onto a rack and leave to cool before serving or packing into an airtight container, where they will keep for about one week stored in a cool place.

● You can make a quicker version of the above by making one large pie instead of small individual ones. Follow the same instructions as in the author's note in walnut pastries, p. 238. Use the date paste filling instead of the walnut one and flatten the paste into one thin layer the size of the baking dish before sandwiching it between the two layers of pastry.

EASTER GALETTES
Kaᶜk el-Eed

Kaᶜk el-eed are delicious ringed biscuits with an unusual taste. When we were children we loved to play with them, wearing them round our fingers before eating them.

MAKES ABOUT 50

233

1 cup fine semolina	7 tablespoons *samneh*, (see
¼ teaspoon finely ground mastic	Lebanese larder, p. 20) or
⅛ teaspoon ground nutmeg	unsalted butter, softened
scant ¼ teaspoon *mahlab*, finely ground	about ¼ cup (2½ oz) golden superfine sugar
⅛ teaspoon Quick Rise or active dry yeast	scant ½ cup milk

One and a half hours in advance
Put the semolina, mastic, nutmeg, *mahlab* and yeast into a mixing bowl and mix together. Add the softened *samneh* (or butter) and rub together with the tips of your fingers until the fat is fully incorporated.

Put the sugar in a small jug, pour the milk over it and stir until the sugar is diluted.

Pour the sweetened milk over the semolina mixture and knead with your hands until you have a smooth and malleable paste. Cover with a damp cloth and leave to rest for 1½ hours.

Finishing and serving
Preheat the oven to 400°F.

Pinch off a small piece of semolina pastry and shape into a ball the size of a small walnut. Roll it into a thin sausage about ½ inch thick and 4½ inches long. Bring both ends together and slightly press one on top of the other to achieve a ring-like galette about 2 inches in diameter. Lift delicately onto a cookie sheet, taking care not to spoil the shape and continue making and arranging the galettes until you have finished the pastry. You should end up with about 50 galettes.

Bake in the preheated oven for 15-18 minutes or until lightly golden. Leave to cool before serving or packing in an airtight container, where they will keep for about two weeks stored in a cool place.

FINGER FRITTERS
Zellabiya

Zellabiya is a speciality of the mountains and is one of the very few exclusively homemade sweets. It is especially prepared for Epiphany (*Ghtass*).

MAKES ABOUT 26

about 2¼ cups (9 oz) all-purpose flour	scant ½ cup (3½ oz) golden superfine sugar
1 tablespoon ground aniseed	½ cup plus 2 tablespoons milk
½ teaspoon ground cinnamon	vegetable oil for frying
scant ½ teaspoon Quick Rise yeast	a bowl of water to dip your fingers in
2 tablespoons extra virgin olive oil	

Sift the flour into a mixing bowl and mix in the ground aniseed, cinnamon and yeast. Make a well in the center, pour in the oil and rub with your fingers until the oil is completely incorporated.

Dilute the sugar into the milk and add to the flour mixture. Knead with your hand until you have a loose dough. Cover with a damp cloth and leave for 1 hour until it has risen well.

Pour enough vegetable oil in a large frying pan to deep fry the fingers and place over a medium heat. When the oil is hot (to test the heat, dip in a piece of dough, and if the oil bubbles around it, it is ready), moisten your fingers in the water and pinch off a little dough, the size of a large walnut. Stretch the dough into a long finger-like shape, about 4 to 6 inches long by 1¼ inches wide and drop it into the oil. Do as many fingers as you can fit comfortably in the pan and fry until golden brown all over. The dough will puff up during frying and the fritters will end up looking like round, brown alien growths out of a science fiction film (ideal for children's parties).

Remove with a slotted spoon and put to drain onto several layers of paper towels. Some people sprinkle the fingers with a little confectioners' sugar or granulated sugar but I find they are sweet enough without the additional sugar. Serve at room temperature.

WALNUT PASTRIES

Maᶜmool bil-Joz

These molded pastries are traditionally made for Easter. They can be filled with walnuts (*joz*) or pistachios (*festu*). The former are made in a round mold, the latter in an oblong one (see Lebanese larder, p. 35).

MAKES ABOUT 30 PASTRIES

1 recipe date pastries pastry, p. 23	*Decoration*
	confectioners' sugar
Filling	*Equipment*
1 cup walnuts or pistachios	special *maᶜmool* mold known
about ¼ cup (2 oz) granulated sugar	as *tabeᶜ* (see p. 35) or small conical tea strainer
½ teaspoon ground cinnamon	
½ tablespoon rose water	
½ tablespoon orange blossom water	

One and a half hours in advance
Prepare the date pastries pastry as in the recipe on p. 231 and leave to rest for 1½ hours.

The filling
Put the walnuts in a food processor and grind until medium-fine. Transfer into a mixing bowl, add the sugar and cinnamon and mix together. Pour in the rose and orange blossom water and mix again. The mixture should be slightly sticky and dark brown in color.

The pastries
Preheat the oven to 400°F.

Pinch off a small piece of pastry and roll it into a ball the size of a walnut. Place it in the cup of your hand and with the index finger of your other hand burrow a hole into the pastry (be careful not to pierce the bottom) while rotating it to make the hollowing out easier and more even. You should produce a pastry shell resembling a topless egg with walls about ¼ inch thick.

236

Fill the hollowed pastry with a teaspoon of the nut mixture and pinch the dough over it until it is tightly stuck together. Carefully shape the filled dough into a ball and press it lightly into the special decorated mold (*tabe*) or a conical tea strainer 2½ inches wide, putting the unpinched side on the inside so that you get a perfect top. Tap the pastry out onto the tip of your fingers and slide it onto the baking sheet. If using the *tabe* scrape the inside every now and then to get rid of the residue pastry from inside the grooves. You can also shape the pastries with your hands and decorate them by lightly dragging a fork over the top of each. Repeat the above process until you have finished both pastry and filling. You should end up with about 30 pastries each measuring approximately 2 inches wide and 1½ inches high. If you have any leftover filling, eat it as a snack; and if you are left with any extra pastry, shape and bake it as dry biscuits.

Put the pastries in the preheated oven and bake for about 12-15 minutes or until cooked but without having acquired any color. If your oven is not large enough to take the baking sheets side by side you will need to allow more time for the bottom tray.

Finishing and serving
Take the pastries out of the oven and transfer them onto a rack. Leave to cool for a few minutes, then sprinkle them lightly with confectioners' sugar (sift the sugar through a tea strainer to get an even dusting). When the pastries are cold, lift them carefully and arrange on a serving dish or pack them in an airtight container where they will keep for about one week stored in a cool place.

237

Author's note
A quicker version for the above recipe is to make flat pastries instead of conical ones.

Divide the dough in two equal pieces. Pinch off a small handful of pastry from one and flatten it on your palm (to a thickness of ½ inch, then lay it on a baking tray measuring 8¼ x 13¾ inches starting in one corner. Smooth it with your hand, pinch off another piece, again flatten it on your palm and lay it next to the first piece, overlapping them slightly so that the pieces do not separate during cooking. Repeat the above procedure until you have covered the bottom of the tray, making sure you spread the pastry evenly and thinly across it.

Spread the filling over the pastry and lay the rest of the dough over it in the same way you have done the bottom layer. This will be a bit more difficult as you will be doing it over chunky bits of filling instead of a flat surface. Cut into 2-inch squares, then cook and finish as in traditional recipe.

● You can make a slight variation called *karabeege* by replacing the walnuts with pistachios. Shape the pastries into fingers with a flat bottom about 2 inches long and 1 inch wide. Do not sprinkle them with confectioners' sugar and serve them with *natef* (see p. 211).

WHITE SHORTBREAD BISCUITS
Gh'raybeh

These are particularly pretty, fragrant biscuits with a lovely fluffy texture. They can be shaped in three different ways, either as described below or in round cakes about 2 inches in diameter and ¾ inch thick; with a slightly depressed centre in which you press an almond or a pistachio nut; or in diamonds the same thickness as before and with 2-inch sides and also with a central nut garnish. All three shapes are quite simple to make.

MAKES ABOUT 36

7 tablespoons unsalted butter, softened	2 tablespoons rose water
	1 cup fine semolina
¾ cup (4½ oz) confectioners' sugar	2 oz raw pistachio nuts (optional)
2 tablespoons orange blossom water	

Preheat the oven to 325°F.

Put the softened butter and confectioners' sugar in a mixing bowl and work together with the back of a wooden spoon until you have a creamy, smooth white paste.

Work in the flour gradually with your hand until it is fully incorporated, then pour in the orange blossom and rose water and knead with your hand until the pastry is soft and smooth.

Pinch off a little pastry the size of a walnut and roll it into a sausage about ½ inch thick and 4 inches long. Bring both ends together, slightly overlapping them, flatten the ringed pastry a little, press a pistachio nut where the ends join and place on a non-stick baking sheet. Continue shaping and garnishing the biscuits until you have finished the pastry and the nuts; you should end up with approximately 36 biscuits.

Bake in the preheated oven for 15 minutes or until cooked but still white. Leave to cool completely before transferring to a serving platter or an airtight biscuit container.

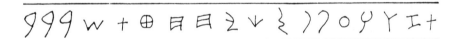

YELLOW CAKES
S'foof

These are basically rather dense sponge cakes made exotic by the addition of turmeric, which imparts a vivid yellow color and a somewhat spicy flavor.

SERVES 4

1 tablespoon tahini	about 1¼ cups (9 oz) golden
about 2¼ cups (9 oz) all-purpose flour	superfine sugar
	scant ¾ cup warm water
½ cup fine semolina	*garnish*
½ teaspoon turmeric	⅛ cup pine nuts or blanched
½ teaspoon baking powder	almonds
5 tablespoons unsalted butter or 5 tablespoons extra virgin olive oil	

Preheat the oven to 350°F and grease a deep baking dish 8¼ x 12¼ x 2 inches with a tablespoon of tahini.

Put the flour, semolina, turmeric and baking powder in a mixing bowl and mix well together. Add the butter (or olive oil) and rub the fat in with your fingers until it is well absorbed.

Put the sugar in another mixing bowl, pour in the water and stir until the sugar is completely diluted. Add the sweetened water to the flour and semolina mixture and blend well together. Pour the mixture into the greased baking dish, scatter the pine nuts or almonds on top and bake in the preheated oven for 35 minutes or until the cake has risen and is cooked inside. Prick the middle of the cake with a toothpick and if it comes out dry, the cake is done.

Remove from the oven, leave to cool, then cut into medium-sized squares or diamonds and serve at room temperature. These cakes will keep for a week if stored in a sealed container in a cool place.

目　日　乙　乚　丰　○　ＰＰ　ｗ　×　与　与　丰　◁　与与

CINNAMON *and* GROUND RICE CUSTARD
Meghli

Meghli is traditionally prepared in large quantities to celebrate the birth of a boy, the male heir who will keep the family name alive. However, there are a few liberal families who will also prepare it for the birth of a girl. Some of it is offered at home and the rest sent off to relatives and friends to announce the happy event.

You can buy a ready-made *meghli* mixture that is an acceptable and quick alternative to the homemade one. The stirring is the main drawback of this fragrant custard-like mixture. It goes on forever, about 1 hour without respite from when it has started boiling until when it is done (*meghli* means "boiled" in Arabic). Some people boil *meghli* for less time, but the result is not as scrumptious as when the ground rice has cooked long enough to absorb all the water and the custard is really creamy and full of taste.

It was one of my favorite puddings when I was young and it always took much convincing before my mother would relent and finally agree to make it, on the condition that I help stir the mixture.

SERVES 4

	garnish
about 10¾ cups water	dried shredded coconut
⅔ cup ground rice (cream of rice)	⅓ cup pine nuts, soaked in
2½ tablespoons ground caraway seeds	boiling water
1½ tablespoons ground anise	⅓ cup walnuts, soaked in
1½ teaspoons ground cinnamon	boiling water then peeled, if you
about 1 cup (7 oz) golden superfine sugar	have the patience
	⅓ cup blanched almond halves, soaked in boiling water

Put the ground rice in a large saucepan. Add the water, ground caraway seeds and anise and place over a high heat. Bring to the boil while stirring constantly and keep stirring for 25 minutes. Then reduce the heat to medium and boil for another 5 minutes, still stirring.

Add the cinnamon and stir for another 20 minutes, then reduce the heat to medium-low, add the sugar and stir for 10 more minutes. Take off the heat and pour into one shallow serving bowl or into 4 or 6 individual custard cups, depending on size.

Leave to cool, then garnish with the shredded coconut and drained nuts and serve chilled or at room temperature.

MILK PUDDING
Muhallabiyeh

Muhallabiyeh can be made with either ground rice or cornflour. There is quite a difference in texture between the two, the one made with cornflour being the finest. The taste of rose and orange flower water might be quite unexpected for those who are not used to scented flavorings in food, in which case use half the quantities given below for your first tasting and then adjust amounts to your liking the second time you prepare the pudding.

SERVES 4

about 4 cups (1 quart) milk	2 teaspoons orange blossom water
4 heaped tablespoons ground rice (cream of rice) or cornstarch	2 teaspoons rose water
about ¾ cup (5 oz) granulated sugar	⅓ cup blanched almonds or coarsely ground pistachio nuts
¼ teaspoon ground mastic (optional)	

Put the milk and ground rice (or cornstarch) in a saucepan, place over a high heat and bring to the boil, stirring constantly. Reduce the heat to low, add the sugar and continue stirring for another 7 minutes or until the liquid has thickened. Add the orange blossom and rose water and simmer, still stirring, for 2 more minutes. Take off the heat, pour into one large shallow bowl (or 4 custard cups) and leave to cool before garnishing with almonds or pistachios. Serve cold.

RICE PUDDING
Rezz bil-Haleeb

The main difference between our rice pudding and the English and American ones is the use of rose and orange blossom water. You might be taken aback by the scented flavoring, and if you find the idea too alien, try using half the quantities given below before deciding whether you like the scented taste or not.

SERVES 4

about ½ cup (3½ oz) white short grain rice	1 tablespoon rose water
scant 1¾ cups water	1 tablespoon orange blossom water
2¾ cups milk	about ¼ cup (2½ oz) granulated sugar

Rinse the rice under cold water and put it in a saucepan. Add the water and place over a medium heat. Bring to the boil, reduce the heat and simmer for 15-20 minutes or until the rice has absorbed all the water.

Pour in the milk, increase the heat to medium and bring back to the boil, stirring occasionally. Cook for 5 minutes, then lower the heat and cook for another 10-15 minutes, stirring the mixture so that the rice does not stick to the bottom of the pan.

Stir in the sugar and cook for a few more minutes, still stirring. Add the rose and orange blossom water and stir for another minute. Take off the heat and pour into individual custard cups or one shallow serving dish. Serve chilled.

WHEAT PORRIDGE
with MIXED NUTS
ˆAmeh

ˆAmeh is prepared for the first teeth of babies as well as for *Eed el-Barbara*, which is our halloween. It makes a delicious, nourishing breakfast, which you can prepare ahead of time reheating it in the morning.

SERVES 4 TO 6

1½ cups wheat or pearl barley

6¾ cups water

1 tablespoon anise seeds, wrapped in a little cheesecloth

seasoning and garnish

granulated sugar

orange blossom water

rose water

⅓ cup pine nuts, soaked in boiling water

⅓ cup walnuts, soaked in boiling water and peeled, if you have the patience

⅓ cup blanched almond halves, soaked

Put the wheat (or barley), water and the small wrap of anise seeds in a large saucepan. Place over a high heat and bring to the boil. Skim the surface clean, cover the pan and boil for 10 minutes. Reduce the heat to medium and boil gently for another 10 minutes, then turn the heat to low and simmer for 40 minutes.

Remove and discard the wrapped anise seeds and serve hot in individual bowls. Stir into each bowl 1 tablespoon orange blossom water, 1 tablespoon rose water and sugar to taste. Mix well and garnish with the pre-soaked nuts before eating.

Ice-cream making is the preserve of professionals in the Lebanon and few people prepare it at home. This is a shame as they are so simple to make and so good. Our ice-cream 'cone' is rectangular in shape and the ice-cream vendors cram it so full that it bulges into a sort of round cup. I have tested the following recipes with cow's milk and cream as well as with goat's milk for friends who do not eat cow's dairy products. Because I could not find goat's cream, I increased the amount of milk to equal that of both milk and cream and thickened it with a little salep (see Lebanese larder, p. 30; use 1 tablespoon Turkish salep [or ½ tablespoon American] per quart) to achieve a similar velvety texture as when using cream.

FIG ICE-CREAM

Boozaï Teen

The color of this ice-cream will vary according to the type of figs you are using (see Fruits entry, pp. 40-1). Any type is suitable as long as the figs are ripe and sweet. You can vary endlessly on this recipe by replacing the figs with any other type of fruit such as mulberry (*toot*), mango (*mangua*), strawberry (*farawelah*), prickly pear (*sobbayr*) or banana (*moz*) and so on. Use the weight given below as a guide line for the amount of fruit pulp you will need.

SERVES 4

scant 1½ cups milk	scant 1½ cups crème fraîche
about 1 lb fresh ripe figs, peeled	¾ cup or a bit more (6 oz) golden superfine sugar

Put the milk in a saucepan, place over a medium heat and bring to the boil. Watch it as it is about to boil so that it does not boil over, then take off the heat and leave to cool. (You can cool it quickly by putting the pan in a bowl of iced water.)

Put the peeled figs in a food processor and process, making sure you do not liquidize them too much, as there should be small chunks of fig in the ice-cream.

Transfer the puréed figs into a mixing bowl, strain the cooled milk over them and add the cream and sugar. Stir until the sugar has melted and the cream is fully incorporated. Then put the bowl in the freezer and whisk every hour or so, for 6-8 hours or until the ice-cream has reached the desired consistency; or if you are using an ice-cream maker, follow the manufacturer's instructions.

MILK ICE-CREAM

Booza ala Haleeb

Milk ice-cream may sound rather boring but I can assure you that it is far from it. The salep and mastic give it a luscious, smooth, chewy texture that stretches the pleasure of savouring it. The secret behind the smooth texture though is in the choice and use of salep (see Lebanese larder, p. 30). The American type seems to dilute less well than the Turkish. The former also leaves a funny dry taste in the mouth and is a stronger thickening agent.

You can vary on the rose water by using orange blossom water or a drop of vanilla extract. You can also leave either one out and only have the mastic as the main flavoring.

SERVES 4

4½ cups milk	about ¾ cup (5 oz) golden superfine sugar
½ teaspoon ground mastic (see Lebanese larder, p. 25)	scant 1½ cups crème fraîche
1 tablespoon Turkish salep or ½ tablespoon American salep (see Lebanese larder, p. 30)	2 tablespoons rose water
	2 tablespoons finely chopped pistachio nuts for garnish (optional)

Put the milk in a saucepan, place over a medium heat and bring to the boil. Strain over a mixing bowl and leave until it is lukewarm. (If you want the milk to cool quickly, put the filled bowl in a larger bowl of iced water.)

Pour a little of the tepid milk over the ground mastic, stir until well blended and set aside.

Pour the tepid milk into a clean saucepan and place over a medium heat. Bring to the boil, stirring constantly, then add the salep gradually, in very small quantities; if not, the powder will clot in the milk. Keep stirring over the heat for about 5-8 minutes, then add the sugar and stir for another 3 minutes.

Remove from the heat and pour into a freezer-proof bowl. If the salep has not diluted well pass the thickened milk through a sieve. Add the diluted mastic, the cream and rose water and stir well together. Leave to cool. If you are putting the mixture in the freezer, whisk it every hour or so for 6-8 hours or until the ice-cream has the desired consistency; if you are using an ice-cream machine, follow the manufacturer's instructions.

Sprinkle with the chopped pistachio nuts (if you are using them) before serving.

● You can make a salep drink (*sahlab*) by preparing the milk as above, but without mastic, cream or rose water plus adding sugar to taste. After you have cooked the milk with the salep and sugar, pour into individual bowls and sprinkle with a little cinnamon. Serve hot with French croissant or sesame bread (see Lebanese larder, p. 16). *Sahlab* used to be our favorite winter drink to cap a long night out in pre-war Beirut. We always stopped on our way home at our regular specialist stall in downtown Beirut to have *sahlab* and croissants before going to bed. There we would meet other friends who had the same idea and the night would get longer until we finally made our way home as the sun was rising and the city was coming to life. An idle youth, but what fun!

CANDIED APRICOT ICE-CREAM

Booza ala ˆAmar el-Deen

'Moon of the religion' is the literal translation of *ˆamar el-deen*, the name of the candied apricot sheets that is the main flavoring of this ice-cream. It has a beautiful pale salmon colour that combines perfectly with the speckled green of the pistachio ice-cream and the pale milk ice-cream if you make all three.

SERVES 4 TO 6

⅔ cup pine nuts	scant ½ cup crème fraîche
2¼ cups milk	about ¼ cup (2½ oz) golden
10½ oz 'moon of the religion'	superfine sugar
(see Lebanese larder, p. 25)	4 tablespoons orange blossom
	water (optional)

Put the pine nuts in a bowl, cover them with boiling water and leave to soak while you are preparing the rest of the ingredients. The idea behind soaking the nuts in boiling water is to soften them and freshen their taste.

Put the milk in a saucepan, place over a medium heat and bring to the boil. In the meantime cut the 'moon of the religion' sheet in medium pieces and put in a large freezer-proof mixing bowl. Watch the milk as it is about to boil, so that it does not boil over and, when it has boiled, take it off the heat. Wait for a few minutes, then strain it over the candied apricot pieces. Make sure you do not pour the boiling milk over the candied apricot, as it will curdle. Stir until the candied apricot has melted in the milk; this will take some time, about 5 minutes, and I suggest you use a whisk towards the end to quicken the disintegration process.

When the 'moon of the religion' is melted, add the cream and stir until well blended. Taste before adding the sugar, in case you find the mixture sweet enough; remember, though, that the iced taste will be less sweet. Add the sugar to taste, pour in the orange blossom water (if you are using it) and stir until the sugar is diluted.

Drain the pine nuts, rinse them under cold water and add to the apricot mixture, reserving a few nuts for garnishing the ice-cream. Blend well and put the bowl in the freezer. Whisk the mixture every hour or so, for about 6-8 hours, or until the ice-cream has reached the desired consistency. If you are using an ice-cream maker, follow the manufacturer's instructions.

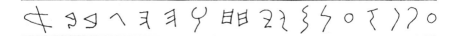

PISTACHIO NUT ICE-CREAM

Booza ala Festu^ Halabi

This ice-cream can be varied by replacing the pistachios with pine nuts, almonds or any other nut of your choice.

SERVES 4

2¾ cups milk	½ tablespoon Turkish salep
1 cup raw pistachio nuts	(see Lebanese larder, p. 30)
(or pine nuts or blanched	about ¾ cup (5 oz) golden
almonds, pre-soaked in boiling	superfine sugar
water and drained)	scant 1½ cups crème fraîche
¼ teaspoon ground mastic	2 tablespoons rose water

Pour the milk into a saucepan, place over a medium heat and bring to the boil. Watch the milk as it is about to boil so that it does not boil over. Take off the heat and leave until tepid. (You can cool it quickly by putting the pan in a larger pan of iced water.)

In the meantime put the pistachio nuts in a food processor (or drained pine nuts or almonds, if you are using either. The idea behind soaking them in boiling water is to soften them and freshen their taste) and process until coarsely ground. You can also grind the nuts finely for a less crunchy texture.

Dilute the ground mastic in a little tepid milk and leave until later.

Strain the rest of the milk into a clean saucepan and place over a medium heat. Bring to the boil, while stirring constantly, then gradually add the salep. Do this in very small quantities or else the powder will clot in the milk. Keep stirring over the heat for about 5-8 minutes, then add the sugar and stir for another 3 minutes.

Pour the thickened milk into a freezer-proof mixing bowl (if the salep has not diluted properly, pour the milk through a sieve) and stir in the diluted mastic. Add the cream, ground nuts and rose water and blend until the cream is fully incorporated.

If you have an ice-cream maker, follow the manufacturer's instructions to ice the mixture; if not, put the mixture in the freezer and whisk every hour or so, for about 6-8 hours, or until the ice-cream has reached the desired consistency.

List of Shops

Damascus Imported Grocery, 5721 Hollywood Blvd., Hollywood, FL 33021, tel. 305/962-4552

International Groceries of San Diego, 3548 Ashford St., San Diego, CA 92111, tel. 619/569-0362

Middle Eastern Bakery & Grocery, 1512 W. Foster Ave., Chicago, IL 60640, tel. 312/561-2224

Sahadi Importing Co., 187 Atlantic Ave., Brooklyn, NY 11201, tel. 718/624-4550

Samiramis Importing Co., 2990 Mission St., San Francisco, CA 94110, tel. 415/824-6555

Shallah's Middle Eastern Importing Co., 290 White St., Danbury, CT 06810, tel. 203/743-4181

Syrian Grocery, 270 Shawmut Ave., Boston, MA 021118, tel. 617/426-1458

Bibliography

Cookery and Reference Books

Agia, Emelie – *"Cooking with Sitto" Middle Eastern Recipes*, St Anne's Melkite Catholic Church, West Paterson, 1982 (2nd ed.)

Al-Faqih, Yaqoot Asᶜad – *Eastern Dishes and Tastes*, Al-Khal, Beirut, Lebanon 1987 (Arabic Edition)

Benghiat, Suzy – *Middle Eastern Cookery*, Weidenfeld and Nicholson 1984

Bissell, Frances – *Sainsbury's Book of Food*, Webster's Wine Price Guide Ltd, 1989

Boulos-Guillaume, Nouhad – *The Lebanese Cooking 99 recipes without meat*, Edifra/Ediframo, Paris 1988

Corey, Helen – *The Art of Syrian Cookery*, Doubleday & Co. Inc. 1962

David, Elizabeth – *Spices, Salt and Aromatics in the English Kitchen*, Penguin Books, 1970

Dawn, Elaine and Anthony, Selwa – *Lebanese Cookbook*, Paul Hamlyn Pty Ltd, Dee Why West, Australia 1978, 2nd ed. Chartwell Books Inc.,

Dowell, Phillip & Bailey, Adrian – *The Book of Ingredients*, Mermaid Books 1991

Farrah, Madelain – *Lebanese Cuisine*, Lebanese Cuisine, Portland, Oregon 1972, 10th ed. 1991

Grieve, Mrs M. F.R.H.S. – *A Modern Herbal*, Jonathan Cape Ltd. 1931

Grigson, Jane – *Vegetable Book*, Michael Joseph 1978
Fruit Book, Michael Joseph 1982

Hamady, Mary Laird – *Lebanese Mountain Cookery*, Godine, Boston Mass. 1987

Haroutunian, Arto der – *Complete Arab Cookery*, Century Publishing Co., London 1982;
Middle Eastern Cookery, Century Publishing Co., London 1982;
Patisserie of the Eastern Mediterranean, Macdonald & Co. Ltd 1988
Sweets and Desserts from the Middle East, Century Publishing Ltd. 1984;
The Yoghurt Book, Food of the Gods, Penguin Books 1983;
Vegetarian Dishes from the Middle East, Century Publishing Ltd
Hourani, Furugh Afnan – *'Laban, Laban': An Essay on Cooking with Yoghurt*, PPC 18, November 1984;
Notes for a Study of Sectarian Cookery in Lebanon, PPC 23, July 1986
Howe, Robin – *Middle Eastern Cookery*, Eyre Methuen, London 1958
Karaoglan, Aida – *A Gourmet's Delight*, Dar el-Nahar, Beirut 1969;
Food for the Vegetarian, Traditional Lebanese Recipes, Interlink, New York 1988
Khawam, Rene – *La Cuisine Arabe*, Albin Michel, Paris 1970
Khayat, Mary Karam and Keatinge, Margaret Clark – *Food from the Arab World*, Khayats 1959
Larousse Gastronomique, Hamlyn Publishing Group, 1988
Lovell, Emily – *Lebanese Cooking Streamlined*, Naylor, San Antonio, Texas 1971
Mallos, Tess – *The Complete Middle East Cookbook*, Paul Hamlyn Pty Ltd, Sydney, Auckland, London, New York 1979
Man, Rosamond – *The Complete Meze Table*, Ebury 1986
de Moor, Janny – *Eating Out in the Ancient Near East*, Oxford Symposium of Food and Cookery, 1992
Mouzannar, Ibrahim – *La Cuisine Libanaise*, Librairie du Liban 1983
Nemir family – *From these Roots and Branches: a Family Cookbook*, Cookbook Publishers, Kansas 1987
Osborne, Christine – *Middle Eastern Food and Drink*, pub. Wayland 1988
Perl, Leila – *Rice, Spice and Bitter Oranges, Mediterranean Foods and Festivals*, The World Publishing Co., Cleveland and New York 1967
Perry, Charles – *Kitab Al-Tibakhah: A Fifteenth Century Cookbook*, PPC 21 November 1985;
Three Medieval Arabic Cook Books, Oxford Symposium of Food and Cookery, 1981;
Couscous and its Cousins, Oxford Symposium, 1989;
Puff Paste is Spanish, PPC 17, June 1984
Rayess, George – *Art of Lebanese Cooking*, Librairie du Liban, Beirut 1991
Roden, Claudia – *A New Book of Middle Eastern Food*, Penguin Books 1986
Rodinson, Maxime – *Recherches sur les Documents Arabes Relatifs à la Cuisine*, Revue des etudes Islamiques, nos 17-18, 1949;
Ghidha, in the Encyclopedia of Islam
Salah, Nahdah – *The Splendors of Arabic Sweets*, World Library, Singapore (Arabic Edition)

Salloum, Mary – *A Taste of Lebanon*, 1st 1988, 2nd ed. Scorpion Publishers, Essex 1989

Scott, David – *Middle Eastern Vegetarian Cookery*, Rider 1981

Smith, Margaret Ruth & Gaden, Eileen – *The Best of Near Eastern Cookery*, Doubleday & Co. Inc. 1964

Smouha, Patricia – *Middle Eastern Cooking*, André Deutsch, London 1955

Stephan, Lily – *Lebanese Dishes Made Delicious*, Rihani Publishing House, Beirut

St Elias Orthodox Church, Toledo, Ohio (c.1970) – *Syrian/Lebanese Cookbook, Festive Foods*

St Mary's Sunday school church guild and the women of St Mary's parish – *Lebanese Cook Book*, Carleton Press, New York 1967

Tannahill, Reay – *Food in History*, Penguin, 1973

Weiss-Armush, Anne Marie – *Arabian Cuisine*, Dar an-Nafaes, Beirut 1984 (2nd ed. 1991)

Yassine, Sima Osman and Kamal, Sadouf – *Middle Eastern Cuisine*, Dar el-Ilm lil-Malayin 1984 rep. 1985

Travellers' Accounts and History

d'Arvieux, Chevalier Laurent – *Mémoires*, 1635 to 1702 Int., notes and index by Antoine Abdelnour, rep. Dar Lahad Khater, Beirut 1982

Berchet, Jean-Claude – *Le Voyage en Orient, Anthologie des Voyageurs Francais dans le Levant au XIX siecle*, Robert Laffont, Paris 1985

Chevallier, Dominique – *La Société du Mont Liban a l'-Époque de la Révolution Industrielle en Europe*, Librairie Orientaliste Paul Geuthner, Paris 1971

Hitti, Philippe – *A Short History of Lebanon*, Macmillan & Co. Ltd, 1965 *Lebanon in History*, Macmillan & Co. Ltd, 1957

Hourani, A. H. – *Syria and Lebanon, A Political Essay*, Oxford University Press, London 1946

Ismail, Adel – *Lebanon, History of a People*, Dar Al-Makchouf, Beirut 1972

Khayat, Marie Karam & Keatinge, Margaret Clarke – *Lebanon, Land of the Cedars*, Khayats, Beirut 1960

Kinglake, Alexander William – *Eothen*, Oxford University Press 1906

Rizk-Allah, Habeeb Effendi – *The Thistle and the Cedar of Lebanon*, James Madden, London 1854 (1st ed. 1853)

Salibi, Kamal S. – *The Modern History of Lebanon*, Weidenfeld and Nicholson 1965

Stark, Freya – *Letters from Syria*, John Murray, London 1942

Stevens, E.S. – *Cedars, Saints and Sinners in Syria*, Hurst & Blackett Ltd. London 1926

Traveller's Dictionary of Quotations, London 1983

Index

INDEX